THE CLEAREST PROMISES OF GOD

AMS Studies in Religious Tradition: No.1
ISSN 1059-7255

Other titles in this series:

2.   Constance J. Post, *"Signs of the Times" in Cotton Mather's Paterna: A Study of Puritan Autobiography.* 1995

THE CLEAREST PROMISES OF GOD

The Development of
Calvin's Eucharistic Teaching

Thomas J. Davis

AMS PRESS
New York

Library of Congress Cataloging-in-Publication Data

Davis, Thomas J. (Thomas Jeffery), 1958-
    The clearest promises of God : the development of Calvin's
eucharistic teaching / Thomas J. Davis.
        (AMS studies in religious tradition, ISSN 1059-7255 : no. 1)
    Revision of thesis (Ph. D.)--University of Chicago.
    Includes bibliographical references and index.
    ISBN 0-404-62531-2 (alk. paper)
    1. Calvin, Jean, 1509-1564--Views on the Lord's Supper. 2. Lord's
Supper--History of doctrines--16th century. 3. Calvinism-
-History--16th century.   I. Title. II. Series.
BX9423.C5D38 1995
234'.163'092--dc20
                                                                91-58297
                                                                    CIP

All AMS books are printed on acid-free paper that meets the guidelines for performance and durability of the Committee on Production Guidelines for Book Longevity of the Council on Library Resources.

AMS PRESS, INC.
56 East 13th Street
New York, NY 10003

MANUFACTURED IN THE UNITED STATES OF AMERICA

Contents

Preface

This work officially began as a doctoral dissertation at the University of Chicago, but its real genesis goes back to a mental image evoked by my earliest readings of Calvin scholarship—the birth of Athena. In Greek mythology, Athena's birth is miraculous. As the story goes, when Zeus's head is split open to get at the cause of his headaches, Athena springs forth fully grown and fully armed. This mental picture summed up for me what I seemed to be reading about Calvin's theology; that it was something that sprang fully grown (and armed!) from Calvin's mind once the wedge of conversion hit him. I finally began, however, to ask the historian's proper question: Was it so? In regard to Calvin's eucharistic teaching, at least, I concluded "no." I decided that, if birthing images were to be used, the natural one applied best to Calvin's eucharistic thought: there is birth, years of growth and development, and, finally, maturity. The purpose of this book is to chart the birth and maturation process of Calvin's eucharistic doctrine. Such a charting activity helps one, I believe, better understand Calvin on this subject.

I have generally used English translations of both primary and secondary sources; however, there are places where I prefer to provide my own translation. When a translation of one of Calvin's works is used, I also provide citations to the *Corpus Reformatorum* and the *Opera Selecta*. When I render a translation of my own, I supply the quotation in its original language in the notes.

1

There are, of course, many people to thank. Teachers at the Divinity School of the University of Chicago were generous in their help; Susan Schreiner, Brian Gerrish, and Martin Marty all provided guidance. The School of Liberal Arts of Indiana University-Purdue University at Indianapolis furnished a grant to help assist with the preparation of the final manuscript; my appreciation goes out especially to Dean John Barlow and Associate Dean Barbara Jackson. My colleagues in the Religious Studies Department of IUPUI have provided a most hospitable environment for a young colleague; I thank Tessa Bartholomeusz, Conrad Cherry, E. Theodore Mullen, William Jackson, Jan Shipps, Rowland A. Sherrill, and James Smurl for their helpful comments and encouragement. Many friends have been kind enough to maintain an active interest in my work; I thank especially Kyle Pasewark, who has heard, if not read, most of this book. Terry Grimm was steadfast in his belief that I could actually pull this work off, even when I had serious doubts. Gratitude goes to Albert E. Hurd, always generous to a fault, for things too many to mention. David Buttrick gave the manuscript a careful and critical reading; for that, and for the extension of hospitality through the years, I am grateful.

Finally, my family has sacrificed much over the years in order to see this work completed. My parents, Paul and Christine Davis, engendered in me a love of learning; here is a debt that can only be acknowledged, never repaid. Carolyn and Charles Fodor have been firm in support; they are (to alter slightly a dedication once used by George Buttrick), parents-in-love as well as in-law. My children, Mave and Gwynne, have constantly and rightly reminded me that there is much joy in life to be had in addition to intellectual pursuits. Most of all, I thank my wife, Melanie Lane. There is simply not enough room to elaborate my debt to her. Let it suffice to say that, thanks to her, I understand better what Edgar Allan Poe meant when he wrote about a couple who "loved with a love that was more than a love." And so to Melanie, my dearest companion, I dedicate this book.

Introduction

Calvin has been characterized as a man of one book.[1] The 1559 edition of the *Institutes of the Christian Religion*[2] has served as the primary source for the study of his theology. Students of his thought have turned to the 1559 *Institutes* for the definitive word on matters related to Calvin's teaching for two reasons. The first is that the 1559 edition of the *Institutes* represents the fullest and most complete expression of Calvin's dogmatic work. Calvin himself made such a claim of "satisfaction" with the completeness of his theological enterprise with the publication of the 1559 edition.[3] The second reason is related to the first; namely, the traditional view of Calvin scholars that the 1559 publication represents the fullest expression of a system of thought that needed only that—fuller expression.[4] Thus, scholars have viewed the growth in size of the *Institutes* from the original "pocket edition" size of 1536 to the massive tome of 1559[5] as nothing more than a process of elaboration, not development.

This characterization should not be taken, however, to mean that sources other than the 1559 *Institutes* have not been examined by those interested in Calvin's thought. However, these other writings have almost always been examined in the light of the 1559 *Institutes*, with this important work serving as the hermeneutical device through which all the other documents have been read and interpreted. Rather than reading, then, for discontinuities, differences, or developments in thought, Calvin scholars have generally examined documents with an eye toward the continuities with and similarities to the 1559 *Institutes*.[6]

3

Such a nondevelopmental method for studying Calvin can be rationalized on the basis of what Calvin himself had said—that he was satisfied with the 1559 *Institutes* as an expression of his thought.[7] However, there are at least three reasons why this methodological procedure should be challenged. The first relates to an emphasis on the integrity of the text as text that I consider helpful in the study of historical works.[8] The author's position as a privileged interpreter of his or her own work is questioned when discrepancies in that author's work warrant such questioning. The text stands on its own as an object of interpretation. Therefore, the author's later judgments should not overshadow the original text itself. If the text presents grounds to question the author's interpretation of it, then one may legitimately do so. One should take an independent stance toward the text over against the author's later interpretive agenda, an agenda that oftentimes arises out of particular historical circumstances subsequent to the original work. This is simply one way of saying that, for example, Calvin's 1536 *Institutes* carry an original intent that should not be clouded by Calvin's authorial intent in later works. It is in this sense that I mean to say that the text itself outweighs the later interpretations of its author.

Moreover, as indicated above, a static reading of Calvin's life work ignores historical circumstances. As the circumstances changed, or as new challenges were issued to his theological endeavors, or as pastoral needs became apparent, Calvin responded from pulpit and printing press. These challenges brought forth from Calvin explanations, developments, and explications that were folded into the more stable structures of his *Institutes* and commentaries. One can read entire passages from his occasional pieces as they have been incorporated into the body of his main theological and exegetical works.[9] Such a process should be seen as historically and developmentally significant for the tone and substance of the *Institutes*.

Finally, a method that deals with Calvin's thought solely on the basis of the 1559 *Institutes* slights something Calvin himself said—that the *Institutes* were meant to be read in conjunction with his biblical commentaries.[10] He viewed his *Institutes* as a theological introduction to the study of Scripture. Thus, when he claimed "satisfaction" with the 1559 *Institutes*, he did not mean that that work was all one needed to know. He meant that the *Institutes* were in a satisfactory form to introduce one to the whole of piety that is required to correctly read the Scripture. Calvin's *magnum opus* was meant as a companion volume to his commentaries. What I will argue, then, is that Calvin was not a "man of one book." Moreover, the '59 *Institutes* cannot properly be understood apart from its developmental context.

There have been scholars who have recognized that the image of Calvin as a "man of one book" is misleading. Ford Lewis Battles, in the preface to his translation of Calvin's 1536 *Institutes*, has indicated such. There is, according to Battles, significant development within the *Institutes* themselves, contrary to what the "histories" of the *Institutes* have said.[11] Moreover, while Battles spoke of the *Institutes*, T. H. L. Parker has spoken of the need to view Calvin's commentaries in a developmental manner. There is, according to Parker, change and development to be charted in the various editions of the commentaries. Parker has at least pointed to some paths one might take in such a charting activity.[12]

While Battles and Parker have written on development in Calvin's work in a rather general manner, there are others who have scrutinized Calvin's teaching on a particular subject in terms of its development. Alexandre Ganoczy, in his treatment of Calvin as a theologian of ministry and the church, has noted the development in Calvin's ecclesiology between the 1536 and the 1559 editions of the *Institutes*.[13] However, he deals with ecclesiology in general and in a rather short section so that the development is more noted than charted. Furthermore, he surveys only the differences between the editions of the *Institutes* and does not deal with ecclesiology in the whole of Calvin's writings.

G. P. Hartvelt's *Corpus Verum* deals with the issue of "true body" in Calvin's eucharistic thought.[14] His work is one of the first to note the substantial development between the '36 and '39 *Institutes* on the matters of eucharistic doctrine. It is the first to take seriously the *difference* between the two editions in terms of, for instance, eucharistic instrumentality. Hartvelt affirms this change as a real development.[15] However, Hartvelt's work operates mostly at the level of looking at the development of Calvin's eucharistic doctrine in terms of the changes that took place between 1536 and 1539.

Thus, there is a paucity in the Calvin scholarship of works that attempt to chart the changes and development of major doctrines of Calvin's over the course of his career and show the difference that method makes in one's interpretation of the 1559 *Institutes*.[16] This project represents such an attempt, and the doctrine of focus is the Eucharist.

Calvin's eucharistic doctrine lends itself to this study for at least two reasons. The first is the recognized importance and place of eucharistic teaching in Calvin's thought. From 1536 until his death in 1564, a year did not go by during which Calvin did not have something of significance to contribute to the discussions on eucharistic doctrine and practice. As for the private life of faith, Calvin's piety seemed to embrace the Eucharist as, indeed, a nourishment and nurturer of faith.[17] The second reason is that approaches to Calvin's eucharistic doctrine exemplify both the general tendencies of Calvin studies mentioned above; namely, to see Calvin as a man of one book and to view his doctrine as unchanging. For an example of the former, one needs look only so far as the last book-length treatment of Calvin's eucharistic teaching, Kilian McDonnell's *John Calvin, the Church and the Eucharist*. The author begins the study with a note as to why only the 1559 *Institutes* are needed to execute a proper study of Calvin's eucharistic teaching.[18] The latter tendency can be attributed to John Calvin himself. Calvin has been allowed the position of "privileged interpreter" on the matter of his eucharistic thought. Expositions of Calvin's eucharistic doctrine generally include Calvin's own statements that his teaching on the Holy Supper never changed.[19] What is clear are the reasons why Calvin would make such a claim in the vicious religious climate of the sixteenth century. What is unclear is why students of Calvin have taken his claim

at face value; yet the claim has more often than not been allowed
to stand.

Conclusion

The procedure, then, for this book will be as follows. After
a review of three key nineteenth-century scholars on Calvin's
eucharistic teaching who set up both the issues and the methodological problems for Calvin studies in the twentieth century,
there will be a chapter devoted to the *Consensus Tigurinus*, its
context, and Calvin's explication of it. This important document
has been viewed in a variety of ways. For this study, the
important point is that Calvin decided that his signature on the
document needed explanation. It is in his defence of the *Consensus* that Calvin states that his views on the Eucharist had never
been different than what they were. He interprets the meaning of
the *Consensus* in light of his current teaching and its relationship
to his "unchanged" thought of past works. His explanation and
interpretations will be held up to scrutiny and will serve as a
hermeneutical device to pose questions of Calvin's work prior to
the *Consensus* and to set the stage to examine his teaching after
the *Consensus*.

There will then follow three chapters arranged chronologi-
cally. The hermeneutical filter that Calvin's explanation of the
Consensus Tigurinus provides will be used to examine the
elements of change and development in his eucharistic teaching.
What will be demonstrated in the execution of these chapters is
that Calvin's eucharistic theology develops from an incomplete
and often ambiguous summary to a much larger project that
incorporates the work of a lifetime into a coherent whole. We
will see Calvin move from denying the Eucharist as an instrument of grace to affirming it as such. We will see Calvin
develop a notion of substantial partaking of the true body and
blood of Christ over his career; an emphasis that is practically

absent, even denied, in his earliest teaching. It will be demonstrated that Calvin moves from a position that posited no eucharistic gift to one that affirms such a gift. There is a special understanding and assurance the Eucharist gives, we will find, that enhances the true partaking of the body and blood of Christ, in degree if not in kind. This special knowledge can be designated as a special gift of the Eucharist. Moreover, these chapters will show the development of such important aspects of Calvin's eucharistic theology as the Holy Spirit as the bond between Christ and the Christian, the Eucharist as an act of accommodation to human weakness, and God's instrumental way of working in the world.

A concluding chapter will examine the final developments in Calvin's "definitive" expression of his eucharistic theology. It will show how a developmental approach to Calvin's eucharistic theology influences the manner in which one reads the content of the 1559 *Institutes*. Finally, the question of how to understand the specific eucharistic gift in Calvin's mature thought will be addressed.

Notes

1. "Calvin was a man of a single book." ("Calvin fut l'homme d'un seul livre.") Luchesius Smits, *Saint Augustin dans l'Oeuvre de Jean Calvin: Étude de critique litteraire*, vol. 1 (Assen: Van Gorcum, 1956), p. 1. For a more detailed explanation of the same sentiment, see Alister McGrath, *A Life of John Calvin* (Oxford: Blackwell, 1990), pp. 145–47.

2. Vols. 3–5 of John Calvin, *Calvini opera selecta*, 5 vols., edited by P. Barth and W. Niesel (Munich: Kaiser Verlag, 1926–1936), hereafter cited as OS; vol. 2 of John Calvin, *Ioannis Calvini opera quae supersunt omnia*, 59 vols., edited by W. Baum, E. Cunitz, and E. Reuss (Brunsvigae: C. A. Schwetscke, 1863–1900), hereafter cited as OC. The best available English edition is *Institutes of the Christian Religion*, 2 vols., edited by John T. McNeill and translated by Ford

Lewis Battles (Philadelphia: Westminster Press, 1960), hereafter cited as *Inst*. Because of the format of the 1559 *Institutes*, the Book, Chapter, and Section designation given after a reference to *Inst*. will serve also as the citation to OC and OS. For Calvin's other writings, however, column numbers will be given for OC, and page numbers will be cited for OS.

3. "Although I did not regret the labor spent, I was never satisfied until the work had been arranged in the order now set forth. . . . For I believe I have so embraced the sum of religion in all its parts, and have arranged it in such an order, that if anyone rightly grasps it, it will not be difficult for him to determine what he ought especially to seek in Scripture, and to what end he ought to relate its contents." John Calvin to the Reader, *Inst*., pp. 3–4.

4. A recent book makes this point particularly well and represents the thought of the majority of historical Calvin scholarship on the idea of the unchanging character of Calvin's thought: "The evidence on which my portrait [of Calvin] is based is drawn indiscriminately from every period in his life for which data are available, and the portrait itself is relatively static." William Bouwsma, *John Calvin: A Sixteenth Century Portrait* (New York and Oxford: Oxford University Press, 1988), p. 4. Bouwsma goes on to say in a note: "Others have looked for development in Calvin and failed to find it." P. 237, n. 19.

5. In 1536, the volume contained 520 octavo pages, was about 6⅛ by 4 inches, and consisted of 6 chapters. The 1559 edition contained 80 chapters, 684 pages in a volume 12½ by 8 inches.

6. This method of reading Calvin has led to three types of treatment that Calvin's life work has received: 1) Since the 1559 edition of the *Institutes* represents Calvin's thought at its most complete, there is no need to review other sources; see, for example, Kilian McDonnell, *John Calvin, the Church and the Eucharist* (Princeton: Princeton University Press, 1967), p. 3. 2) Calvin's thought as expressed in tracts, treatises, commentaries, etc. is considered, but always with an eye toward what is said in 1559. Earlier materials are, thus, read backwards from 1559. This approach reinforces the tradition that an examination of earlier documents proves the overall static quality of Calvin's thought. "Whatever interest and value may attach to his other theological writings, the *Institutes* are the faithful summary of the ideas he expounded in them. Moreover, the *Institutes*—at least in their final form—purport to give a complete account of Christian teaching. They therefore present a synthesis of Calvinist thought, and one that is

sufficient in itself." François Wendel, *Calvin: The Origins and Development of His Religious Thought*, translated by Philip Mairet (London: Collins, 1963), p. 111. 3) Calvin's other works are used to show either "comprehensiveness" or to pull out a particularly well-turned phrase to make evident a point made based on the 1559 work; this method is used particularly in smaller articles that deal with Calvin in a summary fashion. See, for example, Pierre Yves Emery, "The Teaching of Calvin on the Sacrificial Element in the Eucharist," *Reformed and Presbyterian World* 26 (1960): 109–14. Of the nineteen references to Calvin's work, eighteen are to the '59 *Institutes* and one is to the *Short Treatise on the Holy Supper*.

7. "Although I did not regret the labor spent [on earlier editions], I was never satisfied until the work had been arranged in the order *now set forth* (emphasis mine)." John Calvin to the Reader, *Inst.*

8. See, for example, Hans-Georg Gadamer, *Truth and Method* (New York: Crossroad, 1982; first published as *Wahrheit und Methode* in Tübingen by J. C. B. Mohr, 1960). Gadamer makes especially clear the difference between mere repetition of what an author has said and an *interpretation* of what the author has said. *Truth and Method*, p. 300.

9. *Inst.* 4.17.30–34 rely heavily, for example, on the treatises Calvin published against Westphal.

10. John Calvin to the Reader, *Inst.* Calvin's output of biblical commentaries amounts to a much larger percentage of his literary corpus than does his *Institutes*. In relation to the problem, T. H. L. Parker remarks, "The sixteenth century was, above all things, the age of the Bible. How strange, then, that this area of its history has, apart from some well-trodden paths, been neglected." Parker, *Calvin's New Testament Commentaries* (Grand Rapids: Wm. B. Eerdmans, 1971), p. vii.

11. "A problem . . . is the long-held notion that Calvin's theological views never really changed and that what he wrote in the final edition of 1559 of the *Institutes of the Christian Religion* applies more or less indiscriminately to his whole Christian life. This is simply not true; great consistency there is throughout his literary expression of the faith, but also much movement, reconsideration and recasting of his thought." Ford Lewis Battles, Introduction to John Calvin, *Institutes of the Christian Religion: 1536 Edition*, revised edition, edited and translated by Ford Lewis Battles (Grand Rapids: The H. H. Meeter Center for Calvin Studies and Wm. B. Eerdmans, 1986), p. xxi;

hereafter cited as *Inst. '36*. Compare this statement to the position held by Benjamin B. Warfield in his *The Literary History of the Institutes of the Christian Religion by John Calvin* (Philadelphia: Presbyterian Board of Publication, 1909). Warfield is representative of the traditional view that Calvin's theological views never changed over the course of the development of the various editions of the *Institutes*.

12. "One of his [Calvin's] often stressed qualities—desirable or repugnant, according to the point of view—is that he did not change his mind on doctrine between 1539-1559. It is good to record that the same *cannot* (emphasis mine) be said of his exegesis." Parker, *Calvin's New Testament Commentaries*, p. 89. See also Parker's article "Calvin the exegete: change and development," in *Calvinus Ecclesiae Doctor: Die Referate des Internationalen Kongresses für Calvinforschung vom 25. bis 28. September 1978 in Amsterdam*, edited by W. H. Neuser (Kampen: Kok, 1978): 35-46.

13. Alexandre Ganoczy, *Calvin: Théologien de L'église et du Ministère*, Unam Sanctam 48 (Paris: Cerf, 1964), pp. 183-222. The purpose of the cited section is to show "the evolution that saw the accentuation of the invisible church versus the affirmation of the visible, maternal, and ministering church." ("évolution qui va de l'accentuation de l'Eglise invisible vers l'affirmation de l'Eglise visible, maternelle et ministérielle.") Ganoczy, p. 14.

14. G. P. Hartvelt, *Corpus Verum: een studie over een centraal hoofdstuk uit de avondmaalsleer van Calvijn* (Delft: W. D. Meinema N.V., 1960).

15. ". . . it seems to us also proper here to openly point out a definite development that Calvin has gone through, and that is on the instrumental character of the sacrament. We are thinking here of a statement from Inst. I (1536), where Calvin denies the instrumental character of the sacrament. In Inst. II (1539) he has omitted this statement." (". . . lijkt het ons ook juist hier te wijzen ope een bepaalde ontwikkeling die Calvijn heeft doorgemaakt t.a.v. het instrumentele karakter der sacramenten. Wij denken hier aan een uitspraak van Inst. I (1536), waar Calvijn het instumenteel karakter den sacrementen ontkent. Deze uitspraak heeft hij in Inst. II (1539) laten vervallen.") Hartvelt, *Verum Corpus*, p. 78. In support of his statement that Calvin denies the instrumental character of the Eucharist in the '36 *Institutes* he quotes OC 1:115: "Not because such great graces are included and bound to the sacrament, or that the sacrament is an implement or an instrument by which they are conferred to us, but,

simply, it is by this token that the Lord has testified to us his will."
("Non quia sacramento tales gratiae illigatae inclusaeque sint, aut quod
sacramentum organum ac instrumentum sit, quo nobis conferantur, sed
duntaxat, quod hac tessera voluntatem suam nobis Dominus testifica-
tur.")

    16. Perhaps the *Institutes*, for all the sense of "fullness" one may
derive from reading this dogmatic manual, do not contain all that
Calvin would say about a particular subject. Inherent in this argument
is an appeal to take seriously all of Calvin's writings. Indeed, Susan
Schreiner has shown that there can be found in Calvin's sermons
developments and explications that do not appear anywhere else so fully
expounded in the Calvin corpus. Particularly in his preaching on the
book of Job, Calvin expounds a doctrine, the double justice of God, at
greater length and depth of exegesis than can be found anywhere else.
As Schreiner's work shows, Calvin's reference to double justice in *Inst.*
3.12.1. can only be understood by reference to the Job sermons, not
vice versa. See Susan Schreiner, "Exegesis and Double Justice in
Calvin's Sermons on Job," *Church History* 58, no. 3 (September 1989):
322–38. What a surprise this discovery is when dealing with "a man of
one book"! Schreiner's work brings under suspicion one of the primary
claims of McGrath as he argues for the priority of the 1559 *Institutes*:
"In dealing with any given topic in the 1559 edition, the reader can rest
assured that he or she will encounter everything Calvin regarded as
essential to grasping his position on that topic." McGrath, *Calvin*, p.
147. Everything essential to grasp Calvin's position, at least on the
Eucharist, is in fact *not* in the 1559 *Institutes*.

    17. An interesting way one scholar has tried to show the
character of Calvin's eucharistic piety has been to take prosaic lines
from the *Inst.*, give them strophic form, and then let the lines stand as
hymnody. See the "Communion Hymn" Battles has produced from
Inst. 4.17 in *The Piety of John Calvin: An Anthology Illustrative of The
Spirituality of the Reformer*, translated and edited by Ford Lewis
Battles, music edited by Stanley Tagg (Grand Rapids: Baker Book
House, 1978), p. 171.

    18. "It is universally acknowledged among Calvin researchers
that there is little development in his eucharistic doctrine. . . . The
1559 edition of the *Institutes* gives the definitive form of Calvin's
doctrine. This book limits itself to Calvin's doctrine as found in this
edition. His other works are cited to throw light on the doctrine found

in the 1559 edition." McDonnell, *John Calvin, the Church and the Eucharist*, p. 3.

19. Calvin makes several statements in his writings against Westphal that indicate Calvin's belief that his eucharistic doctrine had always been the same. "He writes that my books were highly esteemed and relished by the men of his sect, at the time when they thought that I differed from the teachers of the Church of Zurich. Whence the sudden alienation now? Is it because I have abandoned my opinion? Even he himself does not disguise, nay, he has written on the margins of his book, that everything which our Agreement contains occurs throughout my writings." John Calvin, *Second Defence of the Pious and Orthodox Faith concerning the Sacraments, in Answer to the Calumnies of Joachim Westphal*, in *Selected Works of John Calvin: Tracts and Letters*, edited by Henry Beveridge and Jules Bonnet (hereafter cited as Calvin, *Selected Works*), *Volume 2: Tracts, Part 2*, edited and translated by Henry Beveridge (Edinburgh: Calvin Translation Society, 1849; repr. ed., Grand Rapids: Baker Book House, 1983), p. 247; OC 9:46.

I

The Foundations of the Modern Interpretation of Calvin's Teaching on the Eucharist

John Williamson Nevin

The beginning of the modern historical interpretation of Calvin's teaching on the Lord's Supper in the United States had its genesis in a nineteenth-century debate over the "true meaning" of the Eucharist in Calvin's thought. John Williamson Nevin (1803–1886), professor at the Mercersburg Theological Seminary (Pennsylvania), published in 1846 a book entitled *The Mystical Presence: A Vindication of the Reformed or Calvinistic Doctrine of the Holy Eucharist.*[1] Four years later, in response to criticisms of his understanding of the Eucharist and its proper interpretation within the framework of Reformed theology, Nevin published his "Doctrine of the Reformed Church on the Lord's Supper."[2]

Nevin's work is important for two reasons. The first is that it represents one of the first attempts at a thorough, extended historical analysis of Calvin's eucharistic teaching. Certainly Calvin's teaching on the Lord's Supper had been analyzed at length before this time. However, Nevin's work on Calvin's eucharistic doctrine emerged from a milieu that saw the birth of church history as a field of inquiry.[3] Thus, Nevin's work carries with it a critical insight, a reliance on sources, and an examination of textual evidence that is hard to come by in studies of Calvin's eucharistic teaching before the appearance of *The Mystical Presence*.

The second reason Nevin bears close examination is that his work exhibits problems that have become entrenched in treatments of Calvin's eucharistic doctrine. Most of the references to Calvin's work are to his 1559 *Institutes*, and references not made to that work but to others are read through its lenses. Nevin is at the front of a long tradition of scholarship that takes Calvin's claim that he had never been of a different mind on matters of eucharistic doctrine at face value.[4] Nevin's work is rich with the benefits of historical scholarship that resulted when he addressed the Reformed doctrine of the Eucharist within its historical context. By so doing he treated seriously the developments and changes within the Reformed community. Yet, he never applied the same canons of scholarship to Calvin himself in the sense of taking seriously developments and changes in Calvin's writings.

The Mystical Presence was prompted by Nevin's opinion that the American environment had precipitated a falling away from the true meaning of the Eucharist in the Protestant churches. The book underlines the importance of the Lord's Supper for the life of the church:

> The *Question of the Eucharist* is one of the most important belonging to the history of religion. It may be regarded indeed as in some sense central to the whole Christian system. For Christianity is grounded in the living union of the believer with the person of Christ; and this great fact is emphatically concentrated in the mystery of the Lord's Supper, which has always been clothed on this very account, to the consciousness of the Church, with a character of sanctity and solemnity, surpassing that of any other Christian institution.[5]

This passage outlines the central concern of the book: the living union of the believer with the person of Christ, which the Lord's Supper emphasizes in a special way. The text goes on to explain more fully the "nature of the communion which holds between

Christ and his people . . . as taught by Calvin and the Reformed Church generally."[6] It explains what real communion with Christ is not. It is neither a simple communion of common humanity, nor a moral union, nor a legal union (in the sense of partaking only in Christ's merits and benefits), nor yet a communion only with Christ's divine nature "separately taken" or with the Holy Spirit as the representative of Jesus.[7] Communion with Christ is "a real communion with the Word made flesh; not simply with the divinity of Christ, but with his humanity also."[8] Nevin clarified what he meant: "The participation is not simply in his Spirit, but in his flesh also and blood. It is not figurative merely and moral, but *real, substantial,* and *essential.*"[9] Of course, Nevin's work emphasizes that "real," "substantial," and "essential" have nothing to do with a material eating of the body and blood of Christ. Calvin's view of the Eucharist as a "spiritual" event is noted. Yet, Nevin explained, much as Calvin had to do, what is meant by the term "spiritual communion":

> The communion is spiritual, not material. It is a participation of the Savior's life. Of his life, however, as human, subsisting in a true bodily form. The living energy, the vivific virtue, as Calvin styles it, of Christ's flesh, is made to flow over into the communicant.[10]

The vivifying nature of Christ's flesh, as an objective force, is "the principle of the power itself"[11] that resides in the sacrament's institution. Thus, the union of the believer with Christ is "not natural but sacramental"[12] because of the objective force of divine appointment that binds the sacramental signs to what they represent. This teaching is, according to Nevin, "The Reformed or Calvinistic Doctrine of the Lord's Supper."[13]

Moreover, in his repudiation of the "Modern Puritan Theory" of the Eucharist, Nevin further developed points he considered essential to a true understanding of Reformed teaching. First, he argues for a specific eucharistic gift. "In the old Reformed view," Nevin wrote, "the communion of the believer with Christ in the Supper is taken to be *specific* in its nature, and *different* from all that has taken place in the common exercises of worship."[14] One can deduce from this passage that Nevin believed that in Calvin's view the Lord's Supper includes a eucharistic gift that is different from that which is received in the preached word, or anywhere else.

Second, Nevin contended that the sign and thing signified were inseparable in the old Reformed doctrine. He maintained that, based on the older view of the Lord's Supper, the outward sign and the inward event "by the energy of the Spirit, are made to flow together in the way of a common life."[15] Because of this union between sign and thing signified, Nevin held that the old Reformed doctrine *always* included the idea of an objective force in the Eucharist.[16]

Third, Nevin asserted that the grace of the Eucharist "includes a real participation in [Christ's] *person*."[17] Thus, it is quite appropriate to speak of Christ's real presence in the Eucharist. To speak of the Supper in terms of simply a memorial of Christ's sacrifice is to deny the early church's affirmations that the "very power of the sacrifice itself, as made present in his [Christ's] glorified life"[18] was involved in the sacrament. Nevin thought Calvin supported the ancient church's affirmation: the Eucharist has as its content a present grace won by Christ's sacrifice that Christ shares with believers by sharing his life with them.

Nevin's book concludes with a statement that emphasizes the importance of its subject:

> The mystery of Christianity is here concentrated into a single visible transaction, by which it is made as it were transparent to the senses, and caused to pass before us in immediate living representation.[19]

Nevin believed that he had presented the "fundamentally correct view of this pivotal doctrine"[20] based on the authority of John Calvin and the Reformed tradition.

Charles Hodge (1797–1878), dean of Princeton Theological Seminary, took up the challenge that Nevin had thrown down. The book was so painful to read, according to Hodge, that it took him two years to muster up the required patience to plow through the book for review.[21] In his review, Hodge challenged Nevin on two points: Nevin's interpretation of Calvin's eucharistic doctrine and the appropriateness of having Calvin speak as *the* authority for the Reformed churches.

Nevin responded to Hodge in a series of articles in the German Reformed Church's *Weekly Messenger*. Lack of a publisher other than the church newspaper prompted the founding of the *Mercersburg Review* in 1849. In 1850, the journal published the historical section of Nevin's reply to Hodge. The result was the 128-page essay "Doctrine of the Reformed Church on the Lord's Supper." In what has been called "one of the first significant American contributions to the history of theology,"[22] this essay argues that the doctrine of the Reformed church on the Lord's Supper was Calvin's, as shown through an examination of the national Reformed creeds influenced by his thought. Stated specifically, Nevin's essay begins:

> The object of the following discussion is primarily altogether historical. It proposes simply to answer the question: What was the proper sacramental faith of the Reformed or Calvinistic branch of the Protestant Church in the beginning, as distinguished from Romanism and Lutheranism on the one side as well as from all rationalism and false spiritualism on the other?[23]

Nevin thus wanted to expose the proper historical ties between Calvin's eucharistic doctrine and that of the Reformed family of churches as exemplified in their creeds.

What is it that Nevin finds in the Reformed tradition that he deems to have its highest and best expression in Calvin's exposition of the Eucharist? Exactly those things he had pointed to in *The Mystical Presence*: that the Eucharist carries a specific grace; that the Lord's Supper has a mystical character (that is, a union of the believer with Christ); that the Supper is objective in its force ("something far beyond a mere occasion for the exercise of our faith"); that partaking of the Eucharist involves a real participation in Christ's person through the means of his

flesh and blood (that is, his true human life); and that the Holy
Spirit is the channel through which the event is realized.[24]

What Nevin added in this exposition that is not to be found
in *The Mystical Presence* is an interpretation of the spatial
imagery Calvin uses in his eucharistic theology. Calvin speaks
of Christ's being in heaven as in a place. "What he [Calvin]
means in fact is *sufficiently* plain," Nevin claims. Calvin means
by heaven a higher sphere, and thus the language does not refer
to the sphere of matter and sense. As Nevin explains:

> Neither ascent or descent here are to be taken in any
> outward or local sense; they serve merely to express
> metaphorically the relation of the two orders of spheres of
> existence, which are brought into opposition and contrast.
> The whole *modus* of the sacramental mystery transcends the
> category of space; it belongs to heaven, as a higher order
> of life; but this detracts nothing from its reality or power.
> On the contrary, it is all the more real for this very
> reason.[25]

The "realness" of sacramental life and its importance to proper
Christian worship and life is the point of Nevin's two major
eucharistic treatises. Moreover, he has staked his position on the
Lord's Supper on a eucharistic theology "which he claimed to
find in none other than John Calvin."[26]

The issues that would become standard for scholars of
Calvin's eucharistic thought emerge from Nevin's work.
Scholars after Nevin have had to deal with such concepts as: the
union of the believer with Christ, and how that union is exempli-
fied in the Lord's Supper; whether or not what happens in the
Supper is a special type of union not to be found outside the
celebration of the Eucharist, in other words, the problem of
whether or not there is a specific and special eucharistic gift; the
issue of real presence and participation in the body and blood of
Christ, which relates directly to the problem of objectivity in
Calvin's eucharistic system; the agency of the Holy Spirit in the
Supper and the whole problem of instrumentality in Calvin's
eucharistic teaching; and the spatial imagery Calvin uses in
speaking of the ascended Christ. These emphases in Nevin's

interpretation of Calvin's eucharistic teaching have become part and parcel of Calvin scholarship.

However, the methodological assumptions Nevin made as he studied Calvin's eucharistic teaching have also become part and parcel of Calvin scholarship. One of those assumptions is that Calvin's eucharistic doctrine did not develop over the course of his career. As Nevin states it, "Calvin has written much on the Lord's Supper; and he is always clear, always consistent, always true to himself."[27] More explicitly, in denying any possible development in Calvin's thought, Nevin claims:

> Calvin published the first edition of his *Institutes* in 1536, in the twenty-seventh year of his age, and before he had come into connection with either the Lutheran or Helvetic system of thinking. Here we find very distinctly stated the sacramental doctrine that he contrived to hold to the end of his life.[28]

Such a lack of historical treatment of Calvin's writings on the Eucharist leads to a related problem: the misreading of documents based on mistaken assumptions about both Calvin's development and his power to influence documents that were meant as corporate confessions of faith. One sees this misreading particularly in Nevin's treatment of the *Consensus Tigurinus*. Note the panegyrical lines of Nevin as he speaks of the articles of the *Consensus* and their relation to Calvin: "On the contrary, they show the triumph of Calvinism over what was still defective in the old Swiss view. . . . It is Bullinger who rises above his old position."[29] If Calvin is not, in fact, the author of the twenty-six articles of agreement, according to Nevin, "It turns Calvin into either a fool or a knave."[30] Calvin is turned into the author of a document that is, in fact, uncalvinistic in regard to several important elements of eucharistic meaning.[31] The articles receive a somewhat forced interpretation that pushes them into the accepted mold of the 1559 *Institutes*. As shall be shown in the next chapter, many scholars have trodden this path of inherited error. Thus, Nevin's work is instructive because it sets the stage for the conceptual issues and the methodological problems faced by interpreters of Calvin's eucharistic theology.

J. H. A. Ebrard

Another important work produced by a nineteenth-century scholar on Calvin's eucharistic thought was J. H. A. Ebrard's *Das Dogma vom heilige Abendmahl und seine Geschichte.*[32] While making worthwhile contributions to the study of Calvin's eucharistic thought, this two-volume work also helped solidify the type of methodological error exhibited by Nevin's scholarship.

Since Ebrard's book deals with the entire history of eucharistic dogma, only a portion of the second volume is devoted to Calvin.[33] Yet, one gets the sense that everything before this section is a lead-in to Calvin. In the introduction to Calvin's position, there is a one and one-half page build up to Calvin's very name.[34] The encomium finally ends on a note that brings Calvin into the picture: "the man in himself who executed the process of crystallization of the evangelical teaching [on the Eucharist] was Calvin."[35]

The lines of problematic interpretation that emerged in Nevin become more focused in Ebrard. Ebrard allowed for no influence on Calvin's thought. In defending the independence of Calvin's eucharistic teaching, Ebrard's work vigorously denies that Calvin is in any way a product of Zwingli or Luther, but rather asserts that Calvin "is the product of himself."[36] It baldly denies that Calvin could have received any intellectual influence of substance from either Bucer or Melanchthon.[37] This view of Calvin's independence is tied directly to Ebrard's view of Calvin's unchangability on matters of doctrine. In speaking of Calvin's denial of a substantial reception of Christ's body in the 1536 *Institutes*, the reader is assured by Ebrard that this passage does not contradict later statements by Calvin on the substantial reception of the true body of Christ in the Eucharist. Instead,

Ebrard asserted that Calvin was simply denying the scholastic meaning of substance.[38] That may be so, but a constructive statement by Calvin on what constitutes a proper understanding of substantial reception is totally lacking. So, later meaning is read back into earlier works.

Therefore, based on this view of Calvin's character and intellect, documents are misread. As with Nevin, Ebrard saw the *Consensus Tigurinus* as a complete victory for Calvin.[39] If anything, Ebrard's work states this victory in even stronger terms than Nevin. The book speaks of Bullinger's position in relation to Calvin in these terms: "Everything depended on whether the lesser dealt with humility and self-knowledge well enough to submit itself to the greater. However, that is the greatness of Bullinger, that he did not lack this humility."[40] Ebrard went on to state that the *Consensus* was a full, glorious, public victory of Calvinism over Zwinglianism.[41] This statement misrepresents the actual coming together of the *Consensus Tigurinus* and certainly is no longer recognized as an appropriate way to view the relationship between Calvin and Bullinger. Yet, this view has influenced much of the Calvin scholarship since Ebrard.[42]

One can conclude that in Ebrard one finds firmly entrenched the lines of interpretation that lead to a misreading of Calvin's eucharistic teaching. Amends have been made in the interpretation of Calvin and his proper relationship to the *Consensus Tigurinus* in the most recent scholarship. However, many of the underlying assumptions that led Ebrard to a misreading on this specific matter are still held.

Herman Bavinck

Herman Bavinck's 1887 essay, "Calvijn's Leer over het Avondmaal,"[43] accentuates the methodological problems found in Nevin and Ebrard. Bavinck maintains that Calvin's position on eucharistic doctrine remained unchanged from the 1536 *Institutes* to his last utterances in 1564.[44] He obviously sees the 1559 *Institutes*, Book 4, Chapter 17 as the definitive expression of Calvin's eucharistic teaching. He reads all the earlier eucharistic material through that lens, rather than the other way; that is, reading the '59 *Institutes* as a development based on earlier works and conflicts. As he reminds the reader, the view that Christ is present in the Supper truly and in reality in body and blood is "already" present in the '36 *Institutes*.[45] Thus, seeing no change between 1536 and 1559, Bavinck is able to treat all the eucharistic writings as one piece, including the *Consensus Tigurinus*.

The problem inherent in Bavinck's work that was less noticeable in Nevin and Ebrard is his concentration on the eucharistic concepts apart from the rest of Calvin's theology. His concentration on one chapter in the *Institutes* and on only the eucharistic treatises has the effect of assuming foundations for Calvin's eucharistic teaching that are not made explicit in the eucharistic writings. Those foundations often have their theological support in other parts of Calvin's writings. For instance, the important concepts of instrumentality, accommodation, and the work of the Spirit are assumed as part of the eucharistic formulations when in fact those concepts are worked out in detail in other places and applied to the eucharistic concepts. These concepts, as foundational elements of Calvin's statements in the 1559 *Institutes* on the Lord's Supper, are then read back into the earlier material. One can argue, despite some degree of continuity and similarity of language used in eucharistic doctrine in the 1536 *Institutes*, that that doctrine is not the same as found in the 1559 edition of Calvin's theological *summa*. The concepts of accommodation and instrumentality are practically absent, and no doctrine of the action of the Holy Spirit is presented at all in '36. Without these elements, the foundations of Calvin's mature eucharistic theology are nonexistent. Thus, simply to compare passages where the language of the two editions appears the same is to misread to a degree the documents.

Conclusion

The scholarly literature of the twentieth century on Calvin and the Eucharist has shown a marked tendency to pass on the inherited errors exemplified in the three nineteenth-century scholars that have been examined. The ways modern scholarship appropriates the tradition of inherited error will be laid bare as the *Consensus Tigurinus* is examined.

Notes

1. John Williamson Nevin, *The Mystical Presence: A Vindication of the Reformed or Calvinistic Doctrine of the Holy Eucharist* (Philadelphia: J. B. Lippincott and Company, 1846; repr. ed., Hamden, Conn.: Archon Books, 1963). *The Mystical Presence* also saw reissue in the volume *The Mystical Presence and other Writings on the Eucharist*, edited by Bard Thompson and George H. Bricker, vol. 4 of the Lancaster Series on the Mercersburg Theology (Philadelphia and Boston: United Church Press, 1966). References made are to the Archon Books edition.

2. John Williamson Nevin, "Doctrine of the Reformed Church on the Lord's Supper," *Mercersburg Review* 2, no. 5 (September 1850). Quoted here from *The Mystical Presence and other Writings on the Eucharist*, pp. 267–401.

3. Brian A. Gerrish, "The Flesh of the Son of Man: John W. Nevin on the Church and the Eucharist," in *Tradition in the Modern World* (Chicago: University of Chicago Press, 1978), pp. 55–56. Nevin credits August Neander as his guide into the field of church history and with showing him its importance.

4. See, for example, an imaginary dialogue Nevin has invented where he has Calvin say, "My views now are just what they were clearly stated to be twenty years ago, in the first edition of my *Institutes*." Nevin, "Doctrine of the Reformed Church on the Lord's Supper," p. 355.

5. Nevin, *The Mystical Presence*, p. 51.

6. Ibid., p. 55. Moreover, this communion between Christ and his people, this mystical union, is intimately tied to the Eucharist in Calvin's thought. As Lewis Smedes suggests, "The significance of the sacrament corresponds to the importance of the idea of mystical union. If the latter is indispensable to Christian life, so is the former." Smedes, "Calvin and the Lord's Supper," *The Reformed Journal* 4, no. 7 (July–August 1954): 4.

7. Nevin, *The Mystical Presence*, pp. 55–57.

8. Ibid., p. 58.

9. Ibid.

10. Ibid., p. 61.

11. Ibid.

12. Ibid.

13. The title of the first chapter of the work.

14. Nevin, *The Mystical Presence*, p. 118. Thus, Gerrish says of Nevin, "He clung tenaciously to the notion that something happens in the Lord's Supper which occurs nowhere else." Gerrish, "The Flesh of the Son of Man," p. 63.

15. Nevin, *The Mystical Presence*, p. 118.

16. Ibid., p. 120.

17. Ibid., p. 122.

18. Ibid., p. 137.

19. Ibid., p. 247.

20. Gerrish, "The Flesh of the Son of Man," p. 52.

21. Charles Hodge, "Doctrine of the Reformed Church on the Lord's Supper," *Princeton Review* 20 (April 1848): 227, 275–77, 278, 259 n.

22. James H. Nichols, "The Reformed Doctrine of the Lord's Supper Recovered," in *Romanticism in American Theology: Nevin and Schaff at Mercersburg* (Chicago: University of Chicago Press, 1961), p. 89.

23. Nevin, "Doctrine of the Reformed Church on the Lord's Supper," p. 267.

24. Ibid., pp. 270–71, 276.

25. Ibid., pp. 351–52.

26. Gerrish, "The Flesh of the Son of Man," p. 52.

27. Nevin, *The Mystical Presence*, p. 68.

28. Nevin, "Doctrine of the Reformed Church on the Lord's Supper," p. 315.

29. Ibid.

30. Ibid., p. 325.

31. A claim to be documented in Chapter II.

32. Johann Heinrich August Ebrard, *Das Dogma vom heilige Abendmahl und seine Geschichte*, 2 vols. (Frankfurt: Heinrich Zimmer Verlag, 1845-46).

33. Ebrard, *Das Dogma vom Heiligen Abendmahl*, vol. 2, chapter 5, sections 36-38, and chapter 6, section 39.

34. Ebrard, *Das Dogma vom Heiligen Abendmahl*, 2:403-4.

35. ". . . der Mann, in welchem sich der Krystallisationsprocess der evang. Lehre vollzog—war Calvin." Ibid., p. 404.

36. ". . . er ist das Produkt seiner selbst." Ibid., p. 409.

37. Ibid., p. 464.

38. Ibid., p. 430.

39. Ibid., p. 487.

40. "Darauf kam alles an, ob der kleinere Demuth und Selbst-kenntniss genug befass, um dem Groesseren sich unterzuordnen. Aber das ist das Groesste an Bullinger, dass ihm diese Demuth nicht mangelte." Ibid.

41. The *Consensus Tigurinus* is "ein voller, ehrlicher, offener und auf die reinst Art erfochtener Sieg des Calvinismus über der Zwinglianismus vorliege." Ibid., p. 520.

42. Both of these claims will be documented in Chapter II.

43. Herman Bavinck, "Calvijn's Leer over het Avondmaal," *Vrije Kerk* 13 (1887): 459-86; also found in the author's *Kennis in leven: opstellen en artikelen uit vroegere jaren* (Kampen: Kok, 1922).

44. Thus, one reads sentences that start, "Already he testifies in the first edition of the *Institutes* of 1536 that. . . ." ("Reeds in de eerste uitgave der Institutie van 1536 zegt hij, dat. . . ." Ibid., passim.) Bavinck will start a section with this phrase, and then go on to make undifferentiated use of a variety of Calvin's writings dating from 1536 to 1564.

45. "Already in the first edition of the Institutes of 1536 he [Calvin] testifies that the body and blood of Christ is truly and really communicated to us, but never in a natural manner." ("Reeds in de eerste uitgave der Institutie van 1536 zegt hij, dat het lichaam en bloed van Christus in het avondmaal ons waarlijk en werkzaam, maar niet op natuurlijke wijze wordt medegedeeld.") Bavinck, "Calvijn's leer over het Avondmaal," p. 464. Chapter III will show that this assertion does not bear up under close examination of the 1536 *Institutes*.

II

The *Consensus Tigurinus*[1] and the
Task of Interpretation

In late May of 1549, John Calvin and William Farel traveled through the Swiss countryside from Geneva to Zurich. Once there, they met with Heinrich Bullinger and other representatives of the Zurich church to discuss and sign a doctrinal agreement on the Eucharist. The Reformed churches of Zurich and Geneva were united in eucharistic concord that day in May.[2] Soon, representatives of the other Reformed churches of Switzerland[3] joined their voices of consent to the Agreement of Zurich, termed in Latin the *Consensus Tigurinus*.[4] Years of work and months of intensive negotiations in 1548/49 preceded Calvin's agreement with Bullinger. He signed a eucharistic formula that he believed would unite the Protestant churches in eucharistic concord. Calvin's optimism was short-lived. The Reformed churches of Switzerland did accept the *Consensus* as the basis for doctrinal agreement on the Lord's Supper. However, the document was soon attacked by a group of Lutherans. They viewed the *Consensus* as proof of Calvin's hidden stripes; namely, those of Zwingli's colors. What Calvin had hoped would become a document of union became, as far as the Gnesiolutherans[5] were concerned, an occasion for disunity. Calvin's hopes for eucharistic harmony were dashed on the rocks of reality, and the *Consensus Tigurinus* became the focus of the second "Eucharistic War" of the sixteenth century, a battle fought between Calvin and the representatives of the Gnesio-lutherans.

There was good reason for the Lutherans to be upset with Calvin. The *Consensus Tigurinus* does not, in fact, correspond to some of the things Calvin had written on the Eucharist in previous works. The Lutherans thought Calvin was trying to trick them, or at least playing both ends against the middle. Calvin was incensed that anyone would accuse him of changing his mind or displaying false colors in regard to so important a topic as the Eucharist. Thus, he loudly proclaimed that his doctrine on the Supper as it stood in the *Consensus* was what it had always been.[6]

Yet, the *Consensus* does not fully represent Calvin's views on the Lord's Supper. Rather than being a victory for Calvin, the *Consensus Tigurinus* appears to be the extent to which Calvin was willing to bend his eucharistic opinions in favor of peace among the churches of Switzerland. In fact, Bullinger's influence may overshadow Calvin's to some degree in the actual wording of the articles of the *Consensus*. Thus, it might be proper to think of the agreement as more Bullingerian than Calvinist. The least one can say is that the *Consensus Tigurinus* has the quality of a theological "patchwork" that represented the concerns of all parties at least to the extent that all could agree to sign the document. The fact that later in 1549 (August) Calvin convinced Bullinger to insert two additional propositions so that the *Consensus* consisted of twenty-six articles rather than the original twenty-four shows Calvin's uneasiness with the *Consensus* as it originally stood.

The publication of the Agreement of Zurich in 1551 brought forth attacks, and Calvin felt it imperative that he add to the articles of agreement a short history and an exposition of them. Calvin finished this *Defence of the Sane and Orthodox Doctrine of the Sacraments* probably in November of 1554, and the work was published along with the twenty-six articles of agreement in 1555.[7] The importance of this exposition has been overlooked. Calvin obviously needed to explain his signature on the Agreement. The way he accomplished this explanation was to interpret the articles so they more closely represented his true views on the sacrament. What is available to us, then, is an attempt by Calvin to interpret the *Consensus* on his own terms. There are clues to the development of Calvin's eucharistic thought in this treatise, for it is here that Calvin seeks to correct the Agreement and bring it in line with his previous work. Part of what is involved in this process for Calvin is his emphasizing what he thinks are the important issues and concepts in his teaching on the Eucharist. He renders an interpretation of his earlier work and the *Consensus* so that they appear consistent. However, the same concepts and concerns that he brings forward can be used to read Calvin's works on the Eucharist with an eye toward development and change. In the following pages, I will highlight the history of interpretation of Calvin and the *Consensus Tigurinus*. I will then provide an analysis of the Agreement based on Calvin's first exposition of it. Then, I will present my own exegesis of the document. Finally, I will cull from that analysis the types of questions one may fruitfully ask of Calvin's eucharistic teaching that best elicit evidence of the developmental nature of his work.

History of Interpretation

Chapter I indicated the extent of the nineteenth-century claims that the *Consensus Tigurinus* represented Calvin's victory over Zwinglianism. These claims included accepting the eucharistic doctrine of the *Consensus Tigurinus* as representative of Calvin's eucharistic teaching. Several examples will serve to show the extent to which Calvin scholars in this century have accepted the inherited error of nineteenth-century Calvin scholarship on the Eucharist. For all practical purposes, they view Calvin's relationship to the *Consensus Tigurinus* as that of author.

Hans Grass, a Lutheran, published a book in 1954 that carried the title *Die Abendmahlslehre bei Luther und Calvin*.[8] In his treatment of the *Consensus*, he admits that some scholars were beginning to assert that the Agreement did not fully represent Calvin's point of view.[9] However, Grass argues that the general Calvinistic orientation of the document can be accepted. He asserts that Calvin shared many of Bullinger's viewpoints. Moreover, Grass points out that it was Calvin who pushed for the settlement of the *Consensus*. He also emphasizes that the twenty-six articles of the Agreement were based on the twenty articles Calvin presented to the Bern Synod in March of 1549. Finally, he reminds his readers that Calvin defended the *Consensus* throughout his career.[10] Thus, Grass is able to state, "[Calvin] is himself the chief author of the Consensus Tigurinus."[11] Grass makes it clear that he thinks Calvin responsible for the *Consensus*. While it may not fully represent Calvin's point of view, Grass believes the *Consensus* carries enough of Calvin's imprint to be considered Calvinistic.

To Calvin's left in the Reformation were those who stood in the Zwinglian tradition, led after Zwingli's death in 1531 by Heinrich Bullinger. Yet, even within the historical scholarship of those who trace their confessional roots to the Zurich expression of the Reformed faith, there is never a hint that the *Consensus* does not adequately serve as a true expression of Calvin's eucharistic teaching. André Bouvier, a twentieth-century biographer of Bullinger, claims much for the *Consensus Tigurinus*. While the Calvinist and Lutheran scholars have viewed the agreement as Calvin's victory, thus making it Calvin's document, Bouvier takes a different approach. He sees the *Consensus Tigurinus* as a "truly ecumenical" document, making talk of winners and losers in the process of its coming together inappropriate.[12] He claims that the document is the result of "a veritable interpenetration of ideas . . . a reciprocal fruitfulness of conceptions."[13] This assertion interprets the document as both Calvinistic and Bullingerian,[14] while rising somewhat above both positions. Calvin is made a willing and fully-involved collaborator in the process of the formulation of the *Consensus Tigurinus*. To make the claim that the document does not truly bear

Calvin's imprint, much less to make the claim that one can read it as antithetical to Calvin's views on the Eucharist, is to destroy the foundations for calling it a truly ecumenical document. Thus, some who follow the confessional tradition of Zurich have been inclined not to explore the *Consensus* in terms of its basic discontinuities with Calvin's prior and subsequent eucharistic teachings.

Such an attitude has its roots in Calvin and his successors at Geneva. We have noted how Calvin wanted to claim the *Consensus* as a true expression of his eucharistic teaching, all the while giving it an interpretation that strengthened or even added elements that he felt more clearly represented his point of view. After his death, it fell to his successor, Theodore Beza,[15] to try to hold together the Swiss churches in eucharistic concord. Unity depended on continued acceptance of the *Consensus Tigurinus*. Thus, in his biography of Calvin, Beza introduces the *Consensus* by claiming that it "knit Calvin and Bullinger, Geneva and Zurich, in the closest of ties."[16] However, as will be demonstrated, if one is going to use "needlework" images, the best one can say of the Agreement of Zurich is that it represents a sort of "theological patchwork" wherein the big patches are cut from the fabric of Calvin's and Bullinger's theologies. Furthermore, there may be more Bullinger patches than Calvin patches, and the pattern of the quilt is certainly that designed by Bullinger rather than Calvin.

It may be this very "patchwork" quality, with its jarring juxtapositions of different theologies, that led in the nineteenth century to a change of images for describing Calvin's role in the coming together of the *Consensus* from that of needlework (and cooperation) to that of conquest (Calvin as victor).[17] Three examples will illustrate the pervasiveness of this trend as it continued in twentieth-century Calvin scholarship: Emile Doumergue of France, Alexander Barclay of Scotland, and Wilhelm Niesel of Germany.

Doumergue's biographical work on Calvin, for all its hagiographical aspects, remains a standard work for the study of Calvin. The work is important not just because it still has a grasp of the details of Calvin's life and environment not found elsewhere but because of its attitude toward Calvin that typifies well the attitude twentieth-century Reformed scholars have held toward Calvin. The *Consensus Tigurinus* is, for Doumergue, Calvin's document. The force of this conviction is well-expressed by Doumergue's section on the sacraments in Calvin's thought. What should not surprise us is that Calvin is given such complete credit for the Agreement of Zurich. Doumergue says, "First of all, Calvin pursued and realized the union between the Calvinists and the Zwinglians by the *Consensus Tigurinus*, the Agreement of Zurich, in 1549."[18] What is surprising is that, even given the fact that the *Consensus* is not dealt with at length in this section of Doumergue's work, Bullinger's name is not even mentioned! In the next volume, the events surrounding the *Consensus* are more fully drawn out, so that Bullinger is well-represented in the discussion. However, the argument does not change: the glory, the victory, and the credit go to Calvin.[19]

Neither is it surprising that Alexander Barclay's book presents Calvin as "the winner" of the *Consensus*. As scholars have noted,[20] Barclay relied on both Nevin and Ebrard quite heavily as source books for his own work. Therefore, the problem of inherited error is particularly clear in Barclay. He holds that Calvin won at the meeting with Bullinger in May 1549. He goes beyond Nevin, moreover, in that he spends considerably more energy interpreting the trickier passages of the *Consensus*; that is, those passages that are most at odds with Calvin's own view on the Eucharist. Borrowing from Nevin's store of organic images, Barclay declares, "The so-called 'Zwinglianism' of Zurich recognized Calvinism as its higher and natural development."[21] He completes this thought in encomiastic terms: "Calvin's thought and sincerity awoke the slumbering seed, and brought the Zurichers to recognize that his doctrine was not the negation, but rather the full unfolding of their own incomplete and one-sided teaching."[22] Thus, despite the fact that certain articles are so uncalvinistic that he has to force consistent interpretation,[23] Barclay considers the *Consensus* a thoroughgoing victory for Calvin. "As regards the supposed points of difference with Bullinger, Calvin did not yield an iota."[24]

Three years after Barclay's book, a dissertation was published that launched the career of one of the century's great Calvin scholars, Wilhelm Niesel.[25] The work analyzes the 1559 edition of Calvin's *Institutes* as the last answer to the attacks of Joachim Westphal.[26] Niesel does not limit his work to the last edition of Calvin's *Institutes*, but he does read the significance of all Calvin's earlier works on the Eucharist in light of the 1559 edition. Niesel deals with the other answers to Westphal, but always from the angle of Calvin's last response. What Niesel does not take seriously is Westphal's attack on the *Consensus* and Westphal's (inconsistent) claim that the work is at odds with Calvin's previous teaching.

Niesel does not speak of Calvin as victor in the way Barclay had. He recognizes the ambiguous quality of the *Consensus* as an expression of Calvin's eucharistic teaching. However, neither does he acknowledge Bullinger's influence in regard to the *Consensus* or the uncalvinistic character of the work. In other words, Niesel may not proclaim Calvin as "winner" but neither is he proclaimed "loser." Thus, Niesel does not recognize either the possibility of influence on Calvin or the essential problematic involved in the *Consensus* and the required interpretation Calvin had to give it if Westphal was to be refuted. Instead, Niesel makes several observations.

First, he speaks of "limits" to which Calvin was willing to go in order to maintain eucharistic concord. Niesel views Calvin's relationship to the *Consensus* as similar to Calvin's relationship to the *Augsburg Confession*. He claims, "As Calvin had met the Lutherans halfway, going to the furthermost limit of possibility, in that he signed the Augustana, so he went then to the other side again up to the furthermost limit, in that he professed the *Consensus Tigurinus*."[27] Of course, the parallel is not exact. Calvin's authorship was associated with the *Consensus Tigurinus*, whereas he simply confessed the *Augsburg Confession*, with the proviso that it be interpreted according to the wishes of its author, Philip Melanchthon. Or, if one wants to make a case for the parallel, does that then mean one should read the *Consensus* according to the interpretation of its author? But who is the author? At this point, it becomes clear that, for

Niesel, Calvin is the author and has the *right* to interpret the meaning of the document. Therefore, even in this case where Niesel does not use the "victor" language, the resulting interpretation is that of Calvin as, if not victor, at least rightful interpreter. Niesel makes the above observation to get Calvin off the hook, so to speak, for a misrepresentative agreement, while still claiming its essential character as a Calvinistic document as interpreted by Calvin himself. However, the document and the interpretation are two different things and should be so treated. Niesel treats them as one and the same. He reads for continuity between Calvin's interpretation of the *Consensus* and the document itself. He is able, thus, to dismiss Westphal's claims.

Niesel's second observation is that Calvin's involvement with the *Consensus* was possible only because the Zurich teaching developed beyond its foundation in the early works of Zwingli.[28] Yet, the question arises, in what direction had the development taken place, and under whose influence? Here again, the assumption is that Calvin's influence was of primary importance. There is the hint that Zurich had moved sufficiently toward Calvin's position to make the document representative of his thought. Thus, Bullinger's role in the development of a eucharistic doctrine that moves beyond Zwingli while not becoming Calvinistic is ignored. Implicit in the observation Niesel makes is Calvin's victorious influence.

Therefore, one can see in these examples from twentieth-century scholarship the propagation of inherited error from its origins in the Calvin scholarship of the nineteenth century. Whether explicitly or implicitly, there is the attempt to bring Calvin and the *Consensus Tigurinus* into line with one another, to make Calvin author, victor, and rightful interpreter of the Agreement. Such attempts have at their roots the static reading of Calvin's theology.

However, several works in recent years recognize in a much more pointed way the discontinuity between Calvin's developed thought in 1559 and the statements made in the Agreement of Zurich. For example, in 1950, François Wendel published *Calvin, sources et évolution de sa pensée religieuse*.[29] Herein lies one of the first avowals that the *Consensus* does not represent Calvin, nor is it in any way to be seen as a victory for Calvin. The claim is, however, rather cryptic. Wendel presents no analysis or interpretation. He treats the Agreement in a short paragraph and concludes, "it is unsafe to take the *Consensus Tigurinus* . . . as a basis for an objective study of the real Calvinist teaching."[30] Niesel had said as much, though his interpretation led to a subtle reading of the circumstances that made such an assertion less problematic for the Calvin scholar. Wendel's statement stands without comment or interpretation. Thus, it has been left for others to pick up this thread of thought and provide either an explanation or an analysis of the *Consensus*.

Ulrich Gäbler has provided an essentially political and functional explanation. Part of his argument is that the Bern Articles of March 1549, which share propositions with the points of agreement of the *Consensus*,[31] were written by Calvin and sent to the Synod of Bern in order to strike an agreement with the more moderate Zwinglians in Zurich over against the more radical Zwinglians of Bern (and even Geneva).[32] Gäbler thinks Calvin could have sent the articles to Bern in order to gain the sympathy of the Zurichers in matters eucharistic. Such sympathy, coming from the very home of Zwingli himself, could be used by Calvin to repress the Bernese expression of Zwinglianism. Did Calvin accomplish his task, if that was indeed the task he had set for himself?

The *Consensus Tigurinus* did not result in the repression of extreme Zwinglianism, in Bern or elsewhere, at least not immediately. The more immediate function of the coming together of the *Consensus* lay in how the Swiss viewed Calvin after the document's successful culmination. The Agreement of Zurich functioned to rid the Zurichers and the other Swiss of their mistrust of Calvin.[33] Over the long run, the *Consensus* may have served to suppress the more radical forms of Zwinglianism. It allowed Calvin into the fold of the Swiss churches so that his ideas and influence could effectively and positively operate in the Swiss theological climate. There can be no question, however, of theological synthesis between Calvin and Bullinger, especially not on the basis of the *Consensus*. There remained too many deeply grounded differences between the two.

One can point to a recent essay as an example of the current trend to view the *Consensus Tigurinus* as a compromise rather than a Calvinistic document: Paul Rorem's extensive two-part article, "Calvin and Bullinger on the Lord's Supper." Rorem begins the article by providing an overview of the eucharistic theologies of Calvin and Bullinger. In the introduction, Rorem states that "Calvin's own views of the Lord's Supper were clarified and developed through dialogue, especially with his fellow Swiss pastors and with the German Lutherans who became his opponents."[34] However, Rorem actually does little to chart the development or give any indication as to what he means by such development. In his section on Calvin's theology, he emphasizes those aspects of Calvin's thought that he considers relatively static over the course of the reformer's career.

> The two positions of this 1541 *Short Treatise*—in favor of a full sacramental communion with Christ's body and blood and yet against their local or corporeal presence—characterized Calvin's sacramental theology for the rest of his career. Calvin also knew that these positions seemed incompatible. His complicated resolution of this apparent dilemma is also previewed in his treatise, although only in passing, namely, the liturgical words, *sursum corda*: "lift up your hearts."[35]

After recognizing the possibility of development in Calvin's eucharistic thought, Rorem stresses the continuities in Calvin's doctrine. Moreover, his use of sources indicates the same propensity to read Calvin's works all of the same fabric, using the 1559 *Institutes* as the lens. In his short section on Calvin's teaching, Rorem depends by and large on two sources: Calvin's 1541 *Short Treatise* and Book 4, Chapter 17 of the 1559 *Institutes*. He refers to other sources but always within the context and with reference to these two main sources.[36] He does not deal at all with the 1536 or 1539 editions of the *Institutes*.

Moreover, Rorem ignores material crucial to the theological development of Calvin's ideas on instrumentality and accommodation: the 1540 commentary on the book of Romans.

However, Rorem's point is not to chart the development he mentions in passing but to try to establish a tenet of Calvin's eucharistic doctrine that best demonstrates the point of conflict between Calvin and Bullinger. That point, for Rorem, is Calvin's view of the sacrament as an instrument of grace. During negotiations with Bullinger, Calvin affirms that "the sacrament [is] a means of full communion with Christ's body and blood over against the Zwinglian separation of sacramental sign and reality."[37] By the time of the *Consensus Tigurinus*, Calvin does have in place a view of the sacrament as an instrument. However, it is a view that developed from an earlier perspective that asserted that the sacrament could not serve as an instrument.[38] Thus, Calvin needs to interpret not only the *Consensus* in defence of his signature on it, but he also needs to interpret some of his earlier works on the Eucharist. Still, the first step toward a new interpretation of Calvin's eucharistic teaching depends on a recognition that the *Consensus* is not a fully Calvinistic document, and that is the point Rorem makes so well.

Rorem moves from his section on Calvin to a segment on Bullinger's eucharistic theology to the first substantive dialogue between Calvin and Bullinger, which appears futile. Rorem sketches the process by which Calvin and Bullinger finally are committed to making an agreement, and so he comes to the event of the Zurich Agreement itself. After an analysis of the *Consensus*, he makes some observations in his conclusion that are particularly pertinent to this project.

First, Rorem has clearly laid out evidence that enables him to stand against a sizable tradition of scholarship and declare, "In this light, the *Consensus Tigurinus* can hardly be called Calvin's clear victory in the sixteenth-century Reformed debate over the Lord's Supper, whether over Zwingli's lingering influence or over Bullinger's own substantial position."[39] Therefore, the "Calvin as victor" image in relation to the *Consensus* must be laid to rest.

Second, Rorem moves beyond those who admit the *Consensus* does not represent Calvin's full view on the Eucharist (Niesel) but who still hold that it is not a doctrinal loss for Calvin. He also corrects the opinion that the Agreement symbolizes some kind of closely knit interpenetration of ideas (Bouvier, Beza). Rorem does allow that certain articles can be read as "a finely balanced dialectic between Calvin's concern for the sacraments as God's means or instruments for conferring grace . . . and Bullinger's concern to counteract any transfer of God's saving activity to the saving realm."[40] However, the balancing act may be overbalanced when the absence of several key concepts in Calvin's eucharistic thought of this and later times is considered: there is no reference to the function of the eucharistic action as exhibiting and giving what is signified; the Eucharist is never referred to by the word *instrumentum*; and the Supper is never expressly viewed as an act through which God confers grace.[41] Rorem concludes that the lack of these key expressions of Calvin's may "indicate the extent of Bullinger's success"[42] in terms of the actual wording of the *Consensus*. The Agreement of Zurich became a reality because of Calvin's willingness to omit formulations objectionable to Bullinger.

Third, Rorem appreciates the significance of Calvin's almost immediate interpretation of the wording of the *Consensus* so that it conforms more to his full eucharistic beliefs. Rorem points out that Calvin himself "viewed the May colloquy in Zurich as a compromise by omission on his part."[43] Calvin added a forward, an afterward, and two articles to the *Consensus* almost immediately after its signing. The two new articles stood, but the Zurichers insisted on a new preface.

Calvin agreed to draw up a letter to replace what he had first written. However, the task of interpretation had begun, and Calvin is burdened with the onus of explaining his intentions regarding the *Consensus* for the rest of his life. Rorem notes the need for this interpretation, but he does not pursue its real significance. Neither does he explore how it can be used to construe the development of Calvin's eucharistic doctrine over the course of his career.[44]

Thus, Rorem has laid some of the groundwork; however, the need remains to analyze the *Consensus* as an uncalvinistic document. That analysis will show that Calvin's explanation of the *Consensus* is truly *interpretation* and not simply repetition or clarification. The analysis can then serve as the hermeneutical device to scrutinize the whole of Calvin's eucharistic corpus and its course of development.

Calvin's Interpretation of the Agreement

The *Consensus Tigurinus*, as it originally stood, contained twenty-four articles, not twenty-six. The Agreement signed in May 1549 did not include Articles 5 or 23. Both contain emphases that become "classic" Calvin by Calvin's full treatment of them in the 1559 *Institutes*. Article 5 states:

> How Christ communicates himself to us. Moreover, that Christ may thus exhibit himself to us and produce these effects in us, he must be made one with us, and we must be ingrafted into his body. He does not infuse his life into us unless he is our head, and from him the whole body, fitly joined together through every joint of supply, according to his working, maketh increase of the body in the proportion of each member.[45]

It is remarkable that this article is the only place in the *Consensus* where one of Calvin's favorite words to describe what it is the Eucharist does, *exhibere*,[46] appears. Moreover, this article speaks to Calvin's concept of union with Christ.[47] This union is the basis of Christian existence for Calvin and it is the Eucharist that figures it.

However, the union is not simply "spiritual," if one means by spiritual the union of the believer's spirit and mind with the spirit and mind of Christ. The union is spiritual in that the Holy Spirit serves as the channel by which Christ serves his people by nourishing them with his life-giving flesh. Thus, since Calvin has secured a place for the notions of *exhibere* and communion with Christ, he needs an article that spells out what it means for communion with Christ when the Eucharist exhibits the figure of eating and drinking Christ. Article 23 explains:

> When it is said that Christ, by our eating of his flesh and drinking of his blood, which are here figured, feeds our souls through faith by the agency of the Holy Spirit, we are not to understand it as if any mingling or transfusion of substance took place, but that we draw life from the flesh once offered in sacrifice and the blood shed in expiation.[48]

Communion with Christ is thus not simply a harmony of spirits or a mixing of substances. It is the state in which believers exist as they draw life from the flesh of Christ given on the cross.

Given the importance of these emphases in Calvin's thought, it is no wonder that he could not let the *Consensus* stand without attempting to insert these concerns. Calvin himself would have probably liked to have seen Article 23 placed earlier in the order of things, so that it would not appear to be a matter of secondary concern. Calvin's friend Bucer had misgivings over these omissions in the original document. In his response to one of Bucer's letters, Calvin explains:

> You wish piously and wisely, to explain more clearly and fully the effect of the Sacrament, and what the Lord bestows through it. Nor indeed was it owing to me that they were not fuller on some points. Let us bear therefore with a sigh what we cannot correct.[49]

Yet, Calvin seems to have been aware of the inevitability of the type of criticism Bucer offered, for he was already at work trying to correct the document so that the omission of many of his eucharistic opinions was not so obvious. Perhaps he had the type of criticism Bucer offered in mind when he proposed the new articles to Bullinger. Calvin writes on 6 July 1549 that "nothing is mentioned of the reality itself, especially since no word is said in the entire work about the eating of the flesh."[50]

A month later, Calvin emphasized the need for the new articles based on the apprehension that there would be those who charged him with the sin of theological omission.

> I am persuaded there will be no one among you who would not, of his own accord, desire my additions. And they are of special importance, lest some think we were rather artfully silent, and others justly desire what must necessarily be expressly stated.[51]

To the surprise of some (specifically Bucer), Bullinger and the church at Zurich accepted the two new articles. One reason for the acceptance might be that the articles were worded so that, particularly in the case of Article 23, they might be interpreted differently by the different parties. Another reason for the acceptance would surely be that in Article 23 it is clear that the signs figure the eating and drinking of Christ and are not the thing itself. But, more importantly, the give and take of the negotiations and the *need* for an agreement helped the mood of compromise to prevail. Perhaps the parties involved implicitly understood the trade-offs involved, so that the two new articles Calvin proposed were allowed to stand in the body of the *Consensus* because of Calvin's willingness to drop his original preface to the Agreement on the sacraments. There he had stated that the document "does not contain everything which could usefully and aptfully be said, and which otherwise perfectly fits their [the sacraments'] true understanding."[52] Therefore, from the beginning of the Agreement, as the original preface makes clear, Calvin held some of the same reservations Bucer held in regard to the *Consensus*.

In the public version of the *Consensus*, both as it was circulated to the churches of Switzerland in 1549 and 1550 and as it appeared in published form in 1551, Calvin's 1 August 1549 letter to the clergy of Zurich stood as the new preface to the document. Here (even before the Zurichers had agreed to allow Articles 5 and 23) Calvin declares, much more positively than the original preface, "That we [Geneva and Zurich] are agreed, we can indeed on both sides truly and faithfully declare."[53] Thus, it is obvious that Calvin is willing to bend in the spirit of compromise. However, such a ringing endorsement of the *Consensus* could lead one to take the Agreement, as one modern interpreter has, as "a compact expression of Calvin's sacramental theology."[54] That is exactly how Joachim Westphal took the document. Thus, as Philip Schaff once noted, the *Consensus Tigurinus* became the "innocent occasion of the second sacramental war."[55]

Westphal was a Lutheran pastor at St. Catherine's church in Hamburg. He ardently followed Luther's teachings and opposed the variety of modifications to Luther's theology that were introduced by Melanchthon. He particularly took offense at Article 24 of the *Consensus*, "Transubstantiation and other Follies," where Luther's position is referred to as one of the follies: "For we deem it no less absurd to place Christ under the bread or couple him with the bread, than to transubstantiate the bread into his body."[56]

Westphal responded to the "Zwinglian" agreement with a book entitled *Farrago of Confused and Divergent Opinions on the Lord's Supper Taken from the Books of the Sacramentarians* (1552).[57] A companion volume appeared in 1553 called *The Correct Belief in regard to the Lord's Supper Demonstrated and Secured in the Words of Paul the Apostle and the Evangelists.*[58]

When Calvin's attention (and the attention of all the Swiss churches) was called to the works of Westphal, there is an interesting reversal of attitudes. The Swiss, and Bullinger in particular, did not feel the immediate need to respond to Westphal.[59] Beza counseled caution, stating, "These calumnies are so stupid that they are not worth the trouble of a response."[60] Calvin wanted a reply written in the name of all the Swiss churches and subscribed to by all of them. Bullinger comes around (particularly after reading the second of Westphal's treatises) and agrees Westphal should be answered. Yet, it is Calvin who pushes the response; Calvin who takes it upon himself to draw up a response; Calvin who sends his response to Zurich for approval; and it is Calvin who sees to the publication of the defence, after incorporating some, but not all, of the suggestions of the ministers of Zurich. For the duration of this process, it is the Zurichers who call for moderation, who want to tone down the polemics, who want to see Calvin's blistering remarks excised from the response.[61] Given the history of Zurich-Lutheran relations and Calvin's personal history of ecumenical involvement, particularly his consciously mediating position on the Eucharist, the reversal of attitudes is astonishing.

Yet, maybe Calvin's attitude is not so astonishing. After all, Westphal accuses Calvin of the very thing he had tried to avoid; namely, appearing "artfully silent" on eucharistic matters he held but were not represented in the *Consensus*. Therefore, according to Westphal, Calvin is either a Zwinglian after all, or he is following in the footsteps of his friend Bucer. The Lutherans held the opinion that Bucer bent the real meaning of words so that there appeared to be agreement where there was none. Could it be that, despite the addition of Articles 5 and 23, the *Consensus* still was so far from what Calvin truly thought of the Eucharist that he heard the ring of Bucer's words of admonition in Westphal's sting? Did Articles 5 and 23 address adequately the real question of the clear and full effect of the Eucharist? What is it that Calvin felt he *had to* explain in terms of his eucharistic theology in light of his signature on the *Consensus Tigurinus*?

Calvin's initial response to Westphal serves as his justification for his ecumenical involvement with Zurich. Moreover, it provides an explication for what he considers important in eucharistic theology, despite his signature on the Agreement. Thus, Calvin begins the process of interpreting the *Consensus* that would continue, in some ways, for the rest of his life. In that process, Calvin refines his own thought and doctrine, reinterprets the *Consensus*, and tries to provide a framework through which he would like to see his life work on the Eucharist viewed. I now turn to the first piece of that framework, but not to prove continuity, as Calvin intended. Instead, I will use it as the clue to discontinuity, development, and growth in Calvin's eucharistic teaching.

Calvin's response carried the title *A Defence of the Sane and Orthodox Doctrine of the Sacraments and of Their Nature, Power, End, Use and Fruit.*[62] Here he begins his interpretation of the *Consensus* that, as Timothy George has stated so well, "must have made Bullinger wince."[63] Bullinger's own replies to Westphal must have been written as much to present Bullinger's own interpretation of the *Consensus* as to refute Westphal, which Calvin had already undertaken. One can read the tension between Calvin and Bullinger as Calvin explains his interpretation to Bullinger:

> I fear one thing, that you may judge sometimes more is conceded to them by me than is just. Yet, even this is done on purpose, so that if any still are opposed to us, more odious is their moroseness. However, the learned who have agreed with us, but whom I see to be less courageous than is fitting, may have a more favorable pretext.[64]

Despite the attempt to justify himself on the above grounds, it is clear that Calvin's main reason for writing was his desire to articulate fully what he considered essential to his eucharistic thought that was downplayed in the *Consensus*.

Calvin's *Defence* begins with a letter to the Swiss clergy, dated 28 November 1554. He is eager to establish that the charges that have been leveled against him, the Agreement, and the other Swiss churches are unwarranted. He recognizes the brevity of the *Consensus*. However, he thinks that, in charity, a good interpretation could be put on the Agreement by those who find it short on explanation. He says, "certainly we had inserted enough in that little summary to appease and satisfy all well disposed minds."[65] Calvin takes offense that he has been charged with "finesse and cunning."[66] The letter makes plain that Calvin intends to present a fuller, clearer explanation of what the *Consensus* means.[67] He inserts what was left out of the *Consensus* "due to brevity"!

The letter is followed by the twenty-six articles of the *Consensus* as it was published in 1551. The exposition of the twenty-six headings follows. Here again, as in the letter, Calvin makes a point to start by stating that the problem of interpretation is not inherent in the Agreement but in the uncharitable position of others. As he says:

We felt persuaded that by the publication of this testimony
satisfaction was given to moderate men, and we certainly
thought that no person would be so rigidly scrupulous as
not to rest appeased; for, as we shall afterwards see, it
contains a lucid definition of all the points which were
formerly debated, and leaves no room for any uncharitable
suspicion.[68]

Once again, as if to take away the sting of the accusation of
displaying false colors, Calvin proclaims "that there is scarcely
an individual who can take more pleasure than I do in a candid
confession of the truth."[69] Thus, Calvin's purpose in this work
is to show that "in this matter nothing has been stated by us
obscurely or enigmatically, nothing craftily concealed, in short,
nothing essentially omitted."[70]

What is it that Calvin has to show has not "been omitted"?
First, Calvin points the reader to the end of the Eucharist, its
purpose, which is "to bring us to communion with Christ."[71]
The sacrament serves as the "helps and means by which we are
either ingrafted into the body of Christ, or being ingrafted, are
drawn closer and closer, until he makes us altogether one with
himself in heavenly life."[72]   In relation to communion with
Christ, the Eucharist serves to assist the Christian's salvation by
being one of the ways the believer is "conducted to the very
fountain of life."[73] Therefore, far from considering the sacraments as merely external marks of profession[74] or as void and
empty figures, Calvin claims they are "seals of the divine
promises, testimonies of spiritual grace to cherish and confirm
faith, and . . . instruments by which God acts effectually in his
elect."[75] As an instrument of God, the Eucharist fosters and
increases faith and offers the promise of salvation. Indeed, it
serves as one way in which the Spirit of God effectually works.
"The true effect is conjoined with the external figure, so that
believers receive the body and blood of Christ."[76] Calvin even
says that, when the sacraments are conjoined with the gospel,
they confer "the same advantage upon us in the matter of
salvation. Hence it follows, that what Paul says of the gospel we
are at liberty to apply to them."[77] Calvin attests that there is

nothing one can say of the word that cannot be applied to the sacraments. They are, indeed, "means and instruments of secret grace."[78] That grace is, for Calvin, communion with Christ. In the Eucharist, therefore, the sacrament is conjoined to the reality and effect, though they are not to be confused as one and the same thing.[79]

Calvin then moves to a consideration of the nature of the Christian's communion with Christ in the Supper. Here Calvin emphasizes that it is Christ himself the Christian enjoys, in his flesh and blood, and not simply a communion that results because of the Christian receiving Christ's benefits. In fact, for Calvin, it is only through communion with the life-giving flesh of Christ that his benefits may be bestowed upon the Christian. To believe and to eat are not the same thing for Calvin. To have faith in Christ is not the same thing as to eat Christ. Calvin declares:

> The Lord bids us take bread and wine. At the same time he declares that he gives the spiritual nourishment of his flesh and blood. We say that no fallacious figure of this is set before our eyes, but that a pledge is given us, with which the substance and the reality are conjoined; in other words, that our souls are fed with the flesh and blood of Christ. The term faith is thus used by us not to denote some imaginary thing, as if believers received what is promised only in thought or memory, but only to prevent any one from thinking that Christ is so far prostituted that unbelievers enjoy him.[80]

Thus, Calvin affirms that the habitation of Christ in the Christian's heart is true, not imaginary, and that faith is the way one "ascertains the possession of so great a blessing."[81] It is in this habitation that one is united to Christ in sacred union; it is in this habitation that one draws life from the flesh of Christ; it is in this habitation that one can find common life with Christ.

The communion the elect have with Christ's body and blood involves two related concepts. They receive Christ's life as their own, while also becoming one with Christ. One receives in the Eucharist, then, both Christ and his benefits, but necessarily together, never apart. As Calvin says:

> Let us be contented with this reason, against which no man, unless he is very quarrelsome, will rebel, that the flesh of Christ gives us life, inasmuch as Christ by it instills spiritual life into our souls, and that it is also eaten by us when by faith we grow up into one body with Christ, that he being ours imparts to us all that is his.[82]

As the communion has a twofold aspect, so does the mode of communion. Christ is removed from believers in that his body is in heaven as in a place.[83] Therefore, the very fact of communion with Christ's body and blood becomes for Calvin a miracle effected by the work of the Holy Spirit through which Christ "raises us to heaven to himself, transfusing into us the vivifying vigour of his flesh, just as the rays of the sun invigorate us by his vital warmth."[84] There is also a descending of Christ in Calvin's thought, in that "he infuses life into us from his flesh, in no other way than by descending into us by his energy, while, in respect of his body, he still continues in heaven."[85] Though one might read this twofold process as simply two ways of saying the same thing, I think that this is not the case. Calvin here begins to develop the notion that the descending of Christ and his indwelling in the Christian is the natural state of the Christian's constant communion with Christ in his flesh and blood, a gift given in the Eucharist as in the other instruments of God's grace, such as preaching. However, the ascension to heaven refers to a related, yet distinguishable, function of the Eucharist. Perhaps if one is to look for the eucharistic gift, it is to be found in the dialectical action that takes place between "ascent" and "descent." Certainly one must look for how the notion of mode of communion develops in Calvin's thought and in what context. This twofold aspect of the eucharistic act will be examined more closely as Calvin's thought on the matter further develops.

Calvin concludes his *Defence* with an emphasis on the twofold nature of the instrumentality of the eucharistic act. Here he is most clearly at odds with the Zurichers in his interpretation of the *Consensus*. Calvin contends that the symbol of bread and wine is "not an empty illusory symbol, but one to which its own reality is annexed, so that all who receive the sign with their mouth and the promise by faith become truly partakers of Christ."[86] Once again, there is the characteristic emphasis by Calvin on the need for faith for true reception of Christ in the Eucharist. However, it is coupled with (and preceded by!) the need for the reception of the sign by the mouth for true participation in Christ in the eucharistic act. For Calvin, Christ is received in the Eucharist along with the visible sign. This reception is not to be separated from receiving Christ in the daily walk of faith. However, God does graciously grant Christ himself as the reality and the gift of the Eucharist, along with a special affirmation of that communion through the reception of the sign. Thus ends Calvin's initial explication of the *Consensus*. What are Calvin's emphases and what relation do they bear to the Agreement itself?

The Consensus Tigurinus and Calvin's Defence: An Analysis

The *Defence* makes clear that Calvin asserts that in the Eucharist the sacramental sign is conjoined to the reality and effect of the sacrament. The conjoining is not a loose, accidental, or casual relationship between sign and thing signified. Calvin makes it clear that God has chosen to use the Eucharist as an instrument to join together Christ and his people. Though a distinction must be made between sign and thing signified, Calvin lays heavy emphasis on the fact that what God promises to do with his instruments he fulfills, always and objectively. Of course, the reprobate do not receive the benefits of the Eucharist. However, that is a condition that results from the inability of the reprobate to receive the promises. The gift of union is given in the Eucharist, but only the elect are able to receive the gift.

Such an emphasis is at odds with the general mood of the *Consensus*. In that document, the Eucharist is reduced to a "mere" symbol. There is no emphasis on the sacrament as a channel of grace. There is nothing in the Agreement that approaches Calvin's insistence on the necessity that the act of communing should stand together with faith for the proper working of the Eucharist. Brian Gerrish has analyzed Calvin's thought on the Eucharist by examining the relation of faith, the Spirit, and the word in Calvin's writings. His claim is that the three are always held together; namely, that faith receives the gift of the sacrament (Jesus Christ himself) by the Spirit *through* the sign (sign being a *verbum visibile*).[87] Whereas faith and the Holy Spirit are both heavily emphasized in the Agreement, the notion of the Eucharist as a sign through which the Spirit works is negligible. Faith, Spirit, and sign are distinguished but held tightly together in Calvin's other works. However, in the *Consensus* there is only a loose connection between the sign and faith/Spirit at best. In other words, Calvin's notion of sacramental efficacy is lacking in the document. The Spirit is the efficacious element in Calvin's mature doctrine, but the Spirit uses the signs to do its effective work. This is so because God, according to Calvin, has promised so to do.

With this loosening of effective bonds in the *Consensus* comes the emphasis on the Eucharist as a memorial meal and as an oath of one's Christian commitment. Remembrance is underscored at the expense of substantial partaking. The Eucharist as external badge precedes its function as nourishment and an aid to faith in the *Consensus*. In the *Defence*, Calvin reverses these emphases.

Because of the instrumental nature of the Eucharist, Calvin insists in the *Defence* that what is figured in the Supper is at the same time given and that the effect takes place.[88] The phrasing of Article 13 of the *Consensus* makes the relationship sound much more occasional: "They [the sacraments] are indeed instruments by which God acts efficaciously *when he pleases* (emphasis mine), yet so that the whole work of our salvation must be ascribed to him alone."[89] This phrasing creates Calvin's need to emphasize in the *Defence* the objective force of the sacrament.

Part of the problem with trying to emphasize this objective force is that the Zurich Church had a tradition dating back to Zwingli of collapsing eating and believing. As Timothy George explains, Zwingli thought that to believe is to eat. "To eat the body and to drink the blood of Christ in the Supper, then, simply meant to have the body and the blood of Christ present in the mind."[90] The point of conflict between Calvin and the *Consensus* at this point is that the Agreement relies more heavily upon the Zurich tradition. That tradition emphasized faith in the promise of Christ's testament in such a way that the eating of the Eucharist adds nothing to faith in that promise.[91]

Calvin also emphasizes faith in the promise of Christ's testament in his work, but in a different manner. For Calvin, faith is as much an instrument as the Eucharist and not an end in itself. Faith is an instrument that works with the instrumentality of the Eucharist, both working together to help the Christian achieve union with Christ. However, each has its own function in achieving this goal and so cannot simply be collapsed into one thing. As Calvin makes clear in the *Defence*, true spiritual partaking of Christ is a result of faith and is not faith itself. Moreover, it is the celebration of the Eucharist that enables faith to grasp what it is that is the end of both, that is, union with Christ. If that is indeed the function of the Supper, then its power is more than an occasional one. It may be exercised only when God pleases, but God has bound himself by his word to the sacrament in such a powerful manner that where God promises to reveal himself he does. Thus, the "when he pleases" language must either be seen as antithetical to Calvin's eucharistic intent or else one must read it (as Calvin did) to mean that God *always* pleases to act in the sacrament. However, that emphasis is an interpretation and is not obvious from the context. In fact, the context seems to indicate much more the occasionalism favored by the Zurich church.

Compared to the *Defence*, the *Consensus* has practically nothing to say about the true partaking of the body and blood of Christ. True partaking is, for Calvin, necessary to the process of union with Christ, for it is that partaking that gives the Christian the Christ of the cross in the here and now. To partake of the body and blood of Christ is to receive the body that died to secure salvation for sinners. The body on the cross in the past must be made present through true partaking of the body. Such a clear emphasis in the *Defence* is at best a muted aspect of the Agreement. Furthermore, that emphasis is always presented in ambiguous terms. For example, Article 6 speaks of Christ dwelling in the Christian "by his Spirit."[92] Such a statement sounds as though Christ's Spirit dwells in the Christian. For Calvin, however, Christ dwells in the Christian by power of his Spirit. It is the Spirit who joins together the Christian and Christ and enables true partaking of body and blood, from which the Christian draws life and Christ's benefits. Article 8 emphasizes that the Christian obtains possession of Christ but then seems to equate that possession with "the blessings which were once exhibited on the cross, and which we daily receive by faith."[93] Article 9 stresses that Christians receive Christ spiritually, in such a way that they partake of his Spirit, not his body and blood. Article 19 speaks of Christ's communication to believers but emphasizes that "he had previously imparted himself, and perpetually remains in us."[94] The article does not speak in terms of body and blood, again a concession to Zurich. Article 22 is an exposition of the words "This is my body." It accentuates the figurative nature of the words without the accompanying Calvinistic accent that what is figured is also truly given. Finally, one reaches Article 23, "Of the Eating of the Body." This is one of the articles Calvin had added to the Agreement after the initial meeting. Here the *Consensus*, at last, mentions the eating of Christ's flesh and the drinking of his blood.

> When it is said that Christ, by our eating of his flesh and drinking of his blood, which are here figured, feeds our souls through faith by the agency of the Holy Spirit, we are not to understand it as if any mingling or transfusion of substance took place, but that we draw life from the flesh once offered in sacrifice and the blood shed in expiation.[95]

However, the emphasis of the article is not an explanation of the true partaking of Christ's body and blood but is rather an explanation of what it is not; namely, a mingling of substances. Also, given the exegesis of the period on John 6:35, 51 ("I am the bread of life"), without further explication Article 23 can easily be read in a Zwinglian manner. Not only is the eating of flesh and blood figured in the sacrament but the language itself of eating flesh and blood is also a figure explained by reference to John 6. Thus, eating language becomes synonymous with faith language.[96] The strong accent in the *Defence* is that the body of Christ must be truly communicated to believers in the Supper; indeed, for the believer's salvation Jesus Christ must be the meat and nourishment of his people.[97] Compared to this emphasis, the *Consensus* cannot be said to be at all representative of Calvin's thought.

It is the lack of emphasis in the *Consensus* on true partaking that makes it possible for the mode of Christ's presence in the Eucharist to be completely ignored. As long as the type of communion one has with Christ is muted, there is no need to explain how such a communion can take place. As has been established, in the *Defence* Calvin has a double emphasis on the descent of the Spirit and the ascent through the agency of the Spirit of the human heart to heaven. How is the distance between the human being and Christ to be bridged? How are the two to be joined together? The *Consensus* simply does not say. Article 25 points to the distance that separates Christ from his people. Christ's body is in heaven "as its place." Yet, but for vague references to the work of the Spirit, there is no theory in the Agreement by which the problem of space is overcome in the union of the Christian with the body and blood of Christ. By 1545, Calvin had fully developed the concept that Christ's presence was effected by the Spirit through the signs by lifting the believer's heart up to heaven. Calvin stresses, for instance, in the 1545 Catechism both the Spirit's role and that of the signs as vehicles in this mode of communion.[98] Once again, the Zurich concerns are prominent in that the doctrine of the location of Christ's body in heaven is present in the document. Of course, Calvin also held a view of the exegetical implications of the

Ascension similar to the Zurichers.[99] However, the *Consensus* presents that view without the balancing concepts that bridge the distance, which for Calvin must be bridged. Simple faith or belief and a joining of a purely spiritual type do not represent for Calvin the essence of union with Christ. For Calvin, faith serves as a vehicle for that union; for the Zurichers, that faith tended to represent the union itself.

Finally, a word must be said about the vocabulary itself. It has been noted above that one of Calvin's favorite words when discussing matters eucharistic, *exhibere*, is used only once. Two other favorite words of Calvin's, *instrumentum* and *accommodare*, are not used in the *Consensus* at all.

The absence of the words would not be significant if the concepts they represent were not so muted in the *Consensus*. *Organum*, the word substituted for *instrumentum* in the *Consensus*, is also used by Calvin in the *Defence*. However, everywhere else when he uses instrumental language, he uses *instrumentum*. Of course, the words can be seen as synonyms. Both can be interpreted as "instrument." Calvin himself seems to have preferred *instrumentum*, while Bullinger seems unwilling to have that word used. The difference can be traced to the more specific meaning *instrumentum* can bear, that is, supply, means, assistance, or furtherance. All these concepts are consonant with Calvin's view of the instrumentality of the Eucharist as a means of grace, an assistance to faith, and a furtherance to faith. In other words, it is an instrumentality that adds to faith and works alongside it. *Organum*, meaning more generally "implement," could be taken in a much less "necessary" sense. The word could be seen as an occasional instrument, one that could as easily be replaced by some other means. Therefore, the question arises: What type of instrumentality is at issue in eucharistic doctrine? The substitution of one term for another in the *Consensus* is a clue that prompts the question: What sort of instrumentality does Calvin have in mind when he uses the word?

The concept of accommodation runs as an undercurrent through some of the articles in the *Consensus*. For example, Article 12 speaks of the sacraments as an "adaptation to our weakness."[100] Yet, the word *accommodare* is never used. Calvin expands a bit on the concept in the *Defence*, referring again to the Eucharist as "adapted to our weakness"[101] and as the "inferior means"[102] by which God works through his Spirit. Though the *Defence* brings out the concept of accommodation a bit more, the word still is not used in the *Defence*. This omission is surprising, in light of the development of Calvin's use of the concept where, in the end, even Jesus Christ is an accommodation to human weakness. Perhaps the absence of both the terms *instrumentum* and *accommodare* was an attempt by Calvin to pacify the Swiss clergy, whose support he wanted for the *Defence*. Yet, the concepts are there, and the vocabulary reappears in Calvin's second writing against Westphal. This treatise, however, Calvin published without the approval of the other Swiss clergy.

What should be clear is that the *Consensus Tigurinus* is not Calvin's victory, not Calvin's document, not even a finely balanced juxtaposition of theologies. The *Consensus* did, as Beza claimed, knit Geneva and Zurich in the closest of ties. Yet, these ties were by and large political ties, not theological ones, at least where the Eucharist was concerned. Calvin's *Defence* makes clear that the *Consensus*, in order to be claimed as representative of his views, had to be radically interpreted. There are, given this analysis and despite Calvin's claims to the contrary, few words clearly used in the Agreement.[103]

Conclusion

In summary, then, the following are the points of eucharistic doctrine in the *Consensus* that Calvin interprets in the *Defence* in a manner more consistent with his own thought: the exhibiting function of the Eucharist; union with Christ; true partaking of the body and blood of Christ; the relation of sign and thing signified; the special nourishing function of the Eucharist as opposed to simple faith; the mode of communion;

and the nature of instrumentality and accommodation. These are the very areas of eucharistic doctrine that have been the subject of study by Calvin scholars since Nevin.[104] The methodological question then becomes: What does one do with these points of interpretation? In the past, scholars have taken Calvin's word that these points are consistent with the contents of the *Consensus Tigurinus*. They are not. Could it be, then, that they are not entirely consistent with Calvin's earlier writings, going back to the 1536 edition of the *Institutes*? Could it be that the controversy over Calvin's signing of the *Consensus* led him to clarify his thought on eucharistic matters in relation to what he had written previously to 1549? Furthermore, could it be that the controversy itself led Calvin to develop his eucharistic doctrine beyond what it was in 1549? In the following pages I will argue that this is the case. By applying the same questions to the career of Calvin's eucharistic writings that an analysis of the *Consensus* has raised, the historical development of Calvin's eucharistic theology can be plotted. Only at the end of this process can one then interpret Calvin's eucharistic doctrine in the 1559 *Institutes*; this rather than interpreting the process by the last edition of the *Institutes*. It is the history of the development of Calvin's eucharistic teaching that holds the key to what, in the end, Calvin sees as the proper function of his eucharistic doctrine. The process of questioning the sources properly begins with Calvin's first attempt at summarizing the Christian faith: the 1536 edition of the *Institutes of the Christian Religion*.

Notes

1. The use of the term *Consensus Tigurinus* dates from the nineteenth century. The full title of the document as published in 1551 runs *Consensio Mutua in Re Sacramentaria Ministrorum Tigurinae Ecclesia et D. Ioannis Calvini Ministri Genevensis Ecclesiae*. The text of the twenty-six articles that constitute the Agreement can be found in OC 7:735–44; OS 2:247–53; and in Calvin, *Selected Works* 2:212–20.

2. The exact date is not known, but the meeting probably took place after 25 May 1549.

3. Specifically, the churches of Basel, Neuchatel, St. Gall, the Grisons, and Schaffhausen. The Bernese clergy would not at first publicly state their support for the document. However, after a new introduction and conclusion were added to the Agreement, they gave their approval, although they opposed publication.

4. The object of study in this chapter will be the interpretation of the *Consensus Tigurinus* by Calvin scholars, Calvin, and myself. Thus, the *Consensus* and its exposition and defence by Calvin will be under consideration, whereas the process leading up to the Agreement will not be. For details concerning the negotiations that led to the signing of the *Consensus*, see Ernst Bizer, *Studien zur Geschichte des Abendmahls-streit im 16. Jahrhundert* (Gütersloh: C. Bertelsmann, 1940), pp. 243–70; André Bouvier, *Henri Bullinger, réformateur et conseiller oecuménique, le succeseur de Zwingli* (Neuchatel: Delachaux et Niestlé; Paris: Librarie E. Droz, 1940), pp. 110–49; Ulrich Gäbler, "Das Zustandekommen des Consensus Tigurinus im Jahre 1549," *Theologische Literaturzeitung* 104/5 (1979): 321–32; Timothy George, "John Calvin and the Agreement of Zurich (1549)," in *John Calvin and the Church: A Prism of Reform*, edited by Timothy George (Louisville: Westminster/John Knox Press, 1990), pp. 42–58; Hans Grass, *Die Abendmahlslehre bei Luther und Calvin* (Gütersloh: C. Bertelsmann, 1954), pp. 208–12, 275–78; and Paul Rorem, "Calvin and Bullinger on the Lord's Supper," *Lutheran Quarterly* 2 and 3 (Spring and Summer, 1988): 155–84, 357–89.

5. The Gnesiolutherans were conservative Lutherans who believed they carried on the "legitimate" (*gnesio*) tradition of Luther over against the innovations of Melanchthon and his followers. The party was led by Matthew Flacius (1520–1575) of Madgeburg.

6. ". . . everything which our Agreement contains occurs throughout my writings." Calvin, *Selected Works*, 2:247; OC 9:46.

7. *Defensio Sanae et Orthodoxae Doctrinae de Sacramentis eorumque Natura, Vi, Fine, Usu et Fructu*, OC 9:5/6–36 and OS 2:263–87 for the exposition of the Agreement; OC 7:733/734–48 and OS 2:246–58 for Agreement and the accompanying letters that were published with the *Defence*. For an English translation of the work in its entirety, see Calvin, *Selected Works* 2:200–244.

8. Hans Grass, *Die Abendmahlslehre bei Luther und Calvin: Eine kritische Untersuchung* (Gütersloh: C. Bertelsmann, 1954).

9. "It has been repeatedly emphasized, and not without justice, that this Consensus did not fully hold out the full teaching of Calvin."

("Man hat mehrfach und nicht mit Unrecht hervorgehoben, dass dieser Consensus nicht die volle Lehre Calvins enthält.") Ibid., p. 208.

10. Ibid., pp. 208-11.

11. "Vom Consensus Tigurinus ist er selbst der Haupturheber." Ibid., p. 211.

12. "[The *Consensus*] is the work of an intimate, brotherly, inseparable collaboration between the two [Calvin and Bullinger]." (". . . c'est l'oeuvre d'une intime, d'un fraternelle et indissociable collaboration entre les deux.") Bouvier, *Henri Bullinger*, p. 146.

13. The full quote runs, "Encore une autre preuve du caractère oecuménique de l'oeuvre accomplie, dans une véritable interpénétration des idées, dans la fécondation réciproque des conceptions, et dans la communion, réalisée par sacrifices mutuels, dans un esprit d'amour chrétien." Ibid., p. 144.

14. This sentiment is echoed by Gordon E. Pruett, "A Protestant Doctrine of the Eucharistic Presence," *Calvin Theological Journal* 10, no. 2 (November 1975): 145, who says, "Calvin's and Bullinger's joint document on the Eucharist (1549) illustrates their agreement on the nature of the Supper." See also J. C. McLelland, "Meta-Zwinglian or Anti-Zwinglian? Bullinger and Calvin in Eucharistic Concord," in *Huldrych Zwingli, 1484-1531: A Lively Legacy of Reform*, edited by Edward J. Furcha (Montreal: McGill University Faculty of Religious Studies, 1985), p. 180, who says, "The Zurich Consensus . . . interprets Calvin and Bullinger well."

15. Beza lived from 1519-1605, serving as leader of the church of Geneva from Calvin's death in 1564 until his own death forty-one years later. As Jill Raitt has shown, Beza did not simply take over and maintain Calvin's eucharistic theology (as, in a similar way, has often been claimed in the case of Bullinger as successor to Zwingli) but in fact stood in a critical relationship to that thought. He developed his own eucharistic theology that was to have substantial influence within the Reformed family of churches. See Jill Raitt, *The Eucharistic Theology of Theodore Beza: Development of the Reformed Doctrine*, AAR Studies in Religion, 4 (Chambersburg, Penn.: American Academy of Religion, 1972).

16. Theodore Beza, "The Life of John Calvin," in Calvin, *Selected Works* 1:liv.

17. ". . . the triumph of Calvinism over what was still defective in the old Swiss position." Nevin, "Doctrine of the Reformed Churches on the Lord's Supper," p. 324; for Ebrard's use of "victor" language, see note 41 in Chapter I.

18. "Tout d'abord Calvin poursuivit et réalisa l'union entre les calvinistes et les zwingliens par le *Consensus Tigurinus*, l'accord de Zurich, en 1549." Emile Doumergue, *Jean Calvin: Les hommes et les choses de son temps, t. V: La pensée ecclésiastique et la pensée politique de Calvin* (Lausanne: Georges Bridel et Cie Editeurs, 1917), p. 368.

19. See Doumergue, *Jean Calvin*, t. VI, chapter 4.

20. For example, "[Barclay] borrowed more extensively from Nevin (and Ebrard) than his use of quotation marks would indicate." Gerrish, "The Flesh of the Son of Man," p. 66.

21. Alexander Barclay, *The Protestant Doctrine of the Lord's Supper: A Study in the Eucharistic Teaching of Luther, Zwingli and Calvin* (Glasgow: Jackson, Wylie, and Co., 1927), p. 179.

22. Ibid.

23. See particularly his treatment of Articles 7, 10, 17, and 18, ibid., pp. 166–72.

24. Ibid., p. 172.

25. Wilhelm Niesel, *Calvins Lehre vom Abendmahl, im Lichte seiner letzten Antwort an Westphal* (Munich: Chr. Kaiser Verlag, 1930).

26. The previous writings against Westphal had been: *Defence of the Sane and Orthodox Doctrine of the Sacrament*, which is the exposition of the Heads of Agreement published in 1555; *Second Defence of the Pious and Orthodox Faith concerning the Sacraments, in Answer to the Calumnies of Joachim Westphal*, (*Secunda defensio piae et orthodoxae de sacramentis fidei contra Ioachimi Westphali Calumnias*) published in 1556, OC 9:41–120; and *Last Admonition of John Calvin to Joachim Westphal*, (*Ultima Admonitio ad Ioachimum Westphalum*) published in 1557, OC 9:137–252. Niesel locates Calvin's last answer to Westphal in Book 4, Chapter 17, Sections 20–34 of the 1559 *Institutes*.

27. "So ist er den Lutheranern bis an die aüsserste Grenze des Möglichen entgegengekommen, indem er die Augustana unterschrieb; so ging er nach der anderen Seite wieder bis an die aüsserste Grenze, indem er sich zum *Consensus Tigurinus* bekannte." Niesel, *Calvins Lehre vom Abendmahl*, p. 54, n. 1.

28. "Da hat sie Calvin im *Consensus* geschaffen, zumal sich die Zürcher Lehre über die des 'früheren' Zwingli hinaus entwickelt hatte." Ibid.

29. François Wendel, *Calvin, sources et évolution de sa pensée religieuse* (Paris: Presses Universitaires de France, 1950); translated by

Philip Mairet and published in London by Wm. Collins Sons in 1963 as *Calvin: The Origins and Development of His Religious Thought*; Fontana Library edition published by Collins in 1965. References are to the Fontana Library edition.

30. Wendel, *Calvin*, p. 330.

31. To see how the twenty articles Calvin sent to the Synod of Bern and the articles of the *Consensus Tigurinus* relate to each other, see Grass, *Die Abendmahlslehre bei Luther und Calvin*, pp. 210-11, n. 1.

32. Gäbler, "Das Zustandekommen des Consensus Tigurinus im Jahre 1549," pp. 323-24.

33. "The positive result of the agreement lay in the removal of mistrust that Zurich and the Swiss had brought against Calvin, the student of Bucer. After the Consensus Tigurinus, Calvin was counted by the Swiss as one of their own." ("Der positive Ertrag der Vereinbarung liegt in dem Ausräumen des Misstrauens, welches Zürich und die Schweizer dem Bucerschüler Calvin entgegengebracht hatten. Nach dem Consensus Tigurinus galt Calvin den 'Schweizern' als einer der Ihren.") Ibid., p. 330.

34. Rorem, "Calvin and Bullinger on the Lord's Supper, Part I: The Impasse," p. 155.

35. Ibid., p. 157.

36. There are thirty-two footnotes in Rorem's section on Calvin's eucharistic teaching (pp. 155-161). There are seventeen references to Book 4 of the '59 *Institutes*, ten references to the *Short Treatise*, thirteen references to the anti-Westphal writings, and ten references to other sources scattered throughout Calvin's career, from his early "Two Discourses on the Lausanne Articles" (1537) to *The True Partaking of the Flesh and Blood of Christ in the Holy Supper* (1563). However, the sources are not cited in any order that would indicate development in Calvin's thought.

37. Ibid., p. 161.

38. See note 15 of the Introduction.

39. Rorem, "Calvin and Bullinger on the Lord's Supper, Part II: The Agreement," p. 375.

40. Ibid.

41. Ibid., p. 376.

42. Ibid. However, it is not just a matter of the absence of key expressions from Calvin's thought. For example, Article 7 describes the primary function of the sacraments as serving as badges and marks of the Christian. No where else, *ever*, does Calvin allow the "badge"

function of the Eucharist to stand in first place in understanding the Eucharist. Yet, in the *Consensus*, this function is mentioned and placed before what Calvin considered to be the primary function of the Eucharist; namely, that Christ is the true and only food for the soul, not mentioned until Article 23.

43. Ibid.; see also Gerrish, "Sign and Reality," in *The Old Protestantism and the New: Essays on the Reformation Heritage* (Chicago: University of Chicago Press, 1982), p. 124. "The Consensus did not say all Calvin liked to say about the sacraments, only what he was not prepared to omit."

44. Timothy George's "John Calvin and the Agreement of Zurich" reinforces many of the judgments brought to light in Rorem's article. He states, "The *Consensus* was an unmitigated victory for neither Calvin nor Bullinger; . . . Most Calvin scholars are agreed that the *Consensus* does not represent a complete, or some would say, even an adequate expression of Calvin's eucharistic theology." George, "John Calvin and the Agreement of Zurich," p. 54.

45. Calvin, *Selected Works* 2:213–14; OC 7:736–37; OS 2:248.

46. On *exhibere* in Calvin's eucharistic theology, see Joseph N. Tylenda, "The Ecumenical Intention of Calvin's Early Eucharistic Teaching," in *Reformatio Perennis*, edited by Brian A. Gerrish (Pittsburgh: Pickwick, 1981), pp. 31–32.

47. For an analysis of Calvin's doctrine of union with Christ and its importance, see Wilhelm Kolfhaus, *Christusgemeinde bei Johannnes Calvin* (Neukirchen: 1939).

48. Calvin, *Selected Works* 2:219; OC 7:742; OS 2:252.

49. Calvin, *Selected Works* 5:235; OC 13:439.

50. ". . . nullam . . . rei nominatur, praesertum quum in toto scripto verbum de carnis manducatione non fiat." OC 13:306.

51. Calvin, *Selected Works* 5:243–44; OC 13:348.

52. "Quia nostra haec de sacramentis confessio non omnia complectitur quae utiliter apteque dici poterant, et maxime alioqui ad verbum eorum intelligentiam conveniunt, operae pretium est pauca de consilio nostra praefari." OC 7:XLIX–L.

53. Calvin, *Selected Works* 2:200; OC 7:733/734; OS 2:246.

54. Joseph N. Tylenda, "Calvin and Christ's Presence in the Supper—True or Real?" *Scottish Journal of Theology* 27 (1974): 66.

55. Philip Schaff, *Creeds of Christendom*, 6th edition, 3 vols. (New York: Harper and Brothers, 1931), 1:473.

Battles remarks, "Repeatedly in Calvin's writings, the creative value of controversy is to be marked." Ford Lewis Battles, "Calculus

Fidei," in *Calvinus Ecclesiae Doctor: Die Referate des Internationalen Kongresses für Calvinforschung vom 25. bis 28. September 1978 in Amsterdam*, edited by W. H. Neusner (Kampen: J. H. Kok, 1978), p. 89, n. 7. Thus, though the occasion may be characterized as "innocent," it is nonetheless important in terms of the way the controversy forced Calvin to deal with unclear and unsettled aspects of his eucharistic thought.

56. Calvin, *Selected Works* 2:219; OC 7:742–43; OS 2:253.

57. For fuller treatment and analysis of the Calvin-Westphal polemics, see OC 9:IX–XI, and Joseph N. Tylenda, "The Calvin-Westphal Exchange," *Calvin Theological Journal* 9, no. 2 (November 1974): 182–209.

58. *Recta fides de Coena Domini ex verbis apostoli Pauli et evangelistarum demonstrata ac communita.* As Tylenda notes, it is possible that none of Wetphal's treatises have been translated into English. See "The Calvin-Westphal Exchange," pp. 183–84, n. 3.

59. "Ioachimo Westphalo non arbitror esse respondendum." OC 15:119.

60. "Certe tam crassae sunt istius calumniae ut responsionis labore minime dignus videatur." OC 15:97.

61. See Tylenda, "The Westphal-Calvin Exchange," pp. 192–93; OC 15:273.

62. The work was published in mid-January 1555 by Robert Estienne. The response can be divided into three sections: Calvin's letter to the Swiss ministers, dated 28 November 1554; the reprint of the 1551 publication of the *Consensus*; and the exposition of the points of agreement. In OS, the 1554 letter and the exposition can be found on pp. 263–87, while the 1551 publication appears just before, pp. 246–58. Calvin, *Selected Works* 2:199–244, contains the 1555 defence and maintains the structure of the original (letters, followed by the Agreement, followed by the exposition).

63. George, "John Calvin and the Agreement of Zurich," p. 55.

64. "Unum metuo, ne me interdum plus aequo illis largitum esse iudices. Hoc tamen etiam consulto feci, ut si qui adhuc refragentur, magis odiosa sit eorum morositas, docti vero qui nobis assentiuntur, quos video minus cordatos esse quam deceat, magis favorabilem habeant praetextum." OC 15:255.

65. Calvin, *Selected Works* 2:205; OC 9:5/6; OS 2:263.

66. Calvin, *Selected Works* 2:208; OC 9:9/10; OS 2:265. Of course, Westphal's charge is not without reason. Westphal says that Calvin plays on words. Calvin answers the charge by stating, "For it

is impossible better to commend and prove a good agreement and full conformity than by collecting all these forms of speech which he opposes to each other as quite contrary, while everyone sees that they all come to the same thing." Calvin, *Selected Works* 2:208-9; OC 9:9/10; OS 2:266. Calvin continues, "Surely the words sign, signification, figure, earnest, memorial, representation do not give a contrary meaning, seeing they are so closely connected together that any one draws the other after it." Certainly, such a statement does strengthen the Agreement in the sense that each party to the Agreement can claim it as his own because these different terms are being called synonyms. The Zurichers can subscribe to the Agreement exactly because they can read these terms on the basis of their controlling metaphor, memorial. Meanwhile, Calvin subscribes because he reads the terms on the basis of his controlling metaphors, figure and representation, which for him indicate a true presence of Christ exhibited in the Eucharist.

67. "Now the method which I have here adopted, of giving a fuller explanation of our meaning, has seemed to me the most proper. For the too great brevity of our first writing lays it open to much cavilling, and does not remove scruples which are deeply rooted. I have therefore dilated the summary which was formerly printed, and made the same confession at greater length, to render it more clear." Calvin, *Selected Works* 2:211; OC 9:11/12; OS 2:267.

68. Calvin, *Selected Works* 2:221; OC 9:15; OS 2:268.

69. Calvin, *Selected Works* 2:222; OC 9:16; OS 2:269.

70. Calvin, *Selected Works* 2:222; OC 9:16; OS 2:269.

71. Calvin, *Selected Works* 2:222; OC 9:16; OS 2:269.

72. Calvin, *Selected Works* 2:222-23; OC 9:17; OS 2:269.

73. Calvin, *Selected Works* 2:223; OC 9:17; OS 2:269.

74. Of course, this charge is leveled by Westphal because it is exactly the function of the Eucharist as an external badge that is the first specific function of the Eucharist mentioned in the *Consensus*. As noted earlier, Calvin himself never gives first place to the external badge feature of the Eucharist in any of his other writings.

75. Calvin, *Selected Works* 2:224; OC 9:18; OS 2:271.

76. Calvin, *Selected Works* 2:225; OC 9:19; OS 2:271.

77. Calvin, *Selected Works* 2:225; OC 9:19; OS 2:271.

78. Calvin, *Selected Works* 2:227; OC 9:20; OS 2:273.

79. Calvin emphasizes the need to recognize this distinction in several pages. Calvin, *Selected Works* 2:228-36; OC 9:21-28; OS 2:274-81. However, since this section is not at odds with the position of the *Consensus*, there is no need to deal with that segment here.

80. Calvin, *Selected Works* 2:238; OC 9:30; OS 2:282.
81. Calvin, *Selected Works* 2:238; OC 9:30; OS 2:282.
82. Calvin, *Selected Works* 2:240; OC 9:32–33; OS 2:284.
83. Nevin believed Calvin's spatial language about the ascended Christ could be read metaphorically (Nevin, "Doctrine of the Reformed Church on the Lord's Supper," pp. 351–52). When speaking of Christ in heaven, Nevin asserts, Calvin means that Christ resides in the "heavenly realm," a higher order of existence in relation to earthly existence. Thus, Nevin concludes, Calvin does not mean to imply outward or local space when writing about Christ in heaven. It is not a matter of physical distance to be bridged. Rather, it might be likened more to an existential distance, according to Nevin. There is some support for Nevin's view. Calvin does not simply equate heaven with a sphere of space removed from the earthly orbit. In relation to Christ, "heaven" can refer to Christ's power, glory, and exaltation. Moreover, the phrase about Christ "at the right hand of God" does not mean that Christ must be at a particular place. See Calvin's comments on Ephesians 1:20 (Calvin, *The Epistles of Paul the Apostle to the Galatians, Ephesians, Philippians, and Colossians*, translated by T. H. L. Parker, in the series *Calvin's New Testament Commentaries*, edited by David W. Torrance and Thomas F. Torrance (Edinburgh: Oliver and Boyd, 1965; repr. ed., Grand Rapids: Eerdmans, 1980), pp. 136–37; OC 51:158.) In addition, Calvin admits that the word "heaven" can carry several meanings, one of which is simply "the glorious kingdom of God where the majesty of God has his proper abode." (Comment on Acts 1:11, in Calvin, *The Acts of the Apostles, 1–13*, translated by W. J. G. McDonald, in the series *Calvin's New Testament Commentaries*, p. 34; OC 48:12.) Thus, to a degree, Nevin is correct—there is a metaphorical aspect to Calvin's spatial imagery in relation to his discussion of the ascended Christ.

However, the imagery is not *just* metaphorical. Calvin also explicitly states in his comments on Acts 1:11 that "For when Christ is said to be taken up to heaven, spatial distance is clearly indicated" (*Acts, 1–13*, p. 34; OC 48:12). Calvin thus seems to indicate that, as it relates to Christ's divinity, the concept of space is irrelevant; heaven is a metaphorical term for power, glory, exaltation, etc. But in his humanity, Christ is contained in heaven as a place removed from the world. Calvin hopes to protect both the prerogatives of divinity and the limitations of humanity in relation to Christ *the Mediator*. The first, the prerogatives of divinity, are necessary if the person of Christ is to be salvific. The second, the limitations of being human, are necessary if

Christ's salvific power is to be related to the needs of humanity. Christ must be really human to save humans; thus he must have a real human body bounded by space, even if a heavenly space. Only in such a balance is there true hope of salvation. The implications of Calvin's move toward a "mediator theology" that tries to hold the balance between the divine and human are sketched out by Heiko Oberman in "The 'Extra' Dimension in the Theology of Calvin," in *The Dawn of the Reformation* (Edinburgh: T. & T. Clark, 1986), pp. 234–58, especially pp. 245–55.

84. Calvin, *Selected Works* 2:240; OC 9:33; OS 2:284.

85. Calvin, *Selected Works* 2:240; OC 9:33; OS 2:284.

86. Calvin, *Selected Works* 2:244; OC 9:36; OS 2:287.

87. See Gerrish, "Gospel and Eucharist," in the author's *The Old Protestantism and the New*, pp. 110–14.

88. See, for example, in the letter to the Swiss clergy Calvin's claim, "I pray you, do we leave nothing but empty signs when we affirm that what is figured is at the same time given, and that the effect takes place?" Calvin, *Selected Works* 2:207; OC 9:7/8; OS 2:265.

89. Calvin, *Selected Works* 2:216; OC 7:739; OS 2:250. The word translated as "instrument" is organum, not instrumentum.

90. Timothy George, *Theology of the Reformers* (Nashville: Broadman Press, 1988), p. 153.

91. In the *Consensus*, it is faith that adds to the eating. See Article 18, where the emphasis is on the fact that Christ is received by each person "according to the measure of his faith." Calvin, *Selected Works* 2:217; OC 7:740; OS 2:251.

92. Calvin, *Selected Works* 2:214; OC 7:737; OS 2:248.

93. Calvin, *Selected Works* 2:215; OC 7:738; OS 2:249.

94. Calvin, *Selected Works* 2:218; OC 7:741; OS 2:251.

95. Calvin, *Selected Works* 2:219; OC 7:742; OS 2:252.

96. See, for example, Zwingli's exegesis on the bread of life passages in "The Clarity and Certainty of the Word of God," in the Library of Christian Classics Series, *Zwingli and Melanchthon*, edited by G. W. Bromiley (Philadelphia: Westminster Press, 1953), p. 81. He says, "In this verse [John 6:35] it is quite certain that Christ is speaking of the nourishment of teaching." See also in the same volume pp. 155 and 223. See also Zwingli's *Commentary on True and False Religion*, edited by Samuel Jackson (Durham, N.C.: The Labyrinth Press, 1981), pp. 126–28, especially p. 128. There Zwingli states, "But now I come to the words I quoted [Jn. 6:53] 'Except ye eat,' i.e., except ye firmly and heartily believe that Christ was slain for you." See also p. 205,

where Zwingli says, "in this chapter (Jn. 6) Christ means by 'bread' and 'eat' nothing else than 'the gospel' and 'believe.'"

Calvin will come to believe that there is a teaching function involved in the Eucharist, but he thinks it serves the advancement of spiritual nourishment, which he will come to base on the notion of communion with the body and blood of Christ as his thought develops. Thus, for Calvin, there is a teaching element involved, but it serves to underscore and heighten spiritual eating; thus having faith is not the same as eating the body of Christ. In Calvin's thought as it develops, John 6 will come to be exemplary of the necessity for true participation in the body of Christ that, though such participation also takes place outside of the eucharistic action, is best exhibited in the Lord's Supper (see Chapter V of this work). Therefore, Calvin will come to base the need for true participation in the body of Christ on John 6. Zwingli, however, uses the passage to deny that anything is necessary to salvation other than faith. Zwingli exegetes John 6 in such a way as to undercut the need for a substantial partaking of Christ in the Supper. Thus, Zwingli reads John 6 as a chapter that has much to do with eucharistic theology, though through it he denies the validity of a sacramental eating that contributes to salvation.

Luther, of course, denied that John 6 referred to the Eucharist in any way. Therefore, he denied that it could be used to either support or undercut the notion of substantial partaking in the Supper. Referring to John 6:35 ("I am the bread of life"), Luther reminds his listeners: "In this light I now remind you that these words are not to be misconstrued and made to refer to the Sacrament of the Altar; whoever so interprets them does violence to this Gospel text. There is not a letter in it that refers to the Lord's Supper. Why should Christ have in mind that Sacrament when it was not yet instituted?" Martin Luther, *Sermons of Martin Luther*, 7 vols., edited and translated by John Lenker (1907; repr. ed., Grand Rapids: Baker Book House, 1988), 3:402.

Most sixteenth-century exegetes, however, did view Jesus' statement about himself as the bread of life as pertaining in some way to the Eucharist. For an example to the left of Luther, see Caspar Schwenkfeld, "An Answer to Luther's Malediction," in *Spiritual and Anabaptist Writers*, edited by George H. Williams and Angel M. Mergal (Philadelphia: Westminster Press, 1957), pp. 163–81. For an example of how one of Luther's Catholic opponents asserted the importance of John 6 for eucharistic theology, see Cajetan's "Errors on the Lord's Supper," in *Cajetan Responds: A Reader in Reformation Controversy*, edited and translated by Jared Wicks (Washington, D.C.:

Catholic University Press of America, 1978), pp. 153–73, especially pp. 153–58. "The fact that he [Jesus] spoke . . . of the sacrament itself is clear from the future tense when he said, 'the bread which I will give' [6:51]." P. 154. When speaking of John 6:53, Cajetan says, "What is here drawn together shows that the Evangelist wrote about a spiritual eating and drinking not only of the death of Christ, but as well of the sacrament of Christ's death under the form of food and drink." P. 155.

97. "Holding it as a settled point that Jesus Christ has only a true and natural body, we say that as he was once offered on the cross to reconcile us to God, he is also daily offered in the Supper. For the Lord Jesus, to communicate the gift of our salvation which he has purchased for us, must first be made ours, and his flesh be our meat and nourishment, seeing that it is from it that we derive life." Calvin then concludes this paragraph from his letter to the Swiss clergy (the first part of the *Defence*) with the astounding claim: "Such are the words which we clearly use in our Agreement." Calvin, *Selected Works* 2:208; OC 9:9/10; OS 2:265. Article 23 comes nowhere close to such bold wording, particularly the identification Calvin makes between the body once offered on the cross and the body offered in the Supper.

98. Calvin, *Selected Works* 2:84, 91; OC 6:111–14, 127–30.

99. Calvin's position on the ascension of Christ's body has been briefly spelled out in note 83 above. For Zwingli's view of the ascended body of Christ and how it is bounded by space, see Zwingli, *On Providence and other essays*, edited by Samuel Macauley Jackson (1922; repr. ed., Durham, N.C.: Labyrinth Press, 1983), pp. 51 and 251, where Zwingli states, "But how has he gone away? In a bodily and literal sense, and as he really is by the essence of His humanity." See also Zwingli, "On the Lord's Supper," in *Zwingli and Melanchthon*, pp. 185–238, especially pp. 215–22.

100. Calvin, *Selected Works* 2:216; OC 7:739; OS 2:249–50.

101. Calvin, *Selected Works* 2:227; OC 9:20; OS 2:273.

102. Calvin, *Selected Works* 2:231; OC 9:24; OS 2:276.

103. "Such are the words which we clearly use in our Agreement," Calvin claims in relation to the *Consensus*'s position on the true partaking of the body and blood of Christ. Calvin, *Selected Works* 2:208; OC 9:9/10; OS 2:265.

104. See Chapter I.

III

Calvin's Eucharistic Teaching in
the 1536 *Institutes*

A Harmony of Calvin's Eucharistic Teaching:
Attempts to Resolve Contradiction

Raymond Aron, in his *Introduction to the Philosophy of History*, makes a distinction between "prospective choices" and "retrospective interpretations." The former are made in uncertainty; the latter tend to lean toward determinism. Aron states that "history must be the accidental origin of apparent finalities."[1] He thus reminds his readers that the action of a historical figure, made in some freedom and with the exercise of some choice, can look rather determined as it is assessed. What often appears to be a predetermined historical line seems so only when looking backward. Historians should recognize that what seems to be a set historical path can be just that—an appearance that fades under closer inspection.

The history of thought has been particularly susceptible to this general tendency to read "retrospective interpretations" into the historical record. The "end product" of a line of thought can cause the interpreter to lose sight of the "prospective choices" the thinker has had to make along the way. Such a reading makes the subject's reflections seem to be static rather than dynamic and interactive.

One can see this situation clearly in the way scholars have interpreted Calvin's earliest attempt at a theological *summa*, the 1536 edition of the *Institutes of the Christian Religion*.[2] Herman Bavinck's attitude is illustrative of the way many scholars have approached the '36 *Institutes*:

> When, in a manner yet but very imperfectly known to us, he [Calvin] was converted, this experience was immediately accomplished by such a clear, deep, and harmonious insight into Christian truth as to render any subsequent modification unnecessary. The first edition of the *Institutes* which appeared in March, 1536, was expanded and increased in later issues, but it never changed.[3]

What Bavinck wrote generally of the '36 *Institutes* also has been affirmed specifically for Calvin's eucharistic teaching in the '36 *Institutes*, though in a variety of ways.[4] Some assertions are as bald as Nevin's, who, as we noted in earlier, stated, "Calvin published the first edition of his *Institutes* in 1536. . . . Here we find very distinctly stated the sacramental doctrine that he continued to hold to the end of his life."[5] However, Nevin holds as integral to Calvin's eucharistic doctrine the work of the Holy Spirit as the means by which the "mystical force" of Christ's body is made present to the believer.[6] Yet, the work of the Holy Spirit, so essential for understanding Calvin's mature eucharistic thought, receives practically no attention in the '36 *Institutes*.[7]

Another tactic is to recognize the differences between the '36 *Institutes* and later editions but then to play down their importance. Boniface Meyer speaks of "*only* four emendations" (emphasis mine) that Calvin makes to his eucharistic doctrine in the '39 edition. What are these changes, most of which are characterized as "minor"? They are: the work of the Holy Spirit as the bridge between the believer and Christ in the eucharistic act as the key to Calvin's thinking of Christ's presence in the Eucharist; the spatial specificity of Christ's ascended body in heaven; the development of the "sursum corda" concept; and extended treatment of the problem of unworthy partaking.[8] With these "few and minor" changes in place by '39, Meyer is then able to join the traditional chorus of Calvin scholarship and state:

> The two editions of Calvin's *Institutes* that have been probed for his eucharistic teaching contain substantially the corpus of his theology. The later editions add very little to this content of eucharistic theology except by way of embellishment.[9]

The adoption of such a position leads one to conclude that the biblical scholarship that lay ahead of Calvin and the major conflicts in which he was engaged, such as that with Westphal, had nothing but an embellishing effect on Calvin's eucharistic teaching. I will argue that this view is mistaken and belies the historical working of Calvin's theology.

Another approach to the 1536 *Institutes* is to emphasize the continuities with the 1559 version while ignoring the changes and development. Again, this approach presupposes that the ideas and tendencies present in 1536 *had to* develop in such a way as to prove consonant with the '59 *Institutes*. Bavinck makes much of the eucharistic material held in common between the first and last *Institutes*. One reads sentences like, "Already in the first edition of the Institutes of 1536, he [Calvin] testifies that the body and blood of Christ is communicated to us in the Lord's Supper truly and actively, but not in a natural way."[10] Yet, there is much about the communication of the body and blood of Christ in the Supper that is *not* said in the '36 edition. Thus, I will argue that the road from the earlier to the later edition is marked by great development. Calvin's eucharistic doctrines of 1536 and 1559 simply cannot be equated.

Another course of scholarship takes pains to explain how apparent contradictions in Calvin's eucharistic thought, as presented respectively in 1536 and 1559, can be resolved. These scholars read Calvin so that he does not contradict himself. The desire to make Calvin consistent is especially evident in the way some have dealt with Calvin's notion of "substance" in his eucharistic teaching. Calvin flatly denies substantial reception of the body of Christ in the Eucharist in the 1536 *Institutes*:

> By way of teaching, we say he is in truth and in effective working shown forth, but not by nature. By this we obviously mean that the very substance of his body or the true and natural body of Christ is not given there; but all those benefits which Christ has supplied in his body.[11]

As far back as Ebrard,[12] Calvin scholars have explained this section of the '36 *Institutes* by claiming that Calvin denies here the scholastic meaning of substance. Therefore, there is no contradiction when, in the '59 *Institutes*, Calvin affirms substantial partaking. Note the following passages:

> I say, therefore, that in the mystery of the Supper, Christ is truly shown to us through the symbols of bread and wine, his very body and blood, in which he has fulfilled all obedience to obtain righteousness for us. Why? First, that we may grow into one body with him; secondly, having been made partakers of his substance, that we may also feel his power in partaking of all his benefits.[13]

> But when these absurdities [transubstantiation and ubiquity] have been set aside, I freely accept whatever can be made to express the true and substantial partaking of the body and blood of the Lord, which is shown to believers under the sacred symbols of the Supper—and so to express it that they may be understood not to receive it solely by imagination or understanding of mind, but to enjoy the thing itself as nourishment of eternal life.[14]

Moreover, it is important to recognize that the phrase quoted above from the '36 *Institutes* that denies substantial partaking disappears in the '39 *Institutes*. It is replaced by the phrase that would remain in place there through the '59 edition: "In short, he [Christ] feeds his people with his own body, the communion of which he bestows upon them by the power of his Spirit."[15]

These 1559 passages bring up a question: Does the claim of Ebrard and others that Calvin denies the scholastic meaning of "substance" in 1536 really take care of the problem of contradiction and change in Calvin's thought? Or, to phrase the question differently: What does Calvin *affirm* about the Eucharist in 1536? Moreover, does it coincide with what is maintained in 1559? Aside from denying a false notion of substance, does Calvin put forward a positive notion in 1536? I am suggesting that the focus on Calvin's supposed denial of the scholastic meaning of substance is problematic. Scholars have treated the above passage from the '36 edition as if it ended with such a denial. However, the sentence has a second, affirming part that states that what is received in the Eucharist is not Christ's substance *but his benefits*. Thus, Calvin qualifies his denial of substance with a positive phrase that indicates that what one gets in the Eucharist is not Christ but his benefits, not body and blood but the gains won by Christ for the believer. Such a qualification makes it clear that Calvin thinks Christians receive the benefits of Christ but not Christ himself in the eucharistic act. Interpreted in this manner, the passage certainly contradicts the '59 passages previously cited. The 1559 passage that claims it is only through substantial partaking of Christ's body and blood that the believer is able to receive the benefits Christ won in his body on the cross is particularly at odds with the '36 affirmation.[16] If Calvin had meant merely to reject the scholastic meaning of substance in 1536, he could have qualified the sentence along those lines in '39 and following editions. Yet, he did not. Instead, he replaced the entire sentence with one that emphasizes communion with the body of Christ. In 1559, the standard order of eucharistic meaning for Calvin is Christ first, then his benefits. However, as this exegesis makes clear, that order is not so clearly established in 1536. Yet, interpreters have tried to make it appear so.[17]

Finally, there is an example of scholarship that shows that even when the "idea" of change is accepted by a Calvin scholar, it is still sometimes hard to break through the older stereotypes of a tradition that has seen Calvin as an unchanging mind. As cited above, Battles, in the introduction to his translation of Calvin's 1536 *Institutes*, admitted that over the course of Calvin's life work one finds "much movement, reconsideration and recasting of his thought."[18] Yet, when Battles examines the eucharistic theology of the '36 work, he states that "Calvin's essay on the Lord's Supper sets forth in a briefer fashion the essential points made at greater length in his mature theological expression."[19] He goes on to characterize Calvin's '36 work on the Eucharist in Calvin's own words, asserting that "men have asked the wrong question: 'How do we eat Christ's body?' They should have asked, 'How does Christ's body become ours?'"[20] Yet, to stop with Calvin's own summary of what he considered to be of utmost importance in eucharistic teaching misses the point. Calvin does not, in fact, answer his own question in 1536. The way Christ's body becomes the believer's is through the action of the Holy Spirit. Without a developed theory of the Holy Spirit, which comes after 1536, Calvin can give no answer to his own question. This point shows the extent to which even a scholar who accepted the notion of development could overlook that development.

1536 and 1559: A Comparison

In order to provide an idea of how much more there is in the '59 *Institutes* than the '36 *Institutes* in terms of both size and content, some figures are illuminating. In terms of size alone, there is considerable growth: in '36, there are eight columns in OC devoted to the sacraments in general and a little more than twenty-two columns dedicated to the exposition of the Lord's Supper in particular.[21] By '59, the sacraments in general take up over twenty columns, whereas the eucharistic teaching numbers sixty-four columns.[22]

Size, however, is not the only or even the chief issue. It is not just that Calvin has expanded the '36 material. What is striking is the character of the topics one finds in '59 that are absent from the '36 issue. Those familiar with Calvin's *Institutes* know that the standard method of noting the '59 edition is to make reference to the book number, chapter number, and section number. Sections are generally discrete units of discussion within the larger book and chapter contexts. Thus, for example, Book 4 of the *Institutes* in '59 is on "The External Means or Aims by Which God Invites Us Into the Society of Christ and Holds Us Therein." Chapter 17 within Book 4 is on "The Sacred Supper of Christ, and What It Brings To Us." Within Chapter 17 there are fifty sections, each of which generally deals with a discrete topic. In the original published form of the '59 *Institutes*, the sections were simply numbered; in Battles' translation these numbered sections are given headings that summarize the discussion of these sections.[23]

With this information in mind, the growth of the *Institutes* between 1536 and 1559 is obvious not only in terms of size but also in terms of content. In 1536, Chapter 4 is devoted to the sacraments. The first section is consigned to the sacraments in general, the second section to baptism, the third to the Lord's Supper, and the fourth to the administration of the sacraments. The first section of Chapter 4 of the '36 edition corresponds to Book 4, Chapter 14 of the '59 edition. Using the critical apparati provided by Battles in the translations of the '36 and '59 editions of the *Institutes*,[24] one finds that of the twenty-six sections on the sacraments in general in '59, sixteen of these sections can be identified in the '36 *Institutes*. Thus, ten sections found in the '59 edition have no precedent in the '36 edition; they have been developed over the intervening years.

In the '59 edition, Chapters 17 and 18 of Book 4 represent Calvin's work specifically on the Lord's Supper and correspond to the third section of Chapter 4 of the '36 work. A comparison reveals that twenty-nine sections of the '59 edition are totally absent from the '36 edition. Or, to phrase it positively, forty-one of the seventy sections of the '59 *Institutes* are found in some shape in the '36 work, though often quite abbreviated.[25]

What is the character of the aforementioned sections that are in the '59 *Institutes* but are absent from Calvin's '36 discussion of the sacrament? In terms of the sacraments in general, some of the additions after 1536 are, indeed, embellishments rather than substantive developments. An example would be 4.14.2 in '59, where Calvin provides a short word study of "sacrament." He explains that the Greek word *mysterion* was translated into Latin by the ancients as *sacramentum* particularly when referring to divine things. He quotes passages from Ephesians, Colossians, and 1 Timothy to show how the word means a secret thing, that which "came to be applied to those signs which reverently represented sublime and spiritual things." This section, while adding information of use to the reader, does not represent anything that could be called a substantive addition to Calvin's eucharistic thinking. The same could be said of 4.14.4, where Calvin explains the necessity of the Word to explain the sign. The section is simply a reinforcement of Calvin's insistence in the first part of 4.14.3 (original with '36) that the promise not be lost sight of in the understanding of the sacrament.

However, there is much of substantial import in '59 that is missing from the '36 edition. As indicated, the work of the Holy Spirit is practically nonexistent in Calvin's eucharistic theory in 1536. The substantial passages on the Spirit and the sacrament appear as 4.14.9 and 10 in '59 and are largely original with the '39 *Institutes*. It is a frequently quoted maxim in studies of Calvin's eucharistic teaching that Calvin, when he speaks of the spiritual presence of Christ in the sacrament, means that Christ is made present by the power of the Holy Spirit.[26] That maxim holds well for the '59 *Institutes*. However, with no developed doctrine of the Holy Spirit in general, nor any application of it to the sacraments in particular, it is hard to see how that aphorism can hold for the '36 *Institutes*. As will be demonstrated, such a realization can greatly influence the assessment of Calvin's eucharistic teaching as it stands in the '36 edition.

Another important area of development for Calvin was in the way he thought about the relationship of the New Testament to the Old Testament. Sections 23–25 of Chapter 14, Book 4, 1559 deal with the relationship of the sacraments of the new covenant to those of the old. They discuss the way in which Paul and much of the New Testament should be understood when the sacraments of the old covenant are examined. This material is not included in the '36 edition. Yet, much of Calvin's mature eucharistic theology depends on his view of how God works in the world—specifically, on the concepts of instrumentality and accommodation. Calvin's exegetical work led him to an understanding of God's activity in the world that emphasized the unchanging nature of God's way of revealing himself and communicating himself to his fallen creatures. Much of that understanding hinges on developed notions of instrumentality and accommodation that come forward in Calvin's thought in force as he considers the relationship of the two testaments.[27] These examples illustrate that one cannot simply discount the additions to Calvin's '36 eucharistic writing as "embellishments."

What is more, Battles' marginal notations in his translation of the '36 *Institutes* can mislead the casual reader and cause one to think there is more correspondence between sections of the '36 and '59 editions than there really is. The most astounding example can be drawn from Chapter 4, Paragraph 31 of the '36 *Institutes*. In the right hand margin opposite Paragraph 31 is Battles' reference to 1559 Book 4, Chapter 17, Section 22. This is the only reference provided by Battles to 4.17.22. One might be led to believe that Calvin simply repeated in '59 what he had said in '36, with some embellishment. What is the real correspondence between the two sections noted?

The first line of Chapter 4, Paragraph 31 in '36 reads:

> But if some intransigeant person raises a controversy with us over Christ's words, because he said this is his body, this is his blood, I should like him to ponder here for a little while with me, that we are now discussing a sacrament the whole of which must be referred to faith.[28]

The first line of 4.17.22 in '59 runs: "But if some intransigeant person, blind to all else, so insists upon the expression 'this is' as to regard this mystery as separate from all the others, the answer is easy."[29] Therefore, what one finds is that the first half of the opening sentence of '36 Chapter 4, Paragraph 31 has been incorporated, in a revised manner, as the opening sentence of '59 4.17.22. *That is the entire extent of the correspondence of this '36 material to '59 4.17.22.* Nonetheless, in '59 the subject under discussion, the word "is" in "this is my body," receives extended attention. Besides the paragraphs that fall within 4.17.22, there is a new context. 4.17.22 is surrounded by sections that are essentially new with the '59 *Institutes*. They bear on the words of institution and their interpretation. In fact, the whole point under discussion has been greatly influenced by Calvin's exegetical studies. Calvin's discussion in 4.17.22 in '59 begins with the above-mentioned sentence, then moves to a consideration of how one is to read figures of speech in Scripture. He makes specific reference to Paul's eucharistic passages in 1 Corinthians 10:16. He speaks of the sacraments in general in terms of the way sacramental language is used in passages from Genesis and Exodus. He briefly mentions how his opponents' exegetical rules bring about nonsense if applied literally to John 7:39, where Jesus says that the Holy Spirit has not come because he was not yet glorified. Calvin refers to baptismal language in Titus, and then comes back again to Paul and his letter to the Corinthians, where, in 1 Corinthians 12:12, Paul states that the church is Christ. Calvin's entire treatment of the word "is" in 4.17.22 is new with the '59 *Institutes* except for the first half of the first sentence which comes from '36. Furthermore, this section is surrounded by material not in '36. An idea of the subject matter is indicated by the subject headings: 4.17.19, "How is the presence of Christ in the Lord's Supper to be Thought of?"; 4.17.20, "The words of institution"; 4.17.21, "The figurative interpretation of the decisive words"; and 4.17.23, "The impossibility of a purely literal interpretation." These passages are heavy with the fruits of Calvin's exegetical work. They also reflect (since much of this material is new with the '59 *Institutes*) Calvin's conflict with Westphal.

Thus, it is evident that even the listing given above in reference to the sections that correspond between Calvin's eucharistic sections in '36 and '59 can be greatly misleading. The context and content of the one is so greatly expanded that it simply cannot be equated with the other. It should be quite clear at this juncture that Calvin's eucharistic doctrine in 1536, though not incongruous with the '59 *Institutes*, does not set "forth in a briefer fashion the essential points made at greater length in his mature theological expression."[30] There are too many critically important elements not included in the '36 work to be able to sustain that erroneous assessment.[31]

Calvin's Ambiguous Eucharistic Doctrine

Calvin was just beginning his labors with the '36 *Institutes*. As a twenty-six-year-old man, he still had much to study and learn, think and arrange, when he completed his initial catechetical treatise in 1535. How does the '36 material look when viewed through this frame of mind?

Ganoczy, in examining the young Calvin's 1536 eucharistic teaching as it related to the influence of Zwingli, states, "Calvin's essay on the Supper is ambiguous."[32] Perhaps that is the best characterization of Calvin's overall teaching on the Lord's Supper in 1536—ambiguous. There are strands of thought in this treatise, some contradictory to others, that have not been unified with any overarching vision of purpose. That vision develops over time. Calvin is able to take much of the '36 material and rework it, rearrange it, and surround it by new material. Coherence within his eucharistic thinking develops over time. As things stand in '36, however, such a vision and such clarity is a thing of the future, to be worked on and worked out through a lifetime of conflict, writing, scriptural study, and preaching. The best one can do is to identify strands of thought present in the '36 work and trace what happens to them as Calvin's thought unfolds. In other words, the questions raised at the end of Chapter II as a result of a close reading of the *Consensus Tigurinus* and Calvin's subsequent interpretation of it are by no means answered in Calvin's 1536 *Institutes*. In fact, this analysis of the '36 edition confirms the point of Chapter II: Calvin's assertion that his eucharistic doctrine had always been the same is wrong. Though Calvin interprets his own material in favor of continuity, there is nothing in the language of the 1536 *Institutes* that in and of itself requires one to follow Calvin's interpretation.

A major concept that must be kept in mind as Calvin's eucharistic theology matures is the idea of spiritual nourishment. The term is present in the '36 *Institutes* but the content is not.[33] It cannot be, since there is no emphasis on the life-giving flesh of Christ. It is the concept of life-giving flesh that gives the idea of spiritual nourishment its content; indeed, it is this concept of life-giving flesh that stands at the center of Calvin's mature eucharistic thought.[34] Thus, the Christian must enter into a relationship not only with the spirit of Christ but also with his body and blood. However, as Wendel has noted, this idea is not strongly emphasized until the 1537 *Confession on the Eucharist*.[35] Without this concept of life-giving flesh, Calvin's teaching on spiritual nourishment has no real content. Thus, though the term "spiritual nourishment" may be used in the '36 *Institutes*, its contents is not the same as in '59. Therefore, it cannot serve, in its 1536 form, as the real foundation of Calvin's eucharistic thought. The term is an ambiguous one until Calvin develops his thought in such a way as to give the idea of spiritual nourishment its full range of meaning.[36]

A second concept that appears in the '36 work is the reception of Christ in the Eucharist. Spiritual nourishment is tied to what one *receives* in the Eucharist. Yet, Calvin is uncertain in '36 about what is received in the Eucharist. Is it Christ or Christ's benefits? By 1559, of course, one receives Christ himself, then his benefits.[37] Yet, in 1536 the order is not so clear. Is it Christ's body and blood one receives in the Eucharist, or Christ's benefits gained in his body and blood? Calvin is also ambiguous here.

The '36 *Institutes* do speak of Christ's body and blood in the Eucharist. Consider the following: "to confirm to us that the Lord's body was once for all so handed over to us, as now to be ours, and always forever to be so"[38] and "he testifies that his flesh is food indeed and his blood is drink."[39] The language of substantial reception is present in '36, but it is qualified in such a way as to leave room for doubt. Does Calvin mean such language to be more than an analogy for communion with Christ's spirit, the same spirit that animated Christ as he won benefits for the Christian on the cross?

Tylenda, when he reads Calvin's language about obtaining Christ spiritually,[40] states, "A spiritual reception of Christ's body necessarily implies his presence and Calvin has no doubt in this matter."[41] Yet, without developed concepts of the Holy Spirit's work in the Eucharist and Christ's life-giving flesh, what sort of presence does Calvin mean? The language could as well mean the presence of Christ's spiritually-bestowed benefits as well as a real presence of Christ himself.

This argument for ambiguity in Calvin's approach to what the believer receives in the Eucharist hinges on the way he constantly refers everything back to Christ's benefits. He does so even when talking of Christ's body and blood. As he explains the sacramental analogy of bread and wine, for example, Calvin directs his readers to a reflection on the *benefits* the Christian receives from these elements:

> When we see wine set forth as a symbol of the blood, we must reflect on the benefits which wine imparts to the body, and so realize that the same are imparted to us by Christ's blood. These benefits are to strengthen, refresh, and gladden. For if we sufficiently consider what benefit we have received from the giving of that most holy body, what benefit from the shedding of that blood, we shall clearly perceive that those qualities of bread and wine are, according to such an analogy, excellently adopted to express those things.[42]

Indeed, the very passage Tylenda quotes is followed by a sentence that clouds, rather than clarifies, his assertion that Calvin *must* mean real presence when speaking of obtaining Christ spiritually. Calvin states, "In short, we have enough to obtain him spiritually. For thus we will obtain him as life, because to receive any fruits from the sacrament is to have received him."[43] One can, and people usually have, read this section in such a way as to understand Calvin's meaning to be that to receive anything (any fruits) from the sacrament must be to receive Christ himself. Read this way, Christ is understood as *the* fruit, from which all other fruits flow. However, an alternate reading would be to say that to receive any *benefit* (any fruits) is the same thing as to receive Christ himself. Thus, the reception of Christ's benefits is counted to be same thing as to receive Christ himself. Calvin does not hold this view of the sacrament—to receive Christ's benefits is the same as receiving Christ himself—in '59. Yet, in the '36 edition such an interpretation is altogether feasible. This is so because of the way Calvin explains what he means immediately subsequent to the statement under consideration.

"Because to receive any fruits from the sacrament is to have received him." Calvin proceeds to explain his meaning as follows. Christ's body is offered in the sacrament "truly and effectively." This does not mean, however, a substantial partaking. Christ took on true human flesh. He died in true human flesh. He rose and ascended in true human flesh. Calvin then refutes opinions that would free Christ's body from the restraints of a true human body. Therefore, as a true human body, Christ's body must be in one place—heaven. In heaven, Christ reigns in majesty at the right hand of God. Because he reigns in power, though his body remains in heaven, Christ can exert his power and strength anywhere. It is through this power that Christ lives with his people "as if present in the body."

> In this manner, the body and blood are shown to us in the sacrament; but in the previous manner [ubiquity, substantial partaking] not at all. By way of teaching, we say he is in truth and effective working shown forth, but not in nature. By this *we obviously mean* [emphasis mine] that the very substance of his body or the true and natural body of Christ is not given there; but all those benefits which Christ has supplied us with in his body.[44]

Given this qualifying material, the alternate interpretation I have suggested for the phrase "Because to receive any fruits from the sacrament is to have received him" seems entirely plausible. The reception of Christ's benefits is equated, at least in this section of the '36 *Institutes*, with the reception of Christ himself. Thus, substance and presence of body and blood can refer simply to the fruits of Christ's work on the cross and not to the life-giving substance and presence of Christ's flesh. Because of the ambiguity that the phrase "but all those benefits which Christ has supplied us with in his body" brings about, Calvin drops the phrase in later editions of the *Institutes*.[45] Therefore, a clear-cut answer to the question, "What does one receive in the Eucharist?" is not found in Calvin's 1536 work. This is especially the case since Calvin has not developed at this point a way to put the Christian in communion with Christ's life-giving flesh, that is, a concept of the Holy Spirit's work in the *sursum corda* concept.

This reading leads to another ambiguity: whether or not Calvin shows at least some spiritualizing tendencies in his 1536 work. Of course, there are statements that would argue against that interpretation. Calvin speaks of those who would "weaken the force of the sacraments and completely overthrow their use."[46] He argues against those who speak of the sacraments only as signs, and who then interpret "sign" as simply an oath of allegiance, like the oath of allegiance a military officer would take.[47] Calvin counters with a desire to see the sacraments in their proper light—one neither too exalted nor despised, a desire he will carry with him throughout his eucharistic writings. However, the force of his statements to the contrary cannot completely overcome the weakness of his own position in regard to the relation of matter and sign. Calvin's later position, "distinction without separation," is not missing in '36. Yet, it is extremely muted. The corollary concepts that make "distinction without separation" a real possibility in his thought—particularly the work of the Holy Spirit—are missing. So, one must be forgiven for reading at least traces of sacramental spiritualizing into Calvin's 1536 work.

For example, in his section on the sacraments in general, Calvin has penned lines that remained virtually unchanged throughout the editions of the *Institutes*. They read:

> For first, the Lord teaches and instructs us by his Word. Secondly, he confirms it by the sacraments. Finally, he illumines our minds by the light of the Holy Spirit and opens our hearts for the Word and sacraments to enter in,

which would otherwise only strike our ears and appear before our eyes, but not at all affect us within.[48]

However, in the '36 *Institutes* the passage is ambiguous. How is it that the Holy Spirit opens hearts and illumines minds? Are these three works, word, sacrament, and Holy Spirit separate, or do they work together? Is the confirmation of the sacraments the same thing as an illumination of the mind and heart? In 1559, there can be no doubt that this passage does not carry spiritualizing connotations—it is immediately followed by a section that explains the work of the Holy Spirit in the sacraments, who binds Christ to the Christian (*Inst.* 4.14.9).

Another place where one might read spiritualizing tendencies is where Calvin states, "For the sacraments are messengers which do not bring but announce and show those things given us by divine bounty."[49] Again, by 1559, Calvin has found a way to qualify the statement so that it is less ambiguous: "For the sacraments . . . as messengers . . . do not bestow any grace of themselves, but announce and tells us, and (as they are guarantees and tokens) ratify among us, those things given us by divine bounty." (*Inst.* 4.14.17). Thus, Calvin asserts in 1559 that the sacrament does more than announce; it also ratifies. This assertion is not always clear in 1536.

Moreover, the discussion of what is received in the Eucharist, the deliberation over the meaning of "obtaining Christ spiritually," indicates the possibility that what is received is Christ's benefits rather than Christ. Such material supports the argument that in 1536 Calvin does in fact separate sign and reality, if the reality is Christ himself. Without developed concepts of the life-giving flesh of Christ and the work of the Holy Spirit in joining Christ and the Christian, Calvin's comments on spiritual reception can be read ambiguously, especially if one does not read 1559 back into 1536.

Such an observation brings us to question one of the basic assumptions of Calvin scholars who have tried to summarize Calvin's 1536 teaching: namely, his dependence on Luther. Wendel claims that Calvin, not only in 1536 but as late as 1539, "shows a dependence on Luther that is clear enough."[50] Calvin is a disciple of Luther, not only in 1536 but throughout his career.[51] Yet, this assumption has often been wedded to another, which again Wendel brings to the fore: "But though Calvin thus found in Luther . . . a conception of the Supper with which he could sympathize, the same cannot be said of him in regard to Zwingli."[52] Wendel goes on to describe how Calvin, in his later writings, especially against Westphal, proclaimed his poor opinion of Zwingli. In fact, he states with certainty that "Calvin had such a poor opinion of Zwingli that, during the time that he was writing the first two or three editions of his work, he took good care to avoid even the slightest direct borrowing from him."[53]

Ganoczy points out, however, that such an attitude as Wendel's should, at least, be qualified. He points out where Calvin, at times, seems to prefer Zwingli's terminology to Luther's. Calvin also treats themes that he and Zwingli both held dear: the problem of eating unworthily; the problem of the sacrificial nature of the mass; and an abomination of images that they thought resulted in carnal adoration of earthly elements.[54]

It should be noted, too, that even aside from the close and careful consideration of sources for Calvin's 1536 *Institutes* that Ganoczy presents, there is here some ambiguity about how to view Calvin; and, indeed, how he views himself. Is he a follower of Luther? Is he really such an adamant critic of the whole of Zwingli's eucharistic theology? In the course of his career Calvin will develop a eucharistic theology that is, at least in terms of reality and sign, totally opposed to Zwingli. Yet, that opposition developed over the course of many controversies. It is exactly because of the ambiguities in Calvin's 1536 eucharistic teaching—what is received in the sacrament, how is it received, the meaning of spiritual nourishment—that the relation of Calvin's doctrine to that of Zwingli seems ambiguous.

Finally, one may ask, What is the function of the Eucharist itself in Calvin's 1536 eucharistic thinking? Gerrish has coined the term "symbolic instrumentalism" to describe Calvin's doctrine of the Eucharist.[55] As well as working to present and offer Christ in the most graphic manner, Calvin believes the sacraments through their symbols "are also [a] real means of grace by which the thing symbolized is communicated."[56] Gerrish goes on to say that "the signs are nothing less than pledges of the real presence; indeed, they are the media through which Christ *effects* his presence to his people."[57] Christ is the matter, or the reality, or the substance of the sacraments, but his self-communication takes place through the vehicle of the Lord's Supper. Thus, Gerrish has indicated the Eucharist's function in Calvin's teaching; that is, his mature teaching.

However, after all that has been said in this chapter, the answer to the question, "What is the function of the Eucharist?" cannot be so easily answered "symbolic instrumentalism."[58] Calvin is unclear in 1536 as to the *function* of the Eucharist: is Christ, in fact, communicated in the way Gerrish describes that event? Is the Eucharist in Calvin's 1536 teaching a "means of grace by which the thing symbolized is communicated?" Calvin is ambiguous on what is received in the Eucharist and how it is received. Developed and nuanced principles of instrumentality and accommodation are entirely lacking.[59] Therefore, the questions have no clear-cut answers. In fact, Calvin spends much more space on the denial of the Roman doctrine of the mass, the remembrance of Christ's passion, unworthy participation, and the second and third functions of the Eucharist (outward profession and inducement to brotherly love), than he does on a positive explication of the function of the Eucharist.[60] This fact should come as no surprise. Much of Calvin's thought on the function of the Eucharist depends on concepts that are developed through conflict, pastoral care, and biblical exegesis. What Calvin holds at the beginning of his career as a doctrine of the Eucharist is but a starting point for much determined and dedicated intellectual and spiritual endeavor.

Conclusion

Ganoczy, in the "Preface to the English Translation" of his *The Young Calvin*, retracts his assessment of Calvin as holding a non-Catholic view of the Eucharist in his youth. He states:

> Viewed in a careful manner, the understanding of the sacraments of both the younger and the older Calvin must be acknowledged as in accord with tradition and thus as catholic. By this I mean above all his doctrine of the real presence of Christ in the Lord's Supper through the activity of the Holy Spirit.[61]

Yet, at least for the Calvin of the 1536 *Institutes*, Ganoczy need not have made the retraction. His earlier judgment that the young Calvin did not hold the catholic understanding of the Eucharist stands. He states originally that Calvin's "aversion to anything that seemed to bind grace to carnal elements"[62] led Calvin excessively to separate the human and the divine. In the mature Calvin, it is the Holy Spirit that enables Calvin to make a "distinction without separation" in his eucharistic teaching. The question becomes, of course, how and why did Calvin's eucharistic teaching develop so that it fulfills Ganoczy's require-ment for a "catholic understanding of the Eucharist." How does he develop an understanding of the Lord's Supper that posits a eucharistic gift as the function of the sacrament? The answer to that question will be provided over the course of the next two chapters.

Notes

1. Raymond Aron, *Introduction to the Philosophy of History: An Essay on the Limits of Objectivity* (London: Weidenfeld and Nicolson, 1961), p. 26.

2. Though Calvin had finished the first edition of the *Institutes* by September of 1535, the book was not published until March of 1536. See Alexander Ganoczy, *The Young Calvin*, translated by David Foxgrover and Wade Provo (Philadelphia: Westminster Press, 1987), p. 94.

The original Latin text of the '36 *Institutes* can be found in OC 1:1–252 and OS 1:19–283. A complete English translation with notes has been executed by Ford Lewis Battles. See John Calvin, *Institutes of the Christian Religion, 1536 Edition*, 2d edition, translated with an introduction and notes by Ford Lewis Battles (Grand Rapids: Wm. B. Eerdmans and the H. Henry Meeter Center for Calvin Studies, 1986). All quotations from the '36 *Institutes* will be from this translation, abbreviated *Inst. '36*, followed by page number; corresponding OC and OS references follow.

3. Herman Bavinck, "Calvin and Common Grace," translated by Geerhardus Vos, in *Calvin and the Reformation*, edited by William Park Armstrong (Princeton Theological Review Association, 1909; repr. ed., Grand Rapids: Baker Book House, 1980), p. 111–12. See also J. K. S. Reid, Introduction to *Calvin: Theological Treatises* (Philadelphia: Westminster Press, 1954), p. 13: "There is a massive homogeneity in the thought of Calvin. . . . There is continual amplification, but little change."

4. However, it should be noted that the argument here is that significant development took place in Calvin's eucharistic thought. Statements by scholars such as Bavinck on the nondevelopmental nature of Calvin's work may be more true of other doctrines and aspects of Calvin's thought.

5. Nevin, "Doctrine of the Reformed Church on the Lord's Supper," p. 315.

6. "Right or wrong, Calvin held and taught *all his life* (emphasis mine) that we have in the Lord's Supper something far beyond a mere occasion for the exercise of faith; that it carries itself, *by the Holy Spirit* (emphasis mine), an objective mystical force." Ibid., p. 267.

7. Warfield recognized that there is no explicit doctrine of the work of the Holy Spirit in the '36 *Institutes*, though he thought it implicit in much that Calvin says. He concludes, "It was left, then, to the edition of 1539 to create the whole doctrine [of the Holy Spirit] at, as it were, a single stroke." Benjamin B. Warfield, "Calvin's Doctrine of the Knowledge of God," in *Calvin and the Reformation*, pp. 131–214; the quote on the Holy Spirit is on pp. 208–9. Calvin's doctrine of the Holy Spirit is examined at length in Werner Krusche,

Das Wirken des Heiligen Geistes nach Calvin (Göttingen: Vandenhoeck und Ruprecht, 1957).

8. Boniface Meyer, "Calvin's Eucharistic Theology: 1536–39," *Journal of Ecumenical Studies* 4, no. 1 (1967): 60–63.

9. Ibid., p. 63.

10. "Reeds in de eerste uitgave der Institutie van 1536 zegt hij, dat het lichaam en bloed van Christus in het avondmaal ons waarlijk en werkzaam, maar niet op naturlijke wijze wordt medegedeeld." Bavinck, "Calvijn's Leer over het Avondmaal," p. 464.

11. *Inst. '36,* p. 107; OC 1:123; OS 1:142. Calvin, in an earlier place, objects to those who speak of Christ being "'really' and 'substantially' present" in the Supper. He places those who hold such opinions in a list of eucharistic positions he considers false. See *Inst. '36,* p. 104; OC 1:120; OS 1:139.

12. Ebrard, *Das Dogma vom heiligen Abendmahl,* p. 430. This line of thought has continued well into this century and is essentially the same line of thought one finds in Niesel's explanation of the '36 passage. Niesel adds that it is not only the scholastic meaning of substance that Calvin denies here, but that the denial of substantial partaking is made in terms "of the context of the doctrine of ubiquity." ("So hat er auch 1536 den Substanzbegriff im Zusammenhang mit der Ubiquitätslehre abgelehnt.") Niesel, *Calvin's Lehre vom Abendmahl,* p. 51, n. 103.

13. *Inst.* 4.17.11.

14. *Inst.* 4.17.19.

15. *Inst.* 4.17.18.

16. Thus, Nevin's claim that the 1536 *Institutes* distinctly stated the eucharistic teaching Calvin was to hold his entire life (see note 6 above) is made particularly problematic by this reading. Nevin's dictum, "Christ first, and *then* his benefits. Calvin will hear of no other order but this," (*Mystical Presence,* p. 122) simply does not hold for the 1536 edition.

17. Helmut Gollwitzer, in his work *Coena Domini: Die altlutherische Abendmahlslehre in ihrer Auseinandersetzung mit dem Calvinismus dargestellt an der lutherischen Frühorthodoxie* (Munich: Chr. Kaiser Verlag, 1937), provides a more nuanced reading of "substance" in Calvin's eucharistic teaching than does Ebrard. However, he still misses the point, I think, as he lays out what substance means in Calvin's thought. He also speaks of Calvin's denial of substantial partaking in '36 as a denial of substance in the sense of "real and natural body." Positively, he states that substance can mean Christ

himself as the substance of the sacrament, the Christian's union with Christ himself. But then he also states that substance can mean "The substance of that which we are given when we receive Christ; namely, the life, benefits, the strength proceeding from his body." ("Die Substanz dessen, was wir bekommen, indem wir Christum empfangen: nämlich aus seinem Leibe vita, beneficia, vigor, etc.") Gollwitzer, *Coena Domini*, pp. 120–21. Yet, by 1559 it is well established that Calvin insists that one receives Christ then his benefits. Particularly in the section quoted above, Gollwitzer speaks of substance as the life, benefits, and strength that proceed from Christ's body; as in the mature Calvin, Christ himself and his life precede the reception of benefits. Yet, the 1536 passage emphasizes that it is the benefits won in Christ's body that is the positive side of his denial of a substantial partaking. Thus, the passage from Gollwitzer is misleading if one applies it to the '36 *Institutes* section (see Wendel, *Calvin*, pp. 341–42, for example) where the order of meaning is not present in the manner outlined by Gollwitzer. For a history of the meaning of the word "substance" in Western intellectual history, see Régis Jolivet, *La Notion de Substance: Essai Historique et Critique sur le Développement des Doctrines d'Aristotle a nos Jours* (Paris: Beauchesne, 1929).

18. *Inst. '36*, p. xxi.

19. Ibid., p. lii. Battles also gives the impression that there is no real development in Calvin's eucharistic teaching by the way he charts the growth and development of the *Institutes* in his *Analysis of the Institutes of the Christian Religion of John Calvin*, assisted by John Walchenbach (Grand Rapids: Baker Book House, 1980), pp. 15–16.

20. Ibid., p. liii.

21. OC 1:102–9; OC 1:118–40.

22. OC 2:941–62; OC 2:1002–65.

23. These headings are, by and large, simply translations taken from the section headings of the German edition of the '59 *Institutes* prepared by Otto Weber. See *Inst.*, p. xx.

24. In his translation of the '36 *Institutes*, Battles indicates where the text of the '36 edition corresponds with the text of the '59 edition by placing Book, Chapter, and Section reference to '59 off in the margin of the text in the '36 translation; in the '59 translation Battles, building on the work of earlier critical editions, marks the textual strands in the '59 *Institutes* with superscripted letters: [a] marks material from '36, [b] marks material from '39, etc.

25. The following sections of 4.14 from the '59 *Institutes* are entirely absent from the '36 edition: 2, 4, 9–11, 15–16, 23–25; the

following sections of 4.17 are missing: 6–16, 19–21, 23, 25, 27–28, 31, 34, 39, 45, 49; the following sections of 4.18 are not present: 4, 8, 10–12, 15.

26. See, for example, Jean Cadier, "La doctrine calviniste de la sainte cène," *Études théologiques et religieuses* (1951), p. 53, who says, "We apply now to the Supper and to its efficacy this conception. The presence of the heavenly Christ is given to those who receive the signs of bread and wine by the action of the Holy Spirit. . . . Spiritual presence therefore signifies presence by the Holy Spirit." ("Appliquons maintenant à la Cène et à son efficace cette conception. La présence du Christ céleste est accordée à celui qui reçoit les signes du pain et du vin par l'action du Saint-Esprit. . . . Présence spirituelle veut donc dire: Présence par le Saint-Esprit.") However, the actual situation in 1536 is better summed up by Jean Bosc who, in commenting on the problems involved in using the word "spiritual" in general, states that it is "singularly ambiguous" ("singulièrement ambiguë"). Bosc, "L'Eucharistie dans les Églises de la Réforme," *Verbum Caro* 22, no. 85 (1968): 42.

27. The standard work for Calvin's understanding of the relationship between the two testaments is that of Heinrich H. Wolf, *Die Einheit des Bundes: Das Verhältnis vom alten und neuen Testament bei Calvin*, 2d edition (Neukirchen: Verlag der Buchhandlung des Erziehungsverein, 1958). Much valuable information on the relationship of the two testaments as it informs Calvin's eucharistic theology can be found in Ronald S. Wallace, *Calvin's Doctrine of the Word and Sacrament* (Edinburgh: Oliver and Boyd, 1953; rep. ed., Tyler, Tex.: Geneva Divinity School Press, n.d.), especially chapters 1–6.

28. *Inst. '36*, p. 107; OC 1:124; OS 1:143.

29. *Inst.* 4.17.22.

30. Battles, *Inst. '36*, p. lii.

31. Though of less importance to the argument, there are passages from the '36 *Institutes* that Calvin chose to *eliminate* in later editions. One example is Chapter 4, Paragraph 27, in Battles's translation. There Calvin presents a summary of false opinions on how Christ's body is present in the Eucharist. See OC 1:120–21; OS 1:139.

32. Ganoczy, *The Young Calvin*, p. 153.

33. Tylenda argues that the notion of spiritual nourishment is the "cornerstone" of Calvin's 1536 eucharistic teaching. Tylenda, "Ecumenical Intentions," p. 29. However, Tylenda, in another essay ("Calvin on Christ's True Presence," *The American Ecclesiastical Review* 155 (July–December 1966): 321–33) defines the substantial

communion with Christ, mentioned in the '36 *Institutes*, by citing the '59 *Institutes* 4.17.3. Yet, if the notion of spiritual nourishment in '36 is not congruous with that same notion in '59, as I argue, then Tylenda has no grounds to claim spiritual nourishment as the cornerstone of Calvin's 1536 teaching.

34. See Hartvelt, *Corpus Verum*, p. 96. Hartvelt points out that Calvin interprets John 6 (especially the latter part of verse 51—"the bread which I [Jesus] shall give for the life of the world is my flesh") in such a way that it is confirmed in the act of the Eucharist. (". . . dat wij Joh. 6 bevestigd zien in het avondmaal.") Additionally, Hartvelt asserts that, when talking of communion with the flesh of Christ, Calvin was not simply using an aphorism for the Christian's reception of the benefits of Christ won in his body. "After all that we have cited from Calvin, it seems to us incorrect if we should perceive communion with the flesh and blood of Christ but only as another description for that which Christ has done in his flesh and blood." (Na alles wat wij van Calvijn geciteerd hebben likjt ons onjuist, wanneer wij de gemeen-schap met hat vlees en bloed van Christus alleen maar zouden zien als een ándere omschrijving voor: dátgene wat Christus in zijn vlees en bloed gedaan heeft.") Hartvelt, *Corpus Verum*, p. 97.

35. Wendel, *Calvin*, p. 334. Of course, it should also be pointed out that the *Confession of Faith on the Eucharist* was not simply Calvin's work but an agreement between the ministers of Geneva and Strasbourg. The emphasis on the Christian's relation to Christ's body and blood, and Calvin's appropriation of this concept in his later work, may well have come from the influence of Bucer and the way he (Bucer) appropriated Luther's thought. See Ganoczy, *The Young Calvin*, p. 118.

36. Westphal apparently picked up on this point. Calvin complains, "He infers that if I still continue in the belief which I professed about twenty years ago, there is nothing I less believe than that the body of Christ is given substantially in the Supper." Calvin, *Selected Works* 2:277; OC 9:70.

37. "I say, therefore, that in the mystery of the Supper, Christ is truly shown to us through the symbols of bread and wine, his very body and blood, in which he has fulfilled all obedience to obtain righteousness for us. Why? First, that we may grow into one body with him; secondly, having been made partakers of his substance, that we may also feel his power in partaking all his benefits." *Inst.* 4.17.11. See also 4.17.33, where Calvin again insists that Christ, as the matter

of the Supper, is separate from and is received prior to the effect that follows, that is, all Christ's benefits.

38. *Inst. '36*, p. 102; OC 1:118; OS 1:137.

39. *Inst. '36*, p. 103; OC 1:120; OS 1:138.

40. "In short, we have enough to obtain him [Christ] spiritually." *Inst. 36*, p. 104; OC 1:121; OS 1:140.

41. Tylenda, "Ecumenical Intentions," p. 31.

42. *Inst. '36*, p. 103; OC 1:121; OS 1:140. Most of this section appears in '59 at 4.17.3. Yet, the meaning in '36 is not as clear as in '59. In '59 Calvin precedes 17.3 with 17.1, a section that explicitly spells out the function of Christ's body and blood as the food of the soul. Even so, the passage has not been transferred verbatim; Calvin did make a slight change in the wording of the sentence that directly precedes the passage quoted above. In '36 Calvin states, "Thus, when we see bread set forth to us as a sign of Christ's body, we must at once grasp this analogy: as bread nourishes, sustains, and keeps the life of our body, so Christ's body is the food and protection of our spiritual life." *Inst. '36*, p. 103; OC 1:119; OS 1:138. In '59 the last part of the sentence is clarified so as to read, "so Christ's body is the only food to invigorate and enliven our soul." (4.17.3) Thus, given the preceding material in 4.17.1, this slight change is important: it falls much more in line with Calvin's mature thought on the life-giving flesh of Christ.

43. *Inst. '36*, p. 104; OC 1:121; OS 1:140.

44. *Inst. '36*, p. 107; OC 1:123; OS 1:142.

45. In fact, the questionable paragraph cited at note 44 is dropped completely by 1539, and Calvin inserts instead an explanation that emphasizes that Christ is what one primarily receives in the sacrament through the power of the Holy Spirit, rather than the 1536 emphasis on benefits: "In short, he feeds his people with his own body, the communion of which he bestows upon them by the power of the Spirit." ("Quin denique suo ipsius corpore eos pascat, cuius communionem, spiritus sui virtute, in eos transfundit.") OC 1:1009. This 1539 addition is carried over unchanged in the later editions of the *Institutes*.

46. *Inst. '36*, p. 91; OC 1:106; OS 1:123.

47. *Inst. '36*, p. 90; OC 1:106; OS 1:122.

48. *Inst. '36*, p. 89; OC 1:104; OS 1:121.

49. *Inst. '36*, p. 92; OC 1:107; OS 1:124.

50. Wendel, *Calvin*, p. 331.

51. For a nuanced treatment of Calvin's relationship to Luther, see Brian A. Gerrish, "The Pathfinder: Calvin's Image of Martin Luther," in *The Old Protestantism and the New*, pp. 27–48.

52. Wendel, *Calvin*, pp. 332–33. Though Wendel represents the majority of twentieth-century scholarship on this point, there are those who do not see Zwingli in such a bad light or allow Calvin's polemical posturing in the Westphal treatises to throw them off an examination of Zwingli. One sees a somewhat more positive image of Zwingli in Ebrard, Nevin, and Barclay. All of them, however, read Zwingli in such a way as to make him a rudimentary Calvinist in his eucharistic theology.

Though not of direct interest here, there are certainly those who think Zwingli's eucharistic theology carries definite advantages over Calvin's. Calvin could have learned from a close study of Zwingli. For example, Jaques Courvoisier believes Calvin's eucharistic thought to be too individualistic; Zwingli, by comparison, held to a eucharistic doctrine that emphasized the ecclesial character of the celebration. See Courvoisier, "Réflexions à propos de la doctrine eucharistique de Zwingli et Calvin," in *Festgabe Leonhard von Muralt, zum siebzigsten Geburtstag, 17 Mai 1970, überricht von Freunden und Schulern* (Zurich: Berichthaus, 1970), pp. 258–65.

53. Wendel, *Calvin*, p. 333.

54. Ganoczy, *The Young Calvin*, chapter 14, "Zwingli."

55. Brian A. Gerrish, "Sign and Reality: The Lord's Supper in the Reformed Confessions," in *The Old Protestantism and the New*, p. 128.

56. Gerrish, "Gospel and Eucharist: John Calvin and the Lord's Supper," in *The Old Protestantism and the New*, p. 111.

57. Ibid.

58. In fact, the case could be made that in 1536 Calvin confuses several ways of describing the function of the Eucharist, so much so that one could apply Gerrish's other categories, "symbolic memorialism" (Zwingli's position) and "symbolic parallelism" (Bullinger's position) to certain passages from Calvin's 1536 *Institutes*.

59. As a matter of fact, Calvin explicitly denied the instrumental function of the Eucharist in 1536. See note 15 in the Introduction.

60. In fact, some find that Calvin, throughout his career, spends so much effort opposing transubstantiation that his positive contributions to notions of, for instance, real presence are overshadowed and thus less well-known. See, for example, Henry Chavannes, "La présence réelle chez saint Thomas et chez Calvin," *Verbum Caro* 13, no. 50 (1959): 152. "Calvin's opposition to the doctrine of transubstantiation is known. Less recognized is the force with which he affirmed the real presence." ("On sait l'opposition de Calvin à la

doctrine de la transsubstantiation. On connaît moins la force avec laquelle il affirme la présence réelle.")

61. Ganoczy, *The Young Calvin*, p. 11. Ganoczy's growing appreciation for Calvin's eucharistic thought can be seen, aside from this retraction of an earlier opinion, in his essay, "L'action sacremen-taire de Dieu per le Christ selon Calvin," in *Sacrements de Jésus-Christ*, edited by Joseph Dore (Paris: Desclée, 1983), pp. 109–29.

62. Ganoczy, *The Young Calvin*, p. 237.

IV

Calvin's Eucharistic Teaching from the Lausaunne Disputation of 1536 to the *Short Treatise on the Holy Supper* of 1541

In September of 1536, about a year after he had finished writing the first edition of his *Institutes of the Christian Religion*, Calvin found himself employed as a "Reader of Holy Scripture" by the city of Geneva. The March 1536 publication of his "little book" made for Calvin a reputation among those who sought reform of the Church. William Farel was quick to take advantage of Calvin's talents by encouraging Calvin to help him with the task of continuing reform in the churches of Geneva.[1] Thus, Calvin began his ministry. He would soon become a pastor as well as a teacher, and it is as a pastor that he begins the process of developing his eucharistic teaching. For, as a pastor, he is no longer concerned with just the theological treatise: he must now convey what he understood as the Gospel truth through preaching, writing catechisms, officiating at worship services, explaining Scripture from pulpit and lectern, and through the pastoral work of visitation.

This chapter will trace Calvin's work on eucharistic doctrine from the time he began his work at Geneva (1536) up to the time he returned to Geneva after a three-year period of exile (1541). Calvin's work during this period can be broken down into two sections. The first is from Calvin's arrival in Geneva in 1536 until his departure in 1538; during this period Calvin's primary published work had to do with his parish activities: church organization, confessions of faith, and catechisms. The second section is the Strasbourg years, when Calvin was most at liberty to pursue his scholarly tasks while in a pleasant pastoral environment as he worked with the French refugees in Strasbourg, serving as their pastor. During this time, he also served as professor of exegesis in the new college located in Strasbourg. This period runs from April 1538 until September 1541. While in Strasbourg, Calvin produced some of his best, and most stylistically pleasing, works: the 1539 *Institutes*; his first biblical commentary, a study of Paul's letter to the Romans; the *Short Treatise on the Holy Supper*, an irenic and insightful piece; and the 1541 French translation of his *Institutes*, which has been proclaimed a "masterpiece" of the French language.[2]

During these years, Calvin developed many of the emphases that would become the foundation of his mature eucharistic thought. In this stage of his work, Calvin's concept of the Holy Spirit as the bond between the believer and Christ's body and blood evolved. Calvin came to understand that partaking of Christ is different and prior to the reception of his benefits. The instrumental nature of the Eucharist, and its relation to the way God works in general, began to develop. Finally, there evolved in Calvin's thought the sense of the Eucharist as a *source* of knowledge about God. Understood properly, this knowledge is presented by Calvin as the *highest* source of knowledge about the Christian's relation to God and Christ. First, then, Calvin's eucharistic work will be traced during his first sojourn in Geneva.

Calvin's Church Work in Geneva, 1536–1538

Shortly after Calvin's arrival in Geneva, he took part in a theological disputation at Lausaunne. From 2 October until 8

October 1536, Catholics and Protestants debated issues over which they disagreed. In a sermon, Farel presented ten articles of faith. Two of these articles, Numbers 3 and 4, addressed issues that were later taken up in debate over the Eucharist.[3] During the debates, Calvin twice addressed the articles. The second discourse was basically a denunciation of transubstantiation.[4] However, the first discourse, while ringing true to parts of the '36 *Institutes* in its emphases that were to be developed only at a later point, shows that Calvin had begun to develop more fully certain aspects of his eucharistic thought.

The 5 October discourse by Calvin was a refutation of the accusation that the Reformers rejected the authority of the Fathers in the Protestant rejection of the Roman doctrine of the presence of the glorified Christ in the elements of the Eucharist. Ganoczy finds Calvin's argument weak, insufficient as a theological proof.[5] Regardless of the validity of Calvin's argument, what one does find for the first time is an explicit assertion by Calvin that the Holy Spirit serves as the bond between Christ and the believer in the Eucharist. After denying that Christ's natural body and blood is given in the sacrament, Calvin states:

> We affirm that it is a spiritual communication, by which in virtue and in power he [Christ] makes us participants of all that we are able to receive of grace in his body and blood; or again, to declare better the dignity of the mystery, it is a spiritual communication by which he makes us truly participant of his body and his blood, but wholly spiritually, that is, by the bond of his Spirit.[6]

Now, what keeps one from assuming that here, as it sometimes appeared in the '36 *Institutes*, Calvin means by "Spirit" that the spirit of Christ is given in the Supper? He has preceded the above assertion with the following argument. Christ had a true body, and that true, natural body resides in heaven. Therefore, what one has in the eucharist is a representation of the body through the signs of bread and wine (though Calvin does not use *exhibere* here). Therefore, one can only speak of the bread and wine as body and blood sacramentally. That leads Calvin to the conclusion that "his body which ascended into heaven [had to] be in one place; but his truth is spread over all."[7] Calvin uses this maxim as a springboard for his emphasis on distinction without separation; namely, that one can distinguish between Christ according to his divinity and Christ according to his humanity. Calvin lauds the logic and benefits of such a doctrine.[8] However, once such a distinction is made, Calvin must have a way to bridge Christ and his humanity to the believer, since the emphasis is on the benefit to the believer of Christ retaining a fully human aspect and body. Thus, the Spirit language quoted above is the first step Calvin takes to set up a way for the believer to communicate with the body and blood of the humanity of Christ. The emphasis on the life-giving flesh of Christ is absent; Calvin's insistence on substantial partaking is missing; the Eucharist as a full-blown means of grace through which one receives Christ and all his benefits is not here. Yet, with the line that emphasizes the Spirit as the *bond* between Christ and the believer, one of the elements is in place that will allow for the development of Calvin's mature doctrine of eucharistic symbolic instrumentalism.

By 1537, Calvin had been set apart as a preacher by the town council of Geneva. The year saw the beginning of Calvin's pastoral labors and a concern for the cure of souls. To that end, Calvin participated in the formulation of ecclesiastical articles, a catechism, and a confession of faith for use in Geneva.[9]

The "Articles Concerning the Organization of the Church and Worship of Geneva, Proposed to the Council by the Ministers"[10] were probably not written by Calvin.[11] However, there are points of emphasis here in regard to the Eucharist that Calvin picks up on and develops in his later writings on the Eucharist.

Though not new,[12] the Articles emphasize the church as a eucharistic community and suggest that a church cannot be considered well-ordered if it does not celebrate the Eucharist frequently.[13] The Articles specify by the word "frequently" that "It would be well to require that the communion of the Holy Supper of Jesus Christ be held every Sunday at least as a rule."[14]

Why? Here is the emphasis that becomes important for developments in Calvin's eucharistic thought. For in the Supper, according to the Articles, in accord with the promises of the sacrament, "we are really made participants of the body and blood of Jesus, of his death, of his life, of his Spirit and of all his benefits."[15] Therefore, the Eucharist was "ordained and instituted for joining the members of our Lord Jesus with their Head."[16] It is important to note in this union of the Christian with Christ that the order is explicit: one is joined first of all to the body and blood of Christ, then one participates in his death, life, Spirit, and benefits. This order is a step that will eventually take Calvin away from a simple denial of substantial partaking of the body and blood of Christ (the emphasis of the '36 *Institutes*) toward formulating an understanding of a substantial, life-giving participation in the flesh of Christ.

The catechism and confession of faith[17] date from the same year as the Articles and are a result of the concern expressed in the Articles that the people of the churches of Geneva be adequately trained in true religion. The 1537 Genevan Catechism[18] contains short sections on the sacraments in general, baptism, and the Lord's Supper.[19] Yet, it builds in an important way on Calvin's Lausaunne Discourses and the Ecclesiastical Articles in that the concept of the Holy Spirit as a bond between Christ and the believer is further explicated and developed. This development allows for a fuller understanding of how Christ's flesh can be life-giving.

The 1537 Catechism states that "The sacraments are instituted to this end: to be exercises of our faith as much before God as before men."[20] They exercise faith before God when they confirm to faith God's truth.[21] This confirmation is necessary because of the weakness of believers: they need earthly signs to help them understand and appropriate heavenly truth. Though the signs do not carry of themselves this power of confirmation, God is merciful and thus has marked the signs with signification so that they may serve faith.[22] Thus, Calvin begins the sacramental portion of the 1537 Catechism with an emphasis on God's accommodation to human weakness.[23] Only secondarily does the sacrament serve faith before humanity.[24]

Calvin then moves, after dealing with baptism, to a section on the Lord's Supper. In a strong opening paragraph, Calvin asserts that the purpose of the Supper is to confirm to the believer that the body of the Lord was once given, is now, and always will be given to the believer.[25] With this emphasis on the body of the Lord rather than his benefits, Calvin must discuss how it is that that body, once given, can now be and always be given to the believer.

Calvin's answer, of course, is spiritual communion with Christ. However, in this work Calvin spells out the implications of a spiritual communion that means communion through the work of the Spirit and how that takes place. First, Calvin says, the Savior presents a true communication of his body through the signs of bread and wine, though in a spiritual manner. He insists that such a communication does not require an "enclosed presence either of the flesh under the bread or of the blood under the wine."[26] The reason is, of course, because Christ is in heaven. Yet, despite that, the Christian can be sure that in the Supper "Christ with all his riches is presented to us not less than if he were placed in the presence of our eyes and felt by our hands."[27] Moreover, the fact that the Christian has a type of real communication with the body of Christ, a real body that must maintain its place in heaven, means that Christians have assurance that not only do their spirits have hope of life eternal but that they also can be sure of the immortality of the flesh. How? "Because it [the Christian's flesh] is vivified already by his [Christ's] immortal flesh and transmitted in some manner to his immortality."[28]

Calvin, in the next paragraph, clarifies what he means by this participation in the body and blood of Christ. The signs make the meaning clear: as bread and wine nourish the body, so Christ's body and blood serve as life and nourishment to the Christian.[29] There is a difference and a development here over and above the 1536 *Institutes*. In 1536, Calvin was not clear that it was participation in the body and blood of Christ that was life-sustaining. As was shown in Chapter III, in his '36 *Institutes* Calvin seemed at times to equate the reception of Christ with the reception of his benefits. This is no longer the case in this 1537

Catechism. The emphasis has changed so that it is communication with the life-giving flesh of Christ that is necessary for the reception of Christ's benefits. This development is made clear by Calvin's increased use of realistic language: Christ's flesh is life-giving, the Christian is connected to that very flesh through the work of the Spirit, and the Eucharist is a clear sign that the body of Christ is present to the believer in such a way as to be just as real as if he were seen by the eyes and felt by the hands. This being the case, Calvin ends his section on the Lord's Supper with an emphasis on the union of Christians with one another because of Christians' union with Christ. Thus, the Christian is called by the Eucharist to acts of praise to God and charity toward neighbor.[30]

The final document to consider from this period of Calvin's initial ministry in Geneva is the "Confession of Faith Concerning the Eucharist."[31] It is a doctrinal agreement between Calvin, Farel, Viret, Bucer, and Capito, and thus it cannot be taken as wholly Calvin's work. However, it does strengthen the language of the 1537 Catechism and signals things to come in Calvin's stage of development in Strasbourg; not surprising, since Bucer figures largely in both the 1537 eucharistic confession and Calvin's Strasbourg years.

The 1537 eucharistic confession emphasizes in clearer and bolder language than does the 1537 Catechism the concepts of the vivifying flesh of Christ and the Christian's true participation in that flesh. The first several lines of the confession bear repetition here:

> We confess that the spiritual life which Christ bestows upon us does not rest on the fact that he vivifies us with his Spirit, but that his Spirit makes us participants in the virtue of his vivifying body, by which participation we are fed on eternal life. Hence, when we speak of the communion which we have with Christ, we understand the faithful to communicate not less in his body and blood than in his Spirit, so that thus they possess the whole Christ. Now Scripture manifestly declares the body of Christ to be verily food for us and his blood verily drink. It thereby affirms that we ought to be truly nourished by them, if we

> seek life in Christ. It is no small or common thing that the Apostle teaches, when he asserts that we are flesh of Christ's flesh and bone of his bone. Rather, he points out the great mystery of our communion with his body, whose sublimity no one is able to explain adequately in words.[32]

A careful reading of this section reveals a development of Calvin's eucharistic thought. It comes not in the notion of vivifying flesh, though the concept is stated forcefully; it does not come in the emphasis on the Christian's participation in Christ's body, though that concept is also forcefully stated. Both appeared in the Catechism clearly enough to differentiate them as developments that certainly clarify Calvin's teaching in the '36 *Institutes*, though the language of both concepts is strengthened in the '37 eucharistic confession. Rather, the new development is indicated with the first sentence: it emphasizes that the Christian's participation in the vivifying flesh of Christ is not limited to the eucharistic event but is, in fact, the foundation of the Christian's spiritual life. Thus, when the document states that Christ feeds the believer, the reference is not to the Eucharist but to the totality of Christian life. It is the Spirit that enables such a communion to take place, and so there is a sense that the Spirit works constantly in the life of the believer. Finally, the emphasis on the life-giving body of Christ is so heavy, one finds for the first time Calvin using (or, at least, signing a document that uses) the term "substance" to describe what takes place in spiritual nourishment:

> Hence we acknowledge that his Spirit is the bond of our participation in him, but in such a manner that he really feeds us with the substance of the body and blood of the Lord to everlasting life, and vivifies us by participation in them.[33]

The confession then goes from what it has said about Christian spiritual life in general and ends with a statement regarding specifically the Eucharist: "This communion of his own body and blood Christ offers in his blessed Supper under the symbols of bread and wine."[34]

Thus, one is able to see the developments in Calvin's eucharistic thought as it evolved during the period of his first ministry in Geneva and culminated in the 1537 "Confession of Faith Concerning the Eucharist." These developments bear fruit in the extended discussions of the following topics in the 1539 *Institutes*: communication with the body and blood of Christ in a substantial manner; the life-giving effects of that body and blood; the role of the Spirit in serving as the bond between Christ and the believer; and the Eucharist as a case of the specific presentation of Christ's body and blood drawn from the more general communion with Christ the Christian enjoys as a staple of spiritual life. Of course, these developments do not represent Calvin's full, mature eucharistic teaching—for example, one still has no clear idea if there is a specific eucharistic gift at this stage of Calvin's thought, especially since the '37 eucharistic confession does not limit participation in the body and blood of Christ to the eucharistic act itself. However, they are important building blocks that Calvin will build upon and clarify as he undertakes ministry in the city of Strasbourg.

Calvin's Strasbourg Years, 1538-1541

Calvin's departure from Geneva was occasioned by a disagreement over sacramental ritual between Calvin and Farel, on the one hand, and the Genevan Town Council on the other. The argument was not over sacramental theology proper but over the Council's insistence that Calvin and Farel follow the liturgical lead of the clergy of Bern, who sought to unify and regularize sacramental ceremonies.[35] Calvin and Farel were forbidden to preach by the Town Council because of their unwillingness to act in accord with the wishes of the Council and adopt the Bernese procedures. Despite the order, Calvin ascended to the pulpit on Easter Sunday of 1538. The celebration of the Eucharist was suspended, however, due to the state of mind of the congregation. Because of their action, Calvin and Farel were sent out of the city.

After a short period of time, Calvin settled in the city of Strasbourg at the invitation of Martin Bucer. The atmosphere was most conducive for the young theologian and pastor. Though busy with his ministry to the French refugees of the city, Calvin found the time for both his literary endeavors and the people who would help him along as he thought through the theological and biblical enterprises he undertook.[36]

Almost all of Calvin's published works from his years in Strasbourg contain important statements that represent significant developments in his eucharistic theology. The works to be considered are: the 1539 edition of the *Institutes*, the "Response to the Letter of Sadolet," the *Commentary on Paul's Letter to the Romans*, and Calvin's masterpiece on eucharistic matters from this period, the *Short Treatise on the Holy Supper*. Especially to be considered is the influence of Calvin's exegetical labors on the *Institutes* of 1539. Though Calvin finished the '39 *Institutes* in late 1538 and the commentary on Romans was not published until March of 1540, still the influence of Calvin's biblical scholarship comes to bear on the '39 edition, since much of the work on the Romans commentary occurred as Calvin lectured on Romans in Geneva from 1536-1537.[37]

The 1539 *Institutes* and the 1540 *Commentary on Romans*

What is most obvious about the 1539 *Institutes*,[38] when compared to the '36 edition, is that the 1539 edition represents a large increase simply in terms of size. Of greater importance, however, is the change in *purpose*; the work has evolved from a catechism to a theological handbook for the training of students.[39] Thus, the topics delineated in 1536 receive a much extended treatment in 1539, along with very important doctrinal additions.[40]

Certainly such expansion and addition is apparent in the 1539 sections on the sacraments. The 1536 edition had one chapter entitled, "On the Sacraments." By 1539, there are three chapters devoted to the sacraments: the sacraments in general, baptism, and the Eucharist; Chapters 10, 11, and 12, respectively.

The developments Calvin had worked out in the 1537 materials, or those that he had agreed to with other people, are immediately evident in the 1539 manual. Much of the new data in 1539 has to do with the work of the Holy Spirit in the sacraments in general and the Eucharist in particular. There are also new sections on the concept of the life-giving flesh of Christ and how that flesh is truly communicated to the believer. There is also a greatly expanded section on the idea of the Eucharist as a "sacrifice of praise," first delineated in the '36 *Institutes* but receiving full treatment for the first time in 1539. Finally, there is a new emphasis in the 1539 *Institutes* that relates to the concept of the Eucharist as an instrument of God, a concept that is closely tied to Calvin's developing thoughts on instrumentality as he worked through his *Romans* commentary.

The new material on the work of the Holy Spirit is obvious both in Calvin's section on the sacraments in general and in his section on the Eucharist. In Chapter 10 of the '39 edition, the section on the sacraments in general, Calvin has two new paragraphs on the work of the Holy Spirit: Numbers 6 and 7.[41] Of course, just previous to Paragraph 6, Calvin affirms that "faith is the proper and whole work of the Holy Spirit."[42] He is having to answer accusations that by granting that the sacraments increase faith, he is taking away from the Holy Spirit in its work of faith, saying that it must be augmented. In '36 he answered the accusation by claiming that the blessing of faith came about in a threefold manner: through the teaching of the Word, confirmed by the sacraments, both of which depend on the illumination of the Holy Spirit.[43] In '39, Paragraphs 6 and 7 serve to give content to the concept "illumination of the Holy Spirit."

By adding a full description of what he means by the illumination of the Holy Spirit, Calvin is able to give a much greater force to the work of the sacraments. He begins Paragraph 6 by stating that he assigns the "confirmation and growth of faith . . . to the sacraments."[44] He then goes on to make a distinction between the work of the Spirit and the sacraments:

> Therefore, I thus distinguish between the Spirit and the sacraments that the power of acting resides with the former and simply the ministry is left to the latter, which is empty and frivolous without the action of the Spirit; however, when the Spirit is working within the sacraments, they are fully filled with great energy and put forth his power.[45]

Or, as Calvin indicates in his conclusion to Paragraph 6, without the Spirit the sacraments are of no use, but with the Spirit they function to strengthen faith.[46]

What is interesting, and what Paragraph 7 makes absolutely clear, is that Calvin is here talking about the Spirit's function as the internal testimony that enables one to know with certainty "the good will of our Heavenly Father toward us."[47] Thus, Calvin has developed a section of his doctrine of the Holy Spirit that, on its own, sounds as if for Calvin the function of the Spirit is solely a cognitive one. In other words, he has set things up in Chapter 10 so that, because of the Spirit, the sacraments function as instruments of God in terms of cognitive appropriation of the promises of God.[48] However, that particular work of the Spirit does not function in instrumental terms to bond the Christian with Christ. Calvin discusses this aspect of the Spirit's work in Chapter 12. What this means is that in the sacramental event of the Eucharist the Spirit clearly serves two functions, and it is only in the '39 *Institutes* that this dual action of the Spirit becomes clear.

For besides serving as an internal testimony to God's truth, the Spirit serves as the bond that connects the Christian to Christ. We have seen how this emphasis developed from Calvin's 1537 pastoral work. But here, in his *Institutes*, he has incorporated the material so that there can be no doubt that the concept has truly been worked into his own eucharistic theology, rather than being imposed by outside authors and considerations.

Moreover, this emphasis in the *Institutes* is matched closely by the emphasis on the work of the Spirit in Calvin's commentary on Romans, where the Spirit serves as the effective bond of connection between Christ and his people.

The major section Calvin adds on the Spirit in '39 comes in Chapter 12, Paragraph 13. The section begins with Calvin's denial that there is any type of local presence of Christ in the Supper. He then emphasizes that Christ's body is "limited by the general condition of a human body . . . and is contained in heaven."[49] How does the Christian enjoy participation in Christ, since such a participation is excluded in terms of Christ being under the corruptible elements?

> [T]he Lord bestows this benefit upon us through his Spirit, that we may be made one body, spirit, and soul with him. The bond, therefore, of this connection is the Spirit of the Lord, with whom we are joined by being bound together. This is like a channel through which all Christ is and has is distributed to us. For if we see that the sun projecting its beams upon the earth, casting its substance in a manner upon it in order to beget, nourish, and give growth to its offspring, why should the radiance of Christ's Spirit be less in order to convey to us the communion of his flesh and blood. Because of this, Scripture, where it speaks of our participation with Christ, refers its entire power to the Spirit.[50]

Thus, at least one aspect of what is known as a standard feature of Calvin's mature eucharistic theology has been worked out by 1539—the Spirit as the bond between Christ and the Christian.

One sees, however, that the biblical basis for this position has been developed by Calvin in the *Romans* commentary. Calvin, in fact, refers the reader of the 1539 *Institutes* to Paul's letter to the Romans immediately after the quote given above. What one finds in Calvin's treatment of Paul is a well-cultivated notion of the work of the Spirit as it joins the Christian and Christ. One can find extended treatment of the work of the Spirit in many places throughout the *Romans* commentary, but two are especially important. In his comments on Romans 6:5, where

Paul speaks of being united with Christ, Calvin makes clear that, as he reads Paul, "ingrafting signifies not just conformity to the example [of Christ], but also the secret union through which we grow together with him, in such a way that, invigorating us by his Spirit, he transfers his power to us."[51] Thus, Christians are justified when they possess Christ himself.[52] That union, that possession, is the work of the Spirit: "For as through the Spirit he consecrates us as temples to himself, so by the same Spirit he resides in us."[53] Thus, Calvin affirms that the Spirit not only brings an internal assurance to the believer, but actually joins the believer to the source of salvation, Christ himself.

What these works of Calvin's also make clear is that the Christian is joined to Christ himself, not just his Spirit. In the 1536 *Institutes* Calvin spoke of participation in Christ mostly in terms of the Christian's appropriation of Christ's benefits. Building on the insights of his 1537 pastoral writings, Calvin is loud in proclaiming that what the Spirit joins the Christian to is not Christ's Spirit or Christ's benefits. Rather, the Christian is joined to Christ himself, as mediator, which means in the flesh in which he won salvation for his church. Calvin himself speaks in these very terms in his 1 September 1539 letter to Cardinal Sadolet:

> We loudly proclaim the communion of flesh and blood, which is exhibited to believers in the Supper; and we distinctly show that that flesh is truly meat, and that blood truly drink—that the soul, not contented with an imaginary conception, enjoys them in very truth. That presence of Christ by which we are ingrafted in him, we by no means exclude from the Supper.[54]

This concept, true participation in the body and blood of Christ, with its bold, realistic language, is made possible because of Calvin's developed doctrine of the work of the Holy Spirit in joining the Christian to Christ. It is this concept that Calvin expounds at length in his '39 revision of the *Institutes*. There he adds several new sections on this very thing and expands and develops the concept as it is found in the 1537 material.

Though Calvin was not to publish a commentary on the Gospel of John until 1553, much of his exposition concerning Christ's life-giving flesh and the Christian's participation in it seems to come as an exposition, in part at least, of the sixth chapter John.[55] The tone for his discourse on the subject is set when he begins the newly inserted section with a reference to John 6:51: "The meaning of which is splendidly established by these words: 'The bread which I shall give is my flesh, which I shall give for the life of the world.'"[56] How does Calvin interpret the ramifications of this passage?

"By these [words]," Calvin states, "the Lord doubtless means that his body will be to us for that reason just as bread to the spiritual life of the soul."[57] Calvin sees Christ's flesh, his body, as part of the gift of salvation that enables the Christian to live a spiritual life. However, what is important is that Calvin sees the gift as being given to the Christian through a twofold action: past giving and present gift. For Calvin, Christ did indeed once and for all give up his body to be crucified for the salvation of the world. Yet, simply as a past action, that gift of a crucified body is not sufficient to join the Christian to Christ and his sacrifice. That same body "he gives daily wherever by the word of the Gospel he offers it to us for partaking, to the extent it was crucified."[58] Thus, for the Christian, there must be a present participation in Christ's sacrificed body as well as recognition of the significance of the crucifixion in history. Certainly, the historical action of the crucifixion is the cornerstone of the Christian's salvation. However, it carries life-giving qualities only insofar as the Christian can participate in that flesh in the present.

Such a participation is more than faith; or, at least, it can be distinguished from faith. Calvin claims that partaking of Christ is the fruit of faith, a result or an effect of faith. Eating the bread of life (Christ) follows faith. He makes clear that such a distinction follows from the twofold action of the gift of Christ's body outlined above, the distinction between past and present giving, when he states:

In this manner, by naming himself the bread of life, the
Lord wanted to teach not just that salvation for us rests on
faith in his death and resurrection, but also that, by true
partaking of him, his life passes into us and is made ours.
This is no different than bread, when taken in nourishment,
gives vigor to the body.[59]

Thus, it is Christ himself, in the flesh, who sustains Christian
life by communion with his people. Here is an understanding of
faith that affirms that "by faith we embrace Christ, not as
appearing from afar, but as joining himself to us."[60]

That means, for Calvin, that one cannot, therefore, speak
of partaking of Christ's Spirit only, while "passing over mention
of the flesh and the blood."[61] He accepts at face value John's
statements [John 6:53, 55] that Christ's flesh is truly food and
his blood truly drink. Rather than it being a matter to discuss,
however, it is a matter to be believed, and so "nothing is left
then except breaking forth in wonder at its mystery, which
plainly neither the mind is able to imagine nor the tongue
confess."[62]

Calvin views the life-giving property of Christ's flesh as
absolutely necessary for the Christian because it was in the flesh
that Christ won salvation for his people. Calvin's logic assumes
that, since salvation came about because of the incarnation of the
word of God, the channel of that salvation must be the self-same
flesh. Again, this assertion comes as Calvin comments on John
6:48, 51 in his '39 *Institutes*:

By these words he teaches not only that he is life since he
is the eternal Word of God, who descended from heaven to
us; but also by descending he poured out that power on the
flesh which he assumed so that thence communication of
life might spring forth to us.[63]

Thus, it is only as the *incarnate* word that Christ brings salvation. By taking on the flesh of humanity Christ redeems humanity; however, in order to participate in that salvation one must
participate in the flesh of the savior. It is only by the redemption
of the flesh that humanity can be saved.

Part of the rationale for this line of thought can be seen in Calvin's commentary on Romans. As a student of Pauline theology, Calvin does not use the word "flesh" as simply a synonym for "skin" or "muscles," though the bodily aspect of human existence is certainly included in the word "flesh." However, the word also means more than that for Calvin. In his comments on Romans 3:20, where Paul states that no "flesh" can be justified by the works of the law, Calvin points out that "By flesh, if not especially noted otherwise, he [Paul] signifies men, although it seems to signify a somewhat more general sense. As, for example, it is better phrased when one says 'all mortals' than if one names 'all men.'"[64] To be "in the flesh" is to be human. One can see this emphasis as Calvin comments on Paul in other places. At Romans 7:5, Calvin tells his readers, "And note the customary formula of Scripture, 'to be in the flesh,' which means to be endowed solely with the gifts of nature, without the singular grace with which God makes worthy his elect."[65] At Romans 7:18, Calvin reminds the readers that "Both appellations, therefore, certainly 'flesh' as much as 'spirit,' belong in the soul; but the one belongs to that part which is regenerated, the other to that part which as yet keeps natural affection."[66] Finally, at Romans 8:5 Calvin says, "in the flesh or after the flesh means the same as to be empty of the gift of regeneration. Those who continue in a natural state (to speak commonly) are truly of such a kind."[67] All this is to point out that, for Calvin, the word "flesh" served to designate what it is to be human. Thus, when Christ becomes incarnate, enfleshed, it is a way of saying that, more than simply taking on skin, muscles, and bones (though it is certainly that, as well), Christ becomes truly and fully human. Moreover, it is in that full humanity that Christians participate as they are joined to Christ. Of course, part of what it means to be fully human is to possess a body; thus the Christian also participates in that part of Christ's humanity when joined to him.

Calvin considers his emphasis on the whole of Christ, fully human,[68] to be necessary if the whole of what it is to be human is to be caught up in God's salvation. Calvin speaks of Christ, who "cleaves to us totally by spirit and body."[69] The cleaving of the body is particularly important because "in his humanity he makes known to dwell fullness of life, so that whoever shares in his flesh and blood may at the same time delight in the participation of life."[70] Calvin is able, then, to ask the rather poignant question, "Now who does not see communion in Christ's flesh and blood to be necessary to all who aspire to heavenly life?"[71]

What Calvin makes clear in his next section is that this communion with the body and blood of Christ is an ongoing and necessary element for the life of the Christian. It is not an occasional joining but a permanent one in which the Christian grows more and more into Christ. Therefore, it is not the Eucharist that serves as the only moment or means for union with the body and blood of Christ. In fact, it is the special work of the Eucharist to set forth in the clearest possible way an expression of this state of Christian life that is continual in the life of the Christian—union with Christ. Thus, there is a presence of Christ in the Lord's Supper, but it is not a special kind of presence, in the sense of joining the Christian to Christ in a manner separate from daily Christian life. What the Eucharist does do is present a heightened sense of presence, an awareness of Christ's presence, to the believer. The Eucharist, in Calvin's 1539 teaching, is that which assures the Christian through the symbol of Christ's body that he does, in fact, truly participate in the body of the Lord. As Calvin states, "Because if it is true that a visible sign is offered to us to seal the gift of an invisible thing, when receiving the symbol of the body, let us certainly trust no less that the body itself is also given to us."[72] The gift of the body is given in the Eucharist, but not only there. Thus, the Christian does not receive the body and blood of Christ in a special way in the Eucharist but instead gains along with the general gift of union with Christ a clearer understanding of what it is God does when, by the power of his Spirit, he unites Christ and his people. The experience of union with Christ and the Christian's understanding of that experience are thus intimately linked here in the eucharistic act.[73]

It is exactly this insight into the unity of Christ with his people in full body and blood humanity fellowship that Calvin himself gained after he penned the 1536 edition of the *Institutes*.

In the last chapter, it was pointed out that Calvin added to his denial of the substantial presence of Christ in the Eucharist an affirmation that essentially identified Christ with his benefits. In the '39 edition, he drops the phrase that indicates that in the Eucharist Christ primarily gives, not his true body and blood, but "all those benefits which Christ has supplied us with in his body."[74] By 1539, the emphasis has been switched, as has been shown, to participation in Christ's true body and blood. In 1539, Calvin modifies what he says just before where his 1536 denial had been in such a way that the emphasis is on true partaking. He says, "Indeed, he [Christ], in fact, feeds his people with his own body, the communion of which he pours out on them by the power of his Spirit."[75] Moreover, in this case, he elaborates on what such a communion means. Christ not only imparts the pledge of eternal life to the Christian's spirit, but he renders sure the immortality of the flesh. "Indeed, he is now made alive by his immortal flesh, and in a certain manner he communicates his immortality."[76] In short, this section brings together in one sentence the previous strands of thought that make clear Calvin's newfound insistence that in order for the Christian to attain eternal life the Christian must partake of the life-giving flesh of Christ. Thus, as has been shown, Calvin brings to fruition in this period of his life, the Strasbourg period, the twin seeds that had been planted earlier in the soil of his Genevan pastoral activity: the notion of the life-giving flesh of Christ and the action of the Holy Spirit as the bond between the Christian and that flesh.

These are not the only developments related to the Eucharist, important and central though they are, to show themselves in Calvin's writings during the years 1538–1541. At least two other developments bear attention: the idea of the Eucharist as a sacrifice of praise and the notion of instrumentality in the eucharistic action, which results in a special type of religious knowledge.

Calvin insisted in the first edition of the *Institutes* that the Mass, as practiced by his opponents, corrupted the true use of the Eucharist. They had made the Eucharist, he claimed, into "a sacrifice and offering to obtain forgiveness of sins."[77] In that work, Calvin had countered that the only sacrifice proper in the

Eucharist was a sacrifice of praise.[78] Calvin expands on this notion of thanksgiving as a sacrifice of praise and adds to it a second element in the 1539 *Institutes*.

Much of Calvin's new material on the Eucharist as a sacrifice of praise comes in the form of scriptural explication. He provides a fuller background on the notion of sacrifice in the Old Testament. He then examines how the word "sacrifice" can be understood in two ways: as a sacrifice of praise or as a sacrifice of expiation.[79] For Calvin, the Eucharist can in no way be a sacrifice of expiation, for that sacrifice took place only once on the cross and can never be, nor need be, repeated.[80] So, how does Calvin explain the biblical references to sacrifice?

He relates them back to the first sacrifice of Christ. Christ died once and for all for sin, a sacrifice pleasing to God. Thus, as a result of that "greater sacrifice," Christians are called upon to provide sacrifices of thanksgiving, which honor God for the salvation he has wrought. In other words, in the Eucharist, the only sacrifice Christians claim is that of their own worship, which they give to God out of thankfulness. What is offered to God is not a gift worthy of reward but praise for the gift of his Son, who makes Christians worthy and able to render such glory to God. Thus, Calvin includes in this category of sacrifice in 1536 "all our prayers, praises, thanksgivings, and whatever we do for the worship of God."[81] There is more biblical justification for his position,[82] but the basic position, in terms of worship as sacrifice, remains the same.

However, what is new in 1539 is the notion that it is not only worship of God that is an acceptable sacrifice but also "all the duties of love, when with which we embrace our brothers, we honor the Lord himself in his members."[83] He states that doing good and sharing are themselves sacrifices, going so far as to say "all the good works of the faithful are spiritual sacrifices."[84] Thus, in relation to the Eucharist, Calvin moves to the position that the Eucharist not only joins the elect to Christ but that, because of that union, Christians are also enabled to sacrifice themselves for others in good deeds, just as Christ sacrificed himself for the good of others. Such a sacrifice for others is, in the best Pauline sense, a bodily act, just as Christ's own sacrifice was a bodily act.[85]

Finally, the material from the Strasbourg years shows a much greater development of Calvin's notion of instrumentality, not just in the eucharistic act but in the entirety of God's dealings with his creation. Here the 1539 *Institutes* and Calvin's first edition of the *Romans* commentary serve to illustrate to what degree Calvin's dogmatic and exegetical works are complementary.

While trying to wind his way through the concept of the presence of Christ's body in the sacrament of the Eucharist, Calvin makes the statement that the sacrament should be referred to faith. Calvin states that "the analogy of faith, by which Paul orders all interpretation of Scripture to undergo, in this case, without a doubt, very clearly agrees with me."[86] However, that assertion leads to a consideration of the nature of faith. As that nature is considered, one is led, in Calvin's *Romans* commentary, to a consideration of all God's actions and dealings with human beings.

In commenting on Romans 3:22, Calvin states:

> Therefore, as we are justified, the efficient cause is the mercy of God; Christ is the substance; and the word, with faith, the instrument. Faith is said to justify, therefore, because it is the instrument through which we receive Christ, in whom righteousness is communicated to us.[87]

Faith is an instrument by which God communicates his grace.[88] The work of faith as an instrument is identified with the action of God who wields the instrument. Thus, it is not faith that justifies, but God who uses faith to justify. However, that does not render faith useless or superficial; it is the way God has chosen and promised to work to bring salvation to his people. In fact, Calvin considers them so intimately connected because of God's promises that he is willing to say that faith justifies because God uses the instrument of faith to justify. This is not unlike Calvin's explanation of metonymy in relation to his eucharistic theory: "the body of Christ today is named bread, inasmuch as it is the symbol by which the Lord offers the true eating of his body to us."[89] In other words, God has *chosen* to join the reality to the sign. Thus, just as faith is said to justify, when in fact faith is an instrument through which God works to justify, so the bread of the Eucharist is called Christ's body, because it is the one of the instruments through which God works to offer Christ's life-giving body to his people.

For Calvin, God is the efficient cause of all mercy, which includes the mercy of knowledge of him and his disposition toward humanity. Therefore, what one finds throughout Calvin's *Romans* commentary is that everything related to salvation relies on God as the efficient cause and, in fact, serves him as instruments of his will. This interpretation of God's actions by Calvin does not render the instruments superfluous but invests them with great honor, for they are God's *chosen* instruments. There is no disgrace, in Calvin's eyes, to be called an instrument of God, void of all power without God but filled with might and meaning with God's blessing. This, for Calvin, is simply how God works in the world—he accomplishes his will through instruments of his choosing not because of inherent power in the instruments but because of their status as God's chosen means of expression. In the passage above, Calvin calls faith an instrument—one that relies on God, ultimately, if it is to have any power at all. Calvin says the same, however, not only of faith, but of preaching (the word),[90] and even of Jesus Christ himself. There are those who have accused Calvin of robbing the Eucharist of its force by his insistence that the sign and the matter of the sacrament must be distinguished, though they cannot be separated.[91] The complaint is that Calvin is unwilling to invest material things with the full power of God; it is said that his theology is not fully "incarnational." Therefore, material things are of secondary importance for Calvin. However, this line of reasoning does not recognize that his entire theology is based on the assumption that God actively works through instruments. He enlivens them at each use with his active will. Calvin treats the sacraments no differently than he treats the word or faith, which the commentators who accuse Calvin of Nestorian tendencies usually fail to mention.[92] Moreover, they fail to realize how close much of Calvin's talk about Christ himself resembles his talk of the function of the Eucharist, for Calvin views Christ himself and his work as mediator in instrumental terms. Compare the following:

> This place [Romans 8:32] ought to remind and awaken us to contemplate that Christ conveys to us his riches with himself. For as he is a pledge of God's immense love toward us, so he was not sent to us empty or without gifts but bringing with him all heavenly treasures, so no one possessing him may want for the fullness of happiness.[93]

> We have determined, therefore, the sacraments to be truly named the testimony of God's grace, and they are like images of the benevolence that is felt toward us. By these he seals that good will to us. In this way they encourage, feed, confirm, and increase our faith.[94]

Now, of course, there is a hierarchy of importance and order in terms of how the instruments God uses to be gracious to his people relate to one another—they all work (faith, preaching, the sacraments) to put the Christian in proper relationship to Jesus Christ; however, that relationship itself, though it is the most important and the thing of first order in the scheme of salvation, still serves an instrumental function; namely, to pledge God's good favor to the believer. God relates to humanity instrumentally according to Calvin. Thus, when Calvin insists on distinguishing the instrument of God's action from God,[95] it is not to denigrate the instrument but to uplift God's gracious activity and his position as efficient cause. In fact, that God works through instruments is a part of his graciousness. These instruments are chosen precisely because they serve to bring to believers a true knowledge of God that they can understand and appropriate: "God accommodates to our small measure whatever he makes known about himself."[96] Thus, if one keeps this position in mind, one cannot but be impressed with the tremendous honor Calvin does bestow on the sacraments when he says in the '39 *Institutes*, "To be sure, whatever is clearer, accordingly it is more capable of sustaining faith. And, in truth, the sacraments convey the clearest promises."[97]

The 1541 *Short Treatise on the Holy Supper*

Calvin's assertion about the way the sacrament of the Eucharist functions to present clearly the promises of God—as *the* clearest expression of God's promises—is not limited to this one phrase from the 1539 *Institutes*. In 1541 Calvin published his *Short Treatise on the Holy Supper of Our Lord Jesus Christ*.[98] There one finds this astonishing claim:

> Let us recollect, then, that the Supper is given us as a mirror in which we may contemplate Jesus Christ crucified in order to deliver us from condemnation, and raised again in order to procure for us righteousness and eternal life. It is indeed true that this same grace is offered us by the gospel, yet as in the Supper we have more ample certainty, and fuller enjoyment of it, with good cause do we recognise this fruit as coming from it.[99]

The important development in this treatise of Calvin's is the emphasis he puts on the way the Eucharist provides certainty and assurance: its accommodated nature as a means for knowing the promises of God. The *Short Treatise* is, therefore, an exposition of, above all else, religious *knowledge*. The particular concern of this work is how a Christian knows what Christian life is all about. This is not to say that Calvin does not summarize the whole of his eucharistic doctrine as it has developed up to this point; however, it is to say that, aside from a faithful summary of his eucharistic thought as it had come about up to 1541, the new thing in this treatise is its overriding concern with religious knowledge and certainty. It is here that Calvin begins a process of thought that will lead to a resolution of the problem of what, if anything, constitutes a special eucharistic gift in his mature eucharistic teaching.

One has but to look at how Calvin treats his subject to notice this special emphasis in this work. Most of the content of his eucharistic doctrine is reproduced faithfully but also summarily.[100] However, what runs through his constructive doctrinal passages as well as through the passages that are a critique of Roman doctrine or a historical review of the Protestant dilemma over the Supper is the force with which he pushes the sacred meal as a means of gaining knowledge and certainty about God's salvation through Jesus Christ.

Calvin provides a framework, or an outline, for his treatise. He proposes the following order for considering the Eucharist: the reason for its institution, its fruit and utility, the legitimate use of it, errors concerning its celebration, and a summary of the Protestant disputes over the Eucharist.[101] Yet, on closer inspection, one finds that it is the matter of accommodated knowledge that frames the entire treatise and serves as the one concern that runs throughout the treatise and holds its various tenets together.

Calvin begins the first paragraph of the treatise by voicing his concern over the "errors," "diverse opinions," and "contentious disputes" to which the Eucharist had been subject.[102] Such an environment works to the detriment of "many weak consciences" who, because of the situation surrounding the Eucharist, "cannot fairly resolve what view they ought to take of it."[103] Calvin then asserts that "it is a very perilous thing to have no certainty on an ordinance, the understanding of which is *so requisite for our salvation*" (emphasis mine).[104]

The paragraph may sound as if Calvin's concern is with knowledge *about* the sacrament. And, of course, it is. However, it soon becomes clear that he considers the Eucharist a *source* of knowledge, a way of knowing, that is necessary for Christian existence and is available to the Christian based on prior and proper knowledge about the sacrament. It is this dialectic of knowledge about the sacrament and knowledge that springs from the sacrament that serves as a clue to understanding Calvin's view on the relationship between word and sacrament. The task, then, is to expose the "deep structure" of this treatise, showing that it serves as the foundation for Calvin's more obvious structure.

The treatise begins with the question of knowledge; at least, knowledge about the sacrament. Calvin's framework for considering the Eucharist as a source of knowledge is based on four concepts: the weak nature of humanity in understanding the divine intention, the act of accommodation as an act of grace, the instrumental way God works in accommodating his will to human understanding, and, finally, the result of God's accommodative instrumental actions on behalf of the weak human mind: knowledge of God's good will toward the Christian believer.

As quoted above, Calvin begins his treatise with a concern over "weak" consciences. However, though the phrasing sounds as if he is addressing certain individuals who have problems understanding that others do not have, it soon becomes clear that, from Calvin's viewpoint, human nature is, in its fallen state, weak and incapable of understanding what it should about things divine. This understanding stands at the center of Calvin's eucharistic thought; it is what requires that there be a Eucharist. "For seeing we are so weak that we cannot receive him [Christ] with true heartfelt trust," Calvin states,

> When he is presented to us by simple doctrine and preaching, the Father of mercy, disdaining not to condescend in this matter to our infirmity, has been pleased to add to his word a visible sign, by which he might represent the substance of his promises, to confirm and fortify us by delivering us from doubt and uncertainty.[105]

The Eucharist is to take care of the doubt and uncertainty that arise because, by nature, Christians cannot be sure that they have, indeed, communion with Christ, body and blood. For, even to the Christian mind, such a communion with body and blood is "mysterious" and "incomprehensible."[106] Calvin insists that such communion is not only incomprehensible to the eye "but [also] to our natural sense";[107] it is a "spiritual mystery" that cannot be "comprehended by the human understanding."[108] The faith of Christians is such that it is *always* in the need of help; so the prayer of Christians, as long as they remain in this life, must always be, "Lord, help our unbelief."[109] Calvin is clear that it is this weakness, even in Christian believers, that prompted God in his mercy to institute the sacrament. If there was not such weakness in believers, the sacrament would be "superfluous."[110] Therefore, the Eucharist is seen as a "special remedy" for Christians that "God has given to help our weakness, to strengthen our faith, increase our charity, and advance us in all holiness of life."[111] The weak nature of humanity *requires* an aid to be able to understand communion with the body and blood of Christ as the source of salvation.

Therefore, God, in order to sustain his people, had to accommodate himself and his will such that Christians could grasp the essentials of their salvation and its foundation. This accommodation is to the human understanding: "we on our part are so rude and gross that we cannot understand the least things of God," Calvin claims, and so "it was important that we should be given to understand it [communion with the body and blood of Jesus Christ] as far as our capacity would admit."[112] Calvin does not limit, even in this treatise, the accommodative action of God to the Eucharist; he reminds readers that in the Gospel John the Baptist saw a dove, and in that dove he recognized the work of the Holy Spirit, "because it [the Holy Spirit] was represented to him [the Baptist] according to his capacity."[113]

Calvin uses the metaphor of "mirror" to describe this accommodative process.[114] By this term, he means there are material, earthly signs that God uses to reflect divine truth. These signs are used because, as the human is an earthly creature, so the signs are earthly and readily understandable: there is continuity between the perceiver and the perceived. Earthly existence depends on the senses, and it is with great emphasis upon those senses that Calvin describes the mirror-like process of accommodation. "Now there cannot be a spur which can pierce us more to the quick than when he [God] makes us, so to speak, see with the eye, touch with the hand, and distinctively perceive this inestimable blessing of feeding on his own substance."[115] Inasmuch as human understanding at least *starts* with human perception, God has acquiesced to the level of humanity in the way the truth of Christians' communication with the body and blood of Jesus Christ is presented.

Accommodation to human weakness, however, could be accomplished in more than one way. There are two principles Calvin establishes for this accommodation: that, for true understanding, just as there needs to be a continuity between the perceiver and the perceived, so must there be some continuity between the perceived and that which it signifies. However, that continuity, though important, is not what empowers the sign (that which is perceived through earthly senses). Rather, God's active will controls the signs so that they work effectively; the power of that which is perceived resides in the work of God's Spirit rather than in the sign itself. Therefore, for Calvin, there is a conjunction between sign and thing signified that is exemplified by the nature of the sign's continuity with the spiritual reality. However, the force that enables the conjunction, seals it, and guarantees it is the promise of God, who works through the sign to accomplish his will.

For Calvin, then, God's work of accommodation is instrumental; meaning that the power of the work resides in him who wields the instrument rather than the power residing in the things perceived, that is, the signs. The signs are, in fact, tools in the hands of a controlling force that never transfers the power of control to the elements themselves. However, the continuity between sign and thing signified assures the believer that such a wielding of power is neither occasional nor arbitrary; the continuity assures the believer that what is signified is in fact accomplished because God has promised so to act.

It is through this accommodated instrumentality that God gives Jesus Christ to the believer. Calvin says that, yes, the word is an instrument through which God dispenses Christ. But more, Jesus Christ as the only food for the soul "is distributed to us by the Lord, which he has appointed an instrument for that purpose, that word is also called bread and water."[116] Then Calvin assures his readers that what is said of the word applies as well to the Eucharist, "by means of which the Lord leads us to communion with Jesus Christ."[117] Moreover, these signs ordained by God and controlled by him, the elements of bread and wine, are such that "this name and title of body and blood is given to them because they are as it were instruments by which the Lord distributes them to us."[118]

It should be emphasized again that this accommodated instrumentality that God uses to work his will is not occasional or arbitrary; since the purpose and end of the Eucharist is to give Christians a sure knowledge of their relationship to the body and blood of Jesus Christ, the instrument must inspire confidence. Therefore, Calvin emphasizes in this treatise the conjoining of sign with reality: "It is necessary, then, that the substance should be conjoined with these [the signs], otherwise nothing would be firm or certain."[119] Calvin emphasizes that the sacrament is not a bare figure but is always "combined with the reality and substance."[120] He uses even stronger language when he asserts that, not only should the signs of the Eucharist not be separated from what they signify, but that they also "cannot be at all separated from their reality and substance."[121]

Kilian McDonnell, by concentrating by and large on the 1559 *Institutes*, misses the fact that here, relatively early in Calvin's career, Calvin emphasizes that, though the sign and reality can be distinguished and it is good theology to do so, they properly belong together.[122] As a matter of fact, in this treatise, the emphasis is on the conjoining of the sign and thing signified rather than the distinction between the two. Calvin believes, for instance, that it is when the believer understands the conjunction of the reality with the eucharistic sign that the problem of Christ's presence in the Eucharist is solved.[123] In this treatise, Calvin understands the relationship between sign and thing signified to be so close that he insists that the sign *ought* to have some correspondence to the thing figured.[124] What is more, there is a dialectical relationship between sign and thing signified. Just as the signs assure believers that they really and truly feed off the body and blood of Christ, so that growing assurance enables believers to more fully understand and appropriate the sign. It is through communion with the life-giving flesh of Christ that Christians come to trust more and more the sacramental sign. As Calvin says, "If we have the reality, we are by stronger reason capable of receiving the sign."[125] Through this dialectic of sign and thing signified, through this conjoining of the instrument with the thing it brings, the Christian progresses in Christian faith. Thus, the Eucharist cannot be superfluous, if one understands this relationship.[126] Calvin ends his discussion of the signs of bread and wine by stating that though they are signs, "the reality is conjoined with them."[127] Though Calvin certainly distinguishes sign from reality, there is never a hint in this treatise that they can ever be separated. The emphasis falls wholly on their conjunction.

This emphasis is the only proper one, really, for Calvin's purpose. For this strong conjunction must be inherent in the Eucharist if it is to serve as a source of assurance for the Christian. And that is the point of the treatise—religious knowledge that is sure and trustworthy. If, as Bouwsma indicates, Calvin can serve as a representative "portrait" of the anxious religious man of the sixteenth century, and if his quest is indeed one for certainty,[128] then a great deal of his quest for certainty led him to affirm the Eucharist itself as a source of knowledge as a way of knowing God's good will and intent toward humanity.

As indicated at the start of this interpretation of Calvin's *Short Treatise*, there is a double kind of knowledge involved when dealing with the sacrament of the Lord's Supper: a knowledge *about* the Supper and a knowledge that springs from the Supper properly understood. In Calvin's *Short Treatise*, there is a hermeneutic at work that depends on the dialectical relationship between these two types of knowledge. Proper knowledge about the sacrament is always prior and necessary to the sacrament as a source of knowledge. Much of Calvin's language concerns proper knowledge about the sacrament. As noted above, Calvin begins the treatise with a concern that weak consciences be taught the proper understanding of the sacrament. Indeed, that is the intent of Jesus Christ himself, according to Calvin: "The principal thing recommended by our Lord is to celebrate the ordinance with true understanding. From this it follows that the essential part lies in the doctrine."[129] Of course, for Calvin, this means that the whole is referred to the word, for it is from the word that the sacrament derives its virtue.[130] It is in the word that the Eucharist is fully explained and the promises clearly proclaimed. In other words, through the preaching of the word and the reading of Scripture the Eucharist can be understood for what it is supposed to do: show forth and present to the believer the true communion with the body and blood of Jesus Christ. However, Calvin's concern with knowledge does not stop here with knowledge about the sacrament; there is more.

Once the sacrament is clearly understood, it serves as a source of knowledge; it provides assurance, certainty, a firmness of faith that, finally, Calvin seems to consider more useful to human beings than explication of the word alone. Certainly, the word is prior and necessary to understand the Eucharist.[131] Yet, once the Eucharist is understood for what it is, a visible, tangible expression of the promises of God, it is then a source of knowledge about God, perhaps even more enlightening than the word. Of course, this claim does not mean that the sacrament is inherently better than the word; obviously it is not. Calvin insists repeatedly that it is the word that empowers the sacrament. However, if one is concerned more with the effect the sacrament has on the human beings in their weak nature than with what would or should suffice in a different kind of world,[132] it is clear that Calvin believes, from the perspective of the Christian struggling along in this life, the Eucharist presents "the clearest promises of God." This is so because it is this weak nature that God has taken into account when he accommodated knowledge of himself in the instrument of the Eucharist. Moreover, it is on this exact point that Calvin has the most trouble with Roman doctrine, as is clear when he complains that the mass yields no "edification."[133] This is abominable to Calvin because he has set the Eucharist up as a source of knowledge that "directs," "leads," "certifies," "attests," and "displays." The Eucharist is that "special remedy" that "gives us certainty and assurance."[134] Perhaps it is not so surprising, after this analysis, that Calvin says in this treatise that the Christian receives "more ample certainty, and fuller enjoyment" of grace in the Eucharist than in the Gospel. What is more, given this interpretation of Calvin's *Short Treatise*, it should not be surprising to find that, in a reference to the *sursum corda* concept, Calvin speaks of not only Christian hearts being lifted up to heaven but also of Christian understandings.[135]

Finally, as one leaves Calvin's Strasbourg years behind, it must be recognized that it is here in the *Short Treatise* that one finds the strong foundations laid for what will become one part (along with the reception of Jesus Christ himself as the other part) of a twofold eucharistic gift in Calvin's theology: an *understanding* of communion with Jesus Christ that is not accessible anywhere else for the Christian. What believers receive in the Eucharist that they cannot receive elsewhere (due to human limitations and weaknesses) is the meaning of salvation: full partaking of Jesus Christ, body and blood, with all his benefits. Thus, the eucharistic gift for Calvin, as its foundations are laid here and as it will develop, includes not only a salvific presence of Christ but also a heightened knowledge of Christ's presence.[136] It is this concern with, and emphasis on, knowledge or understanding that serves as the foundation, the deep structure, of everything else Calvin says in this treatise. It makes what he has to say important. Christ is present in the Eucharist—indeed, the Eucharist is an instrument through which presence is effected. But Christ is also present in the word, in prayer, in the totality of the Christian's life. Thus, along with the gift of Christ himself in the Eucharist, God gives the assurance and certainty of Christ's presence and communion with the believer, exhibited and confirmed in the Eucharist as nowhere else.

Conclusion

The foundations, then, of Calvin's eucharistic theology are in place at the end of the Strasbourg period.[137] The concept of the Holy Spirit as the bond between the believer and Christ in body and blood fellowship is firmly in place. Calvin has clearly established that the Christian must receive Christ himself first before he can receive Christ's benefits. The Eucharist as a substantial partaking of Christ is emphasized. The instrumental nature of the Eucharist as a means of grace has begun to shape up—an emphasis that was denied in 1536. Finally, the Eucharist as a source of heightened knowledge, as *the* clearest presentation of Christian life because of its accommodation to the full range of human senses, has been developed. Thus, Calvin has in place the makings of a eucharistic gift in his theology. What remains is for Calvin to implement his eucharistic theology as he serves as pastor in the city of Geneva; to fine-tune his concept of eucharistic instrumentality in his biblical commentaries as it relates to how God has always used secondary instruments to reveal knowledge of himself to his people; and, finally, to refine his notion of how Christ communicates his body and blood to the believer as he engages Westphal in debate. These emphases will be explored in the next chapter.

Notes

1. For accounts of how Calvin came to the city of Geneva, see Ganoczy, *The Young Calvin*, pp. 102–9, and Wendel, *Calvin*, pp. 47–50. Bouwsma is the latest biographer to give out the reminder that the historical account has the ring of a "humanist stereotype," that is, of the scholar pulled into public affairs against his will. See Bouwsma, *John Calvin*, p. 18.

2. Wendel, *Calvin*, p. 116.

3. For the ten articles, see John Calvin, *Theological Treatises*, translated with an introduction and notes by J. K. S. Reid (Philadelphia: Westminster Press, 1954), pp. 35–37; hereafter cited as Calvin, *Theological Treatises*.

4. Ibid., pp. 45–46.

5. Ganoczy, *The Young Calvin*, p. 110.

6. Calvin, *Theological Treatises*, p. 44.

7. Ibid., p. 41.

8. Ibid., pp. 42–44.

9. There also appeared in 1537 an open letter by Calvin, penned in late 1536, entitled "Concerning Fleeing the Illicit Rites of the Impious, and Observing the Purity of the Christian Religion" ("De Fugiendis Impiorum Illicitis Sacris, et Puritate Christianae Religionis Observanda," OC 5:239–78; OS 1:287–28). However, the piece is mostly negative in tone and adds little constructive detail to Calvin's developing eucharistic thought. The main point of the letter is, simply, that the mass is "that chief source of all abominations" ("summum illud abominationum omnium caput, Missa" OC 5:239; OS 1:289) and, as such, serves as a "symbol of denying true religion" ("abiurandae verae religionis symbolum" OC 5:267; OS 1:318).

10. "Articles Concernant L'Organization De L'Église Et Du Culte A Genève, Proposés Au Conseil Par Les Ministres," OC 10a:5–14; OS 1:367–77; these have been translated in Calvin, *Theological Treatises*, pp. 47–55.

11. OC 10a:5, "The wording, as far as one can judge it according to style, does not belong to Calvin." ("La rédaction, autant qu'il est permis d'en juger d'après le style, n'appartient pas directement à Calvin.")

12. See *Inst. '36*, p. 122; OC 1:139–40; OS 1:161.

13. Calvin, *Theological Treatises*, p. 48; OC 10a:5–6; OS 1:369.

14. Calvin, *Theological Treatises*, p. 49; OC 10a:7; OS 1:370. This statement shows early on that Calvin did not wish to replace the Mass with the Sermon. As Raymond Abba says, "Calvin's aim at Geneva was . . . to restore the Sermon to its rightful place in the Supper, thus recovering the original organic unity of Word and Sacrament. His ideal—which the Geneva magistrates refused to allow—was a weekly celebration in which the preaching of the Word was scaled at the Table of the Lord." Raymond Abba, "Calvin's Doctrine of the Lord's Supper," *The Reformed Theological Review* 9, no. 2 (Winter 1950): 1.

15. Calvin, *Theological Treatises*, p. 49; OC 10a:7; OS 1:370.

16. Calvin, *Theological Treatises*, p. 50; OC 10a:8; OS 1:371.

17. On Calvin's authorship of these, see OC 22:11/12–17/18.

18. The actual title of the work is "Instruction and Confession of Faith Given for Use in the Church of Geneva" ("Instruction et Confession de Foy Dont On Use En LEglise Geneve"). OC 22:33–74; OS 1:378–417.

19. The Confession has even shorter sections on the sacraments, and it also has more negative remarks about Roman practices. There is little room for more than extremely cursory constructive statements in

this document. Therefore, the Confession is not as helpful as the Catechism when tracing the development of Calvin's eucharistic teaching. The title of the 1537 Confession is "Confession De La Foy Laquelle Tous Bourgeois et Habitans De Geneve Et Subiets Du Pays Doibvent Iurer De Garder Et Tenir Extraicte De LInstruction Dont On Use En LEglise De La Dicte Ville," OC 22:85–96; OS 1:418–26; translated in Calvin, *Theological Treatises*, pp. 26–33. As the title indicates, this Confession is simply an abstract of the larger Catechism.

20. "Les sacramens sont instituez a ceste fin quilz feussent exercises de nostre foy tant devant Dieu que devant les hommes." OC 10a:68; OS 1:411.

21. "And to be sure, they exercise our faith before God when they confirm it in the truth of God." ("Et certes devant Dieu ilz exercent nostre foy quand ilz la confirment en la verite de Dieu.") OC 10a:68; OS 1:411.

22. OC 10a:68; OS 1:411.

23. In the section "What Is A Sacrament" that immediately follows the opening section on the sacraments, the emphasis there is also on the accommodative function of a sacrament: it "sustains the feebleness of our faith" ("pour soustenir limbecillite de nostre foy"). OC 10a:68; OS 1:411. It is important to note that the sacrament here is also a "testimony of the grace of God" (ibid.) but not an instrument of grace.

24. "But it [faith] is also exercised toward men when it ensues in public confession and is incited to render praise to the Savior." ("Or elle est aussi par les sacramens exercee envers les hommes, quand elle sort en confession publique et est incitee a rendre louanges au Seigneur.") OC 10a:68; OS 1:411.

25. "The promise that is added to the mystery of the Supper declares clearly to what end the Supper has been instituted and to what it aims; that is to say that it confirms to us that the body of the Lord was once given for us in such a way that it is now ours and that it also forever will be so; that his blood was once shed for us so that it will always be ours." ("La promesse qui est adioustee au mystere de la cene declare evidemment a quelle fin il a este institue et a quoy il tend, cest a dire quil nous confirme que le corps du Seigneur a une fois tellement este donne pour nous, quil est maintenant nostre et le sera aussy perpetuellement, que son sang a une fois tellement este espandu pour nous quil sera tousiours nostre.") OC 10a:69; OS 1:412.

26. ". . . une presence enclose ou de la chair soubz le pain ou du sang soubz le vin." OC 10a:69; OS 1:412. Underlying Calvin's

insistence that there need not be an enclosed presence of Christ for there to be a true communication of his body are two factors: Calvin's christological assumptions and his fear of idolatry. Christ's flesh can not be enclosed under the elements because Christ's body is in heaven. Calvin insists that the body *must* be located in a particular place if it is to remain truly human, which it must if it is to be salvific for human beings. Only by retaining its true human nature by being bound by space does Calvin think he can protect both the reality of the incarnation and the hope for the bodily resurrection of Christians. On these assumptions concerning Christ's *caro vero* and the Christian's *spes resurrectionis*, see Oberman, "The 'Extra' Dimension in the Theology of Calvin," pp. 245–55. Calvin's fear that the notion of an enclosed presence of Christ in the eucharistic elements produces idolatry and the worship of earthly elements dates back to the first edition of the *Institutes*. There he considers his eucharistic doctrine as one that "will easily draw us away also from physical adoration." *Inst. '36*, p. 107; OC 1:124; OS 1:143. For Calvin, God alone is to be worshipped in spirit and in truth. Any notion that draws the believer's attention away from God's spiritual reality to a consideration of *only* the earthly signs of God's presence is considered dangerous to the believer's soul and salvation.

27. "Christ avec toutes ses richesses nous y est presente non pas moins que sil estoit mis en la presence de noz yeulx et estoit touche de noz mains." OC 10a:70; OS 1:413.

28. "Car elle est desia vivifiee par sa chair immortelle et communique en quelque maniere a son immortalite." OC 10a:70; OS 1:413.

29. OC 10a:70; OS 1:413.

30. OC 10a:70; OS 1:413.

31. "Confessio Fidei de Eucharistia," OC 9:711–12; OS 1:435–36; translated in Calvin, *Theological Treatises*, pp. 168–69. An analysis of this document as an expression of Calvin's thought has been undertaken by Heinrich Janssen, "Die Abendmahlslehre Johannes Calvin," *Una Sancta* 15, no. 2 (1960): 125–38. Technically, this document is not the last of the period: that would be the 1538 translation Calvin made of the 1537 Catechism. However, as a translation it adds nothing new to Calvin's eucharistic thought. For the sections on the sacraments in the 1538 translation, see OC 5:349–51.

32. Calvin, *Theological Treatises*, p. 168; OC 9:711; OS 1:435.

33. Calvin, *Theological Treatises*, p. 168; OC 9:712; OS 1:435.

34. Calvin, *Theological Treatises*, p. 168; OC 9:712; OS 1:435.

35. For an account of this conflict, see T. H. L. Parker, *John Calvin* (London: J. M. Dent and Sons, 1975; repr. ed., Lion Publishing, 1987), pp. 78-80; and Wendel, *Calvin*, pp. 55-57.

36. "His pastorate in Strasbourg seems to have been a definitive stage in his life. . . . [Calvin] found in Strasbourg an intellectual and religious centre where he could work as he chose, in close collaboration with the theologians resident in the town." Wendel, *Calvin*, p. 65. The direct influence of Bucer on Calvin has been a hotly contested question. For some assessments of the situation, see Jaques Courvoisier, "Bucer et l'oeuvre de Calvin," *Revue de Théologie et Philosophie* 21 (1936): 66-77; Wilhelm Pauck, "Calvin und Butzer," *Journal of Religion* 9 (1929): 237-56; and Henri Strohl, "Bucer et Calvin," *Bulletin d'Histoire du Protestantisme français* 87 (1938): 354-56.

For a fine history of the changes in the eucharistic liturgy in Strasbourg during the sixteenth century brought about by Protestants such as Bucer, see René Bornert, *La Réforme protestante du culte a Strasbourg au XVIᵉ siècle (1523-1598): Approche sociologique et interprétation théologique* (Leiden: E.J. Brill, 1981).

37. Also important to note is that the prefaces to the two works were written within just a few months of each other; the preface to the '39 *Institutes* is dated 1 August 1539, while the *Romans* preface is dated 18 October 1539. For the relation of these two works to one another, see Parker, *John Calvin*, pp. 89-90. A rather cursory summary of the relation is made by Richard C. Gamble when he says, "The material learned by Calvin as he worked on his *Romans* commentary is incorporated in the new edition ['39] and a host of other changes and amplifications occur." Gamble, Preface to *Institutes of the Christian Religion of John Calvin 1539: Text and Concordance*, 4 vols., edited by Richard F. Wevers (Grand Rapids: The Meeter Center for Calvin Studies at Calvin College and Seminary, 1988), 1:vii. For a more detailed examination of the relation between the two works, see Alexandre Ganoczy, "Calvin als paulinischer Theologe," in *Calvinus Theologus: Die Referate des Europäischen Kongresses für Calvinforschung vom 16. bis 19. September 1974 in Amsterdam*, edited by W. H. Neusner (Neukirchen-Vluyn: Neukirchener Verlag, 1976), pp. 43-48.

38. The OC collates the Latin editions of the *Institutes* of 1539-1550. The edition by Wevers, noted above, will be used as the primary reference for the '39 *Institutes*. Wevers provides reference to the OC column numbers in the margins of his work, and they will be given after citations from Wevers for those who find the OC more

readily available. Wevers used the first edition of the '39 *Institutes*, printed in Strasbourg by W. Rihel, as the basis for his text.

39. "The *Institutes* no longer looked like an elaborated catechism; it was now a copious manual of dogmatic theology." Wendel, *Calvin*, p. 61. The change in purpose is clear from the prefatory matter in the two editions. In 1536 the *Institutes* are, according to Calvin, "adapted to a simple and, you may say, elementary form of teaching." *Inst. '36*, p. 1; OC 1:9; OS 1:21. However, in 1539 Calvin states that, ". . . it has been my purpose in this work to prepare and train students in theology." OC 1:255/56. Thus, the change in intent from catechetical to dogmatic is apparent. The expansion of the work was great enough that Calvin could comment in the subtitle of the '39 edition, "Now at last truly corresponding to its title." The subtitle should be read with reference to the subtitle original with 1536 which stated, "Embracing nearly the whole sum of piety, and of whatever is necessary for the obtaining of salvation."

40. Such as predestination, for example; see *Inst. '39*, Chapter 8, pp. 216–39; OC 1:861–902.

41. Material from the '39 *Institutes* will be cited in the following manner: by chapter, paragraph, and line number, followed by page number from the Wevers edition (Wevers added the paragraph and line designations for ease of reference); then reference will be made to the appropriate volume and column number of the OC.

42. ". . . proprium ac solidum spiritus sancti opus fidem esse." *Inst. '39* 10.5.31, p. 263; OC 1:943.

43. *Inst. '36*, p. 89; same material to be found in *Inst. '39* 10.5.34–39, p. 263; OC 1:943–44.

44. The full quote runs, "Quomobrem de confirmatione argumentoque [*sic*] fidei monitum velim lectorem: quod iam minime dubiis verbis expressisse mihi videor, id ministerium sic me sacramentis assignare." *Inst. '39* 10.6.1–3, p. 263; OC 1:944. As indicated by the "*sic*" inserted in the quote, the Wevers edition has given the word "argumentoque"; it should read "augmentoque." See OC 944.

45. "Itaque sic inter spiritum sacramentaque partior, ut poenes illum agendi virtus resideat: his ministerium duntaxat reliquatur. Idque sine spiritus actione inane ac frivolum: illo vero intus agente, vimque suam exerente, multae energiae refertum." *Inst. '39* 10.6.11–13, p. 263; OC 1:944.

46. ". . . the sacraments profit not a trifle without the power of the Holy Spirit; and nothing prevents them from strengthening and increasing faith in hearts already taught previously by that teacher."

("... neque sacramenta hilum proficere sine spiritus sancti virtute: et nihil obstare, quominus in cordibus iam ante a praeceptore illo edoctis, fidem et robustiorem, et auctiorem reddant.") *Inst. '39* 10.6.22-24, p. 263; OC 1:944.

47. "... bonam patris coelestis erga nos voluntatem nobis." *Inst. '39* 10.7.23, p. 264; OC 1:945. See also Calvin's comments on Romans 8:16: "Therefore, Paul means that the Spirit of God renders to us such a testimony that our spirit is assured of the adoption of God when he is our leader and teacher. For our mind would not of its own accord convey this guarantee to us except the testimony of the Spirit preceded it." ("Intelligit autem Paulus, spiritum Dei tale nobis testimonium reddere, ut eo duce et magistro spiritus noster statuat firmam Dei adoptionem. Neque enim sponte mens nostra, nisi praeeunte spiritus testimonio, hanc nobis fidem dictaret.") OC 49:150.

48. This notion of the function of the Spirit as an internal testimony to the truth of God's good will toward the Christian is especially forcefully stated in the *Romans* commentary, particularly as Calvin comments on Romans 5:5—"This knowledge of the divine love towards us is instilled in our hearts through the Spirit of God. For the good things God has prepared for those who worship him are hidden from the ears, eyes, and minds of man. The Spirit alone is able to reveal them." ("Haec divinae erga nos dilectionis notitia cordibus nostris instillata est per spiritum Dei. Nam et ab auribus et oculis et mentibus hominum abscondita sunt, quae praeparavit Deus bona culturibus suis: solus est spiritus qui potest ea patefacere.") OC 49:91-92.

49. "Siquidem ut finitum esse, pro perpetua corporis humani ratione . . . coeloque contineri." *Inst. '39* 12.13.3-5, p. 294; OC 1:1003. The importance of Christ's flesh as *human flesh* is most fully spelled out in Calvin's comments on John 6, to be analyzed in Chapter V of this work. As will be shown in more detail, Calvin considers Christ's flesh to be one of a series of instruments God uses to convey salvation. The function of the instrument of Christ's flesh is to make the work of Christ accessible to the believer. If the flesh of Christ becomes something other than true human flesh, then it can no longer be said that Christ is truly "God with us."

50. "... hoc beneficii per spiritum suum nobis Dominus largitur, ut unum corpore, spiritu, et anima, secum fiamus. Vinculum ergo istius coniunctionis est Spiritus Domini, cuius nexu copulamur: et quidam veluti canalis, per quem quidquid Christus et est et habet, ad nos derivatur. Nam si solem conspicimus radiis in terram emicantem ad

generandos, fovendos, vegetandos eius foetus suam quodammodo substantiam ad eam traiicere: cur inferior spiritus Christi esset irradiatione, ad communionem carnis et sanquinis eius in nos traducendam? Quapropter scriptura, ubi de nostra cum Christo participatione loquitur, vim eius universam ad spiritum refert." *Inst.* *'39* 12.13.8–17, p. 295; OC 1:1003–4.

51. ". . . insitio non exempli tantum conformitatem designat, sed arcanum coniunctionem, per quam cum ipso coaluimus, ita ut nos spiritu suo vegetans eius virtutem in nos transfundet." OC 49:106.

52. Comment on Romans 5:17; OC 49:100.

53. Comment on Romans 8:10 ("And if Christ is in you"): "Nam ut per spiritum sibi nos in templa consecrat, ita per eundem in nobis residet." OC 49:145.

54. Calvin, "Reply to Letter by Cardinal Sadolet to the Senate and People of Geneva," in *John Calvin: Selections from His Writings*, edited by John Dillenberger (Anchor Books, 1971; repr. ed., Missoula, Mont.: Scholars Press, 1975), p. 99; OC 5:400; OS 1:472. The translation of Calvin's Reply to Sadolet used by Dillenberger is taken from Calvin, *Selected Works* 1:25–68.

55. This is not surprising, for though Calvin did not publish a commentary on John until 1553, his first set of lectures in Strasbourg were on the Gospel of John. See Williston Walker, *John Calvin: The Organiser of Reformed Protestantism, 1509–1564* (New York: G. P. Putnam's Sons, 1906; repr. ed., New York: AMS, 1972), p. 228 and 228 n. 2.

56. "Quae sententia verbis illis luculente comprobatur. Panis quem ego dabo, caro mea est: quam ego dabo pro mundi vita." *Inst.* *'39* 12.4.15–16, p. 290; OC 1:994.

57. "Quibus haud dubie Dominus innuit, suum nobis corpus ideo pro pane futurum ad spiritualem animae vitam." *Inst.* *'39* 12.4.16–18, p. 290; OC 1:994.

58. ". . . quotidie dat, ubi participandum, quatenus crucifixum est, Evangelii verbo nobis offert." *Inst.* *'39* 12.4.20–21, p. 290; OC 1:994.

59. "In hunc modum voluit Dominus, panem vitae se nuncupando, non tantum docere in mortis resurrectionisque suae fide, repositam esse nobis salutem: sed vera etiam sui communicatione fieri, ut vita sua in nos transeat, ac nostra fiat. Non secus ac panis, dum in alimentum sumitur, vigorem corpori administrat." *Inst.* *'39* 12.9.34–38, p. 293; OC 1:999.

60. ". . . nos fide complecti Christum, non eminus apparentem: sed se nobis communicantem." *Inst. '39* 12.9.41-42, p. 293; OC 999.

61. ". . . praeterita carnis et sanguinis mentione." *Inst. '39* 12.10.3, p. 293; OC 1:1000.

62. ". . . nihil demum restat, nisi ut in eius mysterii admirationem prorumpam, cui nec mens plane cogitando, nec lingua explicando par esse potest." *Inst. '39* 12.10.17-18, p. 293; OC 1:1000.

63. "Quibus verbis docet, non modo se vitam esse, quatenus sermo est Dei aeternus, qui e coelo ad nos descendit: sed descendendo vim istam in carnem, quam induit, diffudisse: ut inde ad nos vitae communicatio promanaret." *Inst. '39* 12.11.19-22, p. 294; OC 1:1001.

64. "Caro, sine aliqua speciali notatione, homines significat: nisi quod generalius quodammodo significatem videtur prae se ferre. Qualiter plus exprimitur, quum quis dicit omnes mortales, quam si omnes homines nominet." OC 49:57.

65. "Et nota formulam scripturae usitatem, in carne esse, pro eo quod est, solis naturae dotibus esse praeditum, sine singulari gratia, qua electos suos Deus dignatur." OC 49:122.

66. "Utrumque igitur nomen, nempe tam carnis quam spiritus, in animam competit: sed alterum qua parte est regenerata, alterum qua naturalem adhuc affectum retinet." OC 49:132.

67. ". . . in carne vel secundum carnem perinde valere atque esse dono regenerationis vacuos. Tales vero sunt quicunque in puris (ut vulgo loquuntur) naturalibus manent." OC 49:141. Alasdair Heron expresses well the meaning of flesh in this Pauline sense when he says that the realm of the flesh is "the world of men living by their own power and their own standards, their own perceptions and their own light, separate from God." Heron, *Table and Tradition: Toward An Ecumenical Understanding of the Eucharist* (Philadelphia: Westminster Press, 1983), p. 49.

68. For a critique of Calvin that claims that he did not, in fact, understand what it meant for Christ to be fully human, see Max Thurian, "The Real Presence," in *Christianity Divided*, edited by Daniel J. Callahan et. al. (New York: Sheed and Ward, 1961), pp. 210-11.

69. ". . . totus spiritu et corpore nobis adhaereat." *Inst. '39* 12.12.22-23, p. 294; OC 1:1002.

70. ". . . in sua quoque humanitate, vitae penitudinem habitare ostendit: ut quisquis carni suae ac sanguini communicarit, vitae participatione simul fruatur." *Inst. '39* 12.12.8-10, p. 294; OC 1:1001.

71. "Iam quis non videt communionem carnis et sanguinis, necessariam esse omnibus, qui ad coelestem vitam adspirant?" *Inst. '39* 12.12.16–18, p. 294; OC 1:1002.

72. "Quod si verum est praeberi nobis signum visibile, ad obsignandam invisibilis rei donationem: accepto corporis symbolo, non minus corpus etiam ipsum nobis dari, certo confidamus." *Inst. '39* 12.13.39–42, p. 295; OC 1:1003.

73. Though I am here distinguishing the understanding from the experience of union with Christ, the two cannot be separated. Rather, understanding and experience are two sides of the same coin, strengthening and upbuilding one another. Heiko Oberman has pointed out the shift in late medieval thought away from "meta" categories (metaphysical ontology, for example) to "experience" categories as the surest way to get at truth. See Oberman, "The Shape of Late Medieval Thought," in *The Dawn of the Reformation*, p. 28, and "Fourteenth-Century Religious Thought: A Premature Profile," in *The Dawn of the Reformation*, p. 16. If Calvin was influenced by the strands of nominalist thought of which Oberman speaks, then it seems logical that Calvin would link understanding and experience. Experience confirms understanding, understanding strengthens experience. This line of thought develops not only in Calvin's eucharistic theology, which will be shown through the course of this work, but also in Calvin's theology of faith. If we look at material new with the '39 *Institutes*, we find the following: "Faith is dependent not on ignorance, but on knowledge." ("Non in ignoratione, sed in cognitione sita est fides." *Inst. '39* 4.18.3, p. 95; OC 1:473.) ". . . by this knowledge, not by the submission of our feeling, do we obtain entrance into the kingdom of heaven." ("... cognitione, non sensus nostri submissione, ingressum in regnum coelorum obtinemus." *Inst. '39* 4.18.8–9, p. 95; OC 1:473.) "[Paul] . . . requires explicit recognition of the divine goodness in which our righteousness consists." (". . . explicitam requirit divinae bonitatis agnitionem: in qua consistet nostra iustitia." *Inst. '39* 4.18.12, p. 95; OC 1:474.) "For faith rests in the knowledge of God and Christ." ("Fides enim in Dei et Christi cognitione . . . iacet." *Inst. '39* 4.18.17–18, p. 95; OC 474.) Of course, this knowledge is not simply a knowledge of God in general but is "a firm and certain knowledge of the divine benevolence toward us." ("Divinae erga nos benevolentiae firmam certamque cognitionem." *Inst. '39* 4.3.51, p. 86; OC 1:456.) This knowledge, however, is not that which can be gained by humans through ordinary means. It is "so far above human sense that the mind of man properly must go beyond and rise above itself that it may reach

it." ("humanum sensum . . . superior est, ut mentem hominis seipsam excedere et superare oporteat, quo ad illam pertingat." *Inst.* *'39* 4.4.5, p. 87; OC 1:456.) In other words, this knowledge is a gift from God, delivered and sealed by the Holy Spirit. There is thus a mysterious element to faith, just as there is to the Eucharist. However, once given, this gift of faith can become a sure knowledge for the believer, made firm and certain by experience, for it "requires full and fixed certainty, such as from things that are usually discovered and tested." (". . . plenam et fixam, qualis de rebus compertis, et probatis esse solet, certitudinem requirit." *Inst.* *'39* 4.4.24–26, p. 87; OC 1:456.) As in Calvin's doctrine of faith, so in Calvin's eucharistic thought knowledge becomes an important category; it both supports and is supported by the Christian's experience of union with Christ.

74. *Inst.* *'36*, p. 107; OC 1:123; OS 1:142.

75. "Quin denique suo ipsius corpore eos pascat, cuius communionem, spiritus sui virtute, in eos transfundit." *Inst.* *'39* 12.17.18–19, p. 297; OC 1:1009.

76. "Siquidem ab immortali eius carne iam vivificatur, et quoddammodo eius immortalitati communicat." *Inst.* *'39* 12.17.24–25, p. 297; OC 1:1010.

77. *Inst.* *'36*, p. 115; OC 1:132; OS 1:152. Calvin deals with the Catholic concept of the Mass as a sacrifice at length on pp. 115–20 of *Inst.* *'36*; OC 132–37; OS 1:152–58.

78. *Inst.* *'36*, p. 120; OC 1:137; OS 1:158.

79. "Therefore, let us divide our [sacrifices] into two categories. For the purpose of teaching, we may call one category of sacrifice 'praise and reverence' because it consists of veneration and worship of God, which the faithful both owe and give to him. Or, if you prefer, it may be called 'thanksgiving,' seeing that it is presented to God by none but those who, loaded down with his immense benefits, pay him back with their whole selves and all their actions. The other category may be called 'propitiation' or 'expiation.'" ("Proinde et nos in duo genera distribuamus: ac alterum, docendi causa, vocemus #latreutikon et #sebasmion quoniam veneratione cultuque Dei constat, quem illi fideles et debent et reddunt, vel si mavis #eucharistikon, quandoquidem a nullis Deo exhibetur, nisi qui immensis eius beneficiis onusti, se totos cum actionibus suis omnibus rependunt. Alterum propitiatorium, sive expiationis.") *Inst.* *'39* 12.32.18–23; p. 307; OC 1:1030. The siglum in the Wevers edition signals the use of Greek words in the original text.

80. "And [the sacrifice] was accomplished but once, because the efficacy and power of this one by Christ are eternal." ("Et semel quod illius unius a Chrsto peracti efficacia et vis aeterna est.") *Inst.* *'39* 12:32:31–32, p. 307; OC 1:1030.

81. *Inst.* *'36*, p. 120; OC 1:137; OS 1:158.

82. See Calvin's comments at Romans 12:1; OC 49:234–35.

83. ". . . omnia charitatis officia, quibus dum fratres nostros complectitur, Dominum ipsum in membris suis honoramus." *Inst.* *'39* 12.34.1–3; p. 307; OC 1:1032.

84. ". . . omnia fide bona opera, spirituales hostiae." *Inst.* *'39* 12.34.27, p. 308; OC 1:1033.

85. See, once again, Calvin's comments on Romans 12:1.

86. ". . . fidei analogiam, ad quam omnem scripturae interpretationem exigere iubet Paulus hac in parte mihi praeclare constare nihil dubium est." *Inst.* *'39* 12.17.31–33, p. 297; OC 1:1010.

87. "Ut ergo iustificemur, causa efficiens est misericordia Dei: Christus, materia; verbum cum fide, instrumentum. Quare fides iustificare dicitur: quia instrumentum est recipiendi Christi, in quo nobis communicatur iustitia." OC 49:60.

88. Grace, for Calvin, is simply God's favor; therefore it is an attitude or a relation God holds toward humanity rather than being a "thing" or a "substance." See Calvin's comment on "grace" at Romans 1:7: "Nothing is better pleasing than that we have a well-disposed God; that is designated by 'grace.'" ("Nihil prius optandum quam ut Deum propitium habeamus: quod designatur per gratiam.") OC 49:13.

89. ". . . corpus Christi panis hodie nuncupatur: quando symbolum est, quo veram corporis sui manducationem offert nobis Dominus." *Inst.* *'39* 12.8.27–29, p. 292; OC 1:998.

90. Commenting on Romans 11:14, Calvin says, "let us understand, however, preaching to be an instrument for accomplishing the salvation of the faithful. Because, although nothing can be produced without the Spirit of God, yet through its inner working it shows his action most powerfully." (". . . praedicationem tamen intelligamus instrumentum esse peragendae fidelium salutis: quod etsi nihil sine Dei spiritu promovere queat, illo tamen intus operante, suam actionem potentissime exserit.") OC 49:219.

91. See McDonnell, *John Calvin, the Church and the Eucharist*, pp. 367, 369, 370, 375, 379, 381 n. 19.

92. Heiko Oberman discusses Calvin's christology in relation to Nestorius in "The 'Extra' Dimension in the Theology of Calvin," in

The Dawn of the Reformation, pp. 246–55, citing some of those who have charged Calvin with Nestorianism.

93. "Hoc locus admonere nos debet ac expergefacere, quid secum nobis afferat Christus ad contemplandas eius divitias. Nam ut est pignus immensae erga nos caritatis Dei, ita non nudas, aut inanis ad nos missus est: sed coelistibus omnibus thesauris refertus, nequid eum possidentibus ad plenam felicitatem desit." OC 49:163.

94. "Constituimus ergo, sacramenta vere nominari testimonia gratia Dei, ac veluti quaedam benevolentiae, qua erga nos affectus est, sigilla: quae dum ipsam nobis obsignat, fidem nostram ita consolantur, alunt, confirmant, adaugent." *Inst. '39* 10.5.1–4, p. 262; OC 1:942–43.

95. In the *Romans* commentary, see Calvin's comments at 4:11, where he declares, "And even though by themselves they benefit nothing, yet God, who desires them to be the instruments of his grace, through the secret grace of his Spirit promotes the benefit of the elect by their means." ("Ac tametsi, per se nihil iuvant, Deus tamen, qui gratiae suae instrumenta esse voluit, arcana spiritus sui gratia efficit ne profectu careant in electis.") OC 49:74. The same concern runs throughout the '39 *Institutes*: "that the administration of the sacraments that he has ordained may not be unfruitful and empty, we teach that the inner grace of the Spirit, since it is distinct from the outward ministry, ought to be pondered and considered separately." (". . . ne infructuosa sit et inanis quam ordinavit sacrmentorum administratia: Interiorem tamen spiritus gratiam, ut ab externo ministerio distincta est, seorsum reputandam et cogitandam, docemus.") *Inst. '39* 10.12.18–21, p. 266; OC 1:950. One must remember, however, that even the work of Christ himself is of no avail unless the Spirit bonds the Christian to Christ.

96. Calvin's comment on Romans 1:19: "Deus ad modulum nostrum attemperat quidquid de se testatur." OC 49:49:23.

97. "Nempe ut quaeque est manifestior: ita est ad fulciendam fidem magis idonea. Sacramenta vero et promissiones afferunt clarissimas." *Inst. '39* 10.2.16–17, p. 261; OC 1:941. Clarity helps serve the end of the Eucharist as a cognitive aid to faith, which itself at this time begins to take on more of a cognitive cast in Calvin's thought. As Jean-Daniel Benoit states, "in the 1536 *Institutio* Calvin, like Luther, insisted that above all faith was trust and hope. In 1539 he made more of the intellectual nature of faith." Benoit, "The History and Development of the Institutio: How Calvin Worked," in *John Calvin*, edited by G.E. Duffield (Appleford, England: The Sutton Courtenay Press, 1966), p. 104.

98. *Petit Traicté de La Saincte Cene de Nostre Seigneur Iesus Christ*, OC 5:433–60; OS 1:503–30; translated by Henry Beveridge in Calvin, *Selected Works* 2:164–98; quoted here from John Calvin, *Selections from His Writings*, edited by John Dillenberger, pp. 507–41, cited hereafter as *Short Treatise*.

Calvin wrote his *Short Treatise* in Strasbourg, but it was published in Geneva after his return to that city in September of 1541.

99. *Short Treatise*, p. 512; OC 5:437; OS 1:507.

100. Calvin emphasizes those aspects of his eucharistic thought that he had developed throughout the Strasbourg years. The concept of the life-giving flesh of Christ and the necessity of the Christian's partaking of it runs throughout the treatise. This concept controls the institution of the Eucharist for Calvin. The Supper was instituted, according to Calvin, "first, in order to sign and seal in our consciences the promises contained in his gospel concerning our being made partakers of his body and blood, and to give us certainty and assurance that therein lies our true spiritual nourishment." *Short Treatise*, p. 510; OC 5:35–436; OS 1:505. Therefore, "the substance of the sacraments is the Lord Jesus." *Short Treatise*, p. 513; OC 5:437; OS 1:507.

101. *Short Treatise*, p. 508; OC 5:433–34; OS 1:503–4. For an analysis of this treatise using Calvin's explicit framework for the piece, see Tylenda, "Ecumenical Intentions," pp. 37–40. Tylenda's interpretation is the best of the standard ways of expounding the doctrinal elements served up in Calvin's outline. The reader is referred to Tylenda here because the bulk of my argument is with the issue of knowledge rather than an explication of all the important elements of this treatise.

102. *Short Treatise*, p. 507; OC 5:433; OS 1:503.

103. *Short Treatise*, p. 508; OC 5:433; OS 1:503.

104. *Short Treatise*, p. 508; OC 5:433; OS 1:503.

105. *Short Treatise*, p. 510; OC 5:435; OS 1:505.

106. *Short Treatise*, p. 510; OC 5:435; OS 1:505.

107. *Short Treatise*, p. 514; OC 5:439; OS 1:508.

108. *Short Treatise*, p. 515; OC 5:439; OS 1:509.

109. *Short Treatise*, p. 521; OC 5:444; OS 1:514.

110. *Short Treatise*, p. 522; OC 5:445; OS 1:515.

110. *Short Treatise*, p. 522; OC 5:445; OS 1:515.

111. *Short Treatise*, p. 522; OC 5:445; OS 1:515.

112. *Short Treatise*, p. 511; OC 5:435; OS 1:505.

113. *Short Treatise*, p. 515; OC 5:439; OS 1:509.

114. *Short Treatise*, p. 511; OC 5:437; OS 1:506.

115. *Short Treatise*, p. 516–17; OC 5:440; OS 1:510.

116. *Short Treatise*, p. 510; OC 5:435; OS 1:505.

117. *Short Treatise*, p. 510; OC 5:435; OS 1:505.

118. *Short Treatise*, p. 514; OC 5:439; OS 1:508.

119. *Short Treatise*, p. 513; OC 5:437; OS 1:507.

120. *Short Treatise*, p. 515; OC 5:439; OS 1:509.

121. *Short Treatise*, p. 515; OC 5:439; OS 1:509.

122. "However, even given Calvin's dialectic, and given his norm of distinction but not separation, it is distinction and not union which has the preponderance . . . more tension than union." McDonnell, *John Calvin, the Church and the Eucharist*, p. 367.

123. *Short Treatise*, p. 531; OC 5:452; OS 1:522.

124. "It is a general rule in all sacraments that the signs which we see must have some correspondence with the spiritual thing which is figured." *Short Treatise*, p. 529; OC 5:451; OS 1:520.

125. *Short Treatise*, p. 523; OC 5:446; OS 1:516.

126. Calvin, in the section quoted above, is answering those who would call the eucharistic celebration "superfluous" in light of communion with Jesus Christ. I think this section, if one understands the dialectic at work between sign and thing signified and how it works in a unique way to bring to Christians sure knowledge of their salvation, also refutes Calvin's modern readers who would also label the Eucharist "superfluous" in relation to his broader religious thought. See Wendel's characterization of the problem, *Calvin*, p. 353.

127. *Short Treatise*, p. 540; OC 5:459; OS 1:529.

128. See Bouwsma, *John Calvin*, p. 4 and chapter 2.

129. *Short Treatise*, p. 533; OC 5:454; OS 1:524.

130. *Short Treatise*, p. 534; OC 5:454–55; OS 1:524.

131. Though, for the purpose of analysis, word and Eucharist have been separated to some extent, it is best to think of them as a "double instrument" ("duplex instrumentum") as does W. F. Dankbaar, *De Sacramentsleer van Calvijn* (Amsterdam: H.J. Paris, 1941), p. 29.

132. Mary Potter Engels has clarified this situation extremely well in regard to Calvin's anthropology in her *John Calvin's Perspectival Anthropology*, AAR Academy Series 52 (Atlanta: Scholars Press, 1988). She has shown that it depends upon which perspective (divine or human, for example) one looks at a doctrine as to how one assesses its standing. This method works extremely well at just this point in Calvin's eucharistic theology.

133. *Short Treatise*, p. 535; OC 5:456; OS 1:525.

134. *Short Treatise*, passim; these words and phrases are easily found throughout the treatise, and all have been quoted in fuller context previously.

135. *Short Treatise*, p. 536; OC 5:456; OS 1:526.

136. Therefore, one can call this knowledge a special gift or grace. What one must keep in mind is that there can be a special grace without a special presence. The mistake of confusing the two leads one to deny a eucharistic gift in Calvin. See, for example, Ronald N. Gleason, "Calvin and Bavinck on the Lord's Supper," *Westminster Theological Journal* 45, no. 2 (Fall 1983): 296, where Gleason makes this very mistake: he cites Calvin's insistence on a perpetual eating of Christ as evidence that the specific eucharistic act lacks a special grace. This is so only if special grace and special presence are synonymous. However, they are not.

137. There is, of course, another very important publication that comes from Calvin's Strasbourg years—the 1541 French edition of his *Institutes*. However, despite its standing as a "masterpiece" of French literature, the 1541 edition adds nothing new to the developments charted during the Strasbourg years.

V

Calvin the Pastor, Expositor, and Polemicist: Eucharistic Developments from 1541 to 1557

With the completion of the *Short Treatise on the Holy Supper*, the foundation for Calvin's mature eucharistic thought is in place. However, the edifice that can be called Calvin's mature doctrine of the Eucharist, while obviously resting on that foundation, cannot simply be equated with it. The walls and roof of Calvin's eucharistic theology must still be built before the final "structure" of Calvin's eucharistic teaching can be discussed.

This chapter will proceed in more of a survey fashion than the previous chapters. Since ambiguity and development in Calvin's early thought (1535–1541) have been shown and the foundation of Calvin's eucharistic thought has been exposed as it has developed, this chapter will proceed thematically. An examination of three themes will show how Calvin's mature eucharistic theology reached its fullest and most developed expression.

First, the theme of "knowledge" will be explored. This section will document that Calvin's concern for the Eucharist as a source for religious knowledge that came to the fore in the explication of the 1541 *Short Treatise* continues. This concern is present throughout Calvin's pastoral, instructional, and exegetical works. Thus, this section will concern itself with the materials Calvin prepared for public worship and celebration of the Eucharist; with specifically educational literature Calvin prepared in his duties as pastor, that is, the catechism; with works that are heavily instructional in intent, such as the 1543 *Institutes*; and with Calvin's New Testament commentaries. One sees with the 1543 *Institutes* in particular the extent to which Calvin further expounded his concept of the Eucharist as a source of knowledge, in that much of the new material in 1543 relates specifically to this topic.

Second, Calvin's polemical treatises against Westphal and his commentary on the gospel of John will be analyzed. Calvin's first treatise against Westphal already has been examined in Chapter II. This chapter will continue that examination and include Calvin's second and third responses to Westphal. In these works, Calvin deals especially with Christ's flesh, feeding on that flesh, and the mode of its communication in the Eucharist. The mode of communication was a topic he had deigned to ignore in some of his earlier works.[1] Calvin's dependence on the Westphal conflict as the spur to his developing thought on eucharistic eating will be shown. Moreover, this influence is intertwined with Calvin's New Testament exegesis of passages having to do with Christ's presence and union with believers, especially his exegesis of the gospel of John.

Third, Calvin's treatises and commentaries from the 1550s will be explored in relation to the concept of "accommodative instrumentality." The biblical commentaries along with his treatises against Westphal disclose Calvin's ideas on how God reveals himself to his creatures and how God puts himself in contact with his people. In other words, these works show how Calvin thinks God makes himself and his will known to his people and at what level it can be said God is "in communion" with his elect.

Once these themes have been explored, we will be in a position to examine the 1559 *Institutes* from the perspective of its full developmental context. First, however, we will begin the examination of the three topics—knowledge, true partaking of Christ's flesh, and accommodated instrumentality—by beginning with the emphasis of the 1541 *Short Treatise*, namely, Calvin's emphasis on the Eucharist as a source of religious knowledge, certainty, and assurance.

The Eucharist as a Source of Knowledge in Calvin's Pastoral, Instructional, and Exegetical Works, 1541–1556

Calvin returned to the city of Geneva in September of 1541. He was supposedly on temporary loan from Strasbourg for six months. Calvin, of course, spent the rest of his life laboring in this "temporary" position. He had learned much from his Strasbourg years; perhaps he learned most of all how to be a pastor. Indeed, one could well attribute the developments in his eucharistic teaching during the Strasbourg years, especially the last mentioned—religious knowledge and certainty—to his need to provide proper "cure of souls" for his parishioners. Moreover, the lutheranizing force of Bucer's influence was substantial. Calvin picks up where he left off in Strasbourg when, in Geneva, he focuses his attention on the needs of the church and its members. The period of 1541–1545, to be discussed in the first section, is exemplary of Calvin's pastoral concerns in regard at least to the Eucharist, for much of his writing on matters of the Eucharist falls within "pastoral" types of writing—particularly the refinement of the Genevan Catechism and the writing of liturgies for Sunday worship. This section will show how Calvin incorporated the gains he made in the development of his eucharistic teaching, particularly the Eucharist as a gift of meaning and knowledge, assurance and certainty, into material adapted for congregational use. Then the developments in his eucharistic teaching in the 1543 Latin edition of his *Institutes* will be shown to be directly related to his concern for the type of sacramental epistemology he developed in the 1541 *Short Treatise*. Finally, in a third section, I will lay bare the biblical bases for Calvin's emphasis on the Eucharist as a way of gaining right knowledge of Christian life. All of these analyses will show the plausibility of the interpretation given the *Short Treatise*—that is, that the *Treatise*'s underlying structure is that of religious knowledge—because of the way the concern for the Eucharist as knowledge is exhibited in these writings.

Pastoral Writings, 1541–1545: Catechisms and Liturgies

Calvin's concern for the celebration of the Eucharist is apparent as he and fellow ministers drafted a set of ecclesiastical ordinances almost immediately upon his return to Geneva. Calvin, with others, worked on the draft during September and October of 1541, with acceptance of a revised set of articles coming by the Town Council in November. Calvin thought the Eucharist should be celebrated frequently—every Sunday. However, because of circumstances—the Town Council's unwillingness to have Communion celebrated so frequently—it was decided that the Eucharist would be celebrated four times per year in each parish church.[2]

Part of the preparation for participation in the Eucharist revolved around the catechism Calvin drew up for the church of Geneva. This catechism was a radical revision (if not an altogether new work) of the 1537 French and 1538 Latin catechism. Calvin prepared the French version in 1541 and published it in 1542, with a Latin translation made and published in 1545. The format was changed in 1541 from the prose format of the earlier catechism to the format of question and answer.

The catechism starts out with a short question and answer that has come to characterize much of the Reformed tradition. "What is the principal end of human life?" the teacher asks. The terse but all-encompassing answer is, simply, "To know God."[3] Much of what follows that short answer is, however, amplification on what it means to know God, how God is known, what is known about God, and what difference it makes.

Calvin's concern for the Eucharist as a specific source of religious knowledge appears in the section on the sacraments.[4]

Their purpose is to "better confirm their truth [God's promises] to us."[5] He explains the need for the sacraments in relation to human weakness. Because human beings have bodies and are not purely spiritual beings like the angels, Calvin claims that "we need figures or mirrors to exhibit a view of spiritual and heavenly things in a kind of earthly manner; *for we could not otherwise obtain them* (emphasis mine)."[6] Calvin is able thus to conclude that "it is [in] our interest to have all our senses exercised in the promises of God, that they may be the better confirmed to us."[7] Faith is, of course, important and necessary. However, Calvin recognizes that faith is such in human beings that it must be helped, for, indeed, all believers labor under "a weakness of faith."[8] Therefore, God uses secondary instruments such as the sacraments, which he enlivens by his Spirit, to aid the believer in the journey of faith, making it sure. It is by these means that the Christian can be said to be "going forward" in Christian life.[9]

When Calvin discusses the Supper in particular, the language of knowledge and certainty is also heavily used. In fact, Calvin speaks of Christ's communication of body and blood as a means of teaching the Christian about the "hope of eternal life."[10] That communication of body and blood, as Calvin had established by this time, is absolutely essential to Christian life. The language of the catechism is bold to answer in the affirmative when the question is asked, "Do we therefore eat the body and blood of the Lord?"[11] The reason Calvin gives is that one must receive Christ in order to receive his blessings. Thus, though the foundation of salvation is Christ's death and resurrection, still Calvin insists that for that event to be salvific, the believer must "now receive him."[12]

Of course, Calvin believes that communion with Christ comes through the Gospel as well as the Supper. The question is asked, "Do we obtain this communion by the Supper alone?" The answer is clear: "No, indeed. For by the Gospel also, as Paul declares, Christ is communicated to us."[13] Why, then, is the Supper necessary? It is because communion with Christ, offered through the Gospel, is "confirmed and increased" in the Supper. This means, for Calvin, that the Eucharist functions in such a way that "we may certainly know that reconciliation belongs to us."[14] It is important, therefore, not only that Christ dwell in the Christian, united as one flesh; it is also important for the Christian's growth in the Christian life to "recognise that he [Christ] dwells in us, and that we are united to him by a union the same in kind as that which unites the members to the head, that by virtue of this union we may become partakers of all his blessings."[15] In other words, proper knowledge and recognition of the source of salvation is a constituent part of growth into that salvation. That recognition is brought about in a heightened way by the Eucharist, in the act of which "our minds must be raised up to heaven."[16] Thus, Calvin's logic is impeccable when, in talking of the "office of teaching" in the church, he declares that "to feed the Church with the doctrine of piety and administer the sacrament, are united together by an indissoluble tie."[17] This is so because, as shown in Chapter IV, proper doctrine (knowledge) about the sacrament leads to the sacrament itself becoming a source of knowledge that presents the clearest promises of God. That knowledge, however, leads to believers' growth in Christian piety, which enables them better to grasp proper doctrine. Thus, there is a dialectical relationship between word and sacrament that leads to the one building up the other.

Such an understanding of the Eucharist's special function in providing knowledge and certainty, understanding and assurance, is underlined in the eucharistic liturgy Calvin writes for the use of the Genevan church in 1542.[18] The *sursum corda* aspect of Calvin's eucharistic thought is well-known. Less well-remarked, but certainly important for this discussion of religious knowledge, is Calvin's exact phrasing in the liturgy. He does, indeed, exhort the eucharistic participants to "lift up your hearts." The exact wording, however, runs, "With this view, let us raise our hearts and minds on high, where Jesus Christ is, in the glory of his Father, and from whence we look for him at our redemption."[19] Because the special gift of the Eucharist is a particular type of knowledge, Calvin is clear that one's mind must be lifted up as well as one's heart; this activity is the function of the Eucharist, as an instrument of God and his Spirit.

This emphasis is underlined in the liturgy Calvin wrote for use in the church of Strasbourg, which was published in 1545. There, in his instructions for its use, he is explicit in his concern that the celebration of the Eucharist serve as a source of knowledge. He states that, in preparation for communing, the people should be instructed by the pastors about four things. The first is that human beings are sinful by nature, heirs to Adam's sin, and therefore unable, because of being "in the flesh," of inheriting the Kingdom of God. Calvin then asserts that the people should be taught that only Christ and his death can bring about remission of sin. Third, Calvin says the people should be instructed to know that Christ gives himself in the sacrament of the Supper, and that by partaking of him the Christian gains all his benefits. Calvin states, "He therefore truly gives his body with the bread and his blood with the cup." " Why?" he asks. "For the remission of sins, and the confirmation of the new testament"[20] is the answer he gives. Calvin associates this confirmation with growth in the Christian life, as when he says, "these two things are given to us for two reasons: for the remission of sin and in order to increase the life of Christ in us—that is, so to speak, the confirmation of the new covenant."[21] Finally, the people should be taught to give thanks for God's great gifts.

These four points of instruction are important for Calvin because they provide the proper understanding and context for the celebration of the Eucharist. With this knowledge about the Eucharist fully explained, the Eucharist is in a position to serve its chief end and goal: to proclaim the forgiveness of sins that results from communion with Christ. The Eucharist, then, is celebrated, at least in part, "in order that we *know* (emphasis mine) how much it is necessary that Christ live in us, and we in him."[22] Therefore, the Eucharist serves as an assurance for the Christian believer, both cognitively and experientially.[23]

Calvin's Instructional Writing: the 1543 *Institutes*

Calvin's concern that the Eucharist serve as a source of knowledge for the Christian is also apparent in the edition of his *Institutes* issued in 1543. In this work, he expands the notions developed in the *Short Treatise* and incorporates them into the sections on the sacraments in general and the Lord's Supper in particular. Indeed, in large part, the additions of 1543 have to do with religious knowledge, patterned after the paradigm explicated above.

In regard to the sacraments in general, it is here that Calvin inserts new material that speaks to proper knowledge about the sacraments. Chapter 16 of the 1543 edition presents new explanations of the word "sacrament"[24] and why a visible sign is required: because souls are connected to bodies. Thus, pure incorporeal expressions of truth are impossible for humans to appropriate.[25]

However, Calvin makes it clear that the visible presentation of the signs alone do not fulfill the criteria for the visible presentation of God's truth. The word must be added to the visible sign to make a true sacrament.[26] In other words, there must be proclaimed doctrine *about* the sacrament in order for the sacrament to function properly. Yet, the word alone is not sufficient either for the Christian believers as they find themselves laboring in this world under the bondage of the flesh. The word is meant to empower the sacrament so that it might serve its proper function as a source of knowledge about divine things. Thus, Calvin proclaims, "Therefore, when we hear mention made of the sacramental word, let us understand the promise, which, preached with a clear voice by the minister, leads the people by the hand *where the sign aims and directs us* (emphasis mine)."[27]

Calvin explicitly notes for the first time in 1543 what had been implicitly stated in earlier works: that the sacrament serves a dual function, requiring a dual action by the Holy Spirit. The two functions work together in a dialectic that helps the Christian make progress in the Christian life. Calvin states:

Therefore, in as much as we are sometimes helped by their [the sacraments'] ministry to support, confirm, and increase a true understanding of Christ in ourselves, at other times to more fully possess him [Christ] and enjoy his riches, to such a degree they are efficacious among us. Moreover, that happens as we recognize in true faith that which is offered there.[28]

Thus, we see that Calvin distinguishes the function of the sacrament as a means of knowledge (or, it might be called an accommodated instrument of gracious knowledge) from its function as an instrument of grace that enriches and strengthens the Christian's communion with Christ. Both parts are necessary for the proper working of the Sacrament. However, the first, the sacrament as a means of knowledge, carries an accommodated function that is not replicated to the same degree elsewhere and is thus particular to this sacrament.[29] Certainly, the word is also an accommodated instrument of gracious knowledge. However, the Eucharist is unique in that it appeals to more of the human senses, thus allowing its message to be grasped more fully and experientially. The second function, that of union, is held in common with other means of grace that present and give Jesus Christ to the believer, such as preaching or prayer. The first and second functions are complementary, however, and serve to strengthen one another. Thus, greater union leads to greater understanding; greater understanding leads to greater union. The knowledge presented by the sacrament is of a special order and is a special gift that helps the Christian appropriate the more general gift of union with Christ, which is a state of Christian existence confirmed and increased by several means.

In the final section of Chapter 16, Calvin compares the sacraments of the Old Testament with those of the New. Here again, Calvin insists that it is the function of the sacraments to provide religious knowledge and certainty; a certainty that is particular to the New Testament sacraments. In baptism and the Eucharist, Calvin insists, God's good will and his grace are offered to the believer through Jesus Christ. However, the presentation is of such a sort that, compared to the old sacraments given the Hebrew children, the New Testament sacraments are "clearer and brighter."[30] Thus, they are "more majestic in signification, more preeminent in power."[31] With this prior and necessary information regarding the sacraments in general properly in place and understood, Calvin is then in a position to refer to the function of the Eucharist in particular as a source of religious knowledge.

The religious knowledge brought about by the Eucharist functions within the realm of sanctification. In 1543, Calvin is clearer than he had been before in either the 1539 *Institutes* or the *Short Treatise on the Holy Supper* when, in Chapter 18 (the chapter on the Eucharist), he distinguishes the task of the Eucharist as a source of knowledge and assurance for those who have been justified through the hearing of the word. Here again, the word is prior. Calvin speaks of the Eucharist as representing that food that "sustains and preserves us in that life into which he begets us by his word."[32] The word alone (as an instrument used by the Spirit) produces the faith that puts one in the state of justification before God. However, once justified, the Christian has another means in addition to the word to grow in faith. For it is the special work of the Eucharist to "confirm for us that the body of the Lord was once for all sacrificed for us so that we may now feed on it, and by feeding we perceive in ourselves the efficacy of that singular sacrifice."[33] In the eating of bread and the drinking of wine in the eucharistic act, believers "may certainly be assured that the power of his [Jesus'] life-giving death now lives in us."[34] Calvin is then able to conclude that, in the Supper, Christians "have this testimony that, as Christ is joined to us, as we in turn are engrafted into him, we are thus joined with him in one body so that whatever is his we may call ours."[35] Therefore, the Supper serves the function of assuring Christians that they indeed have received Christ and all his benefits.[36]

In fact, the witness of the Supper is so strong that, in speaking of appropriating Christ as the true food and drink of the soul, Calvin is able to say, "That happens not only through the Gospel but also more clearly through the Holy Supper, where he offers himself to us with all his benefits, and we receive him by faith."[37] Why is this recognition of the basis of Christian existence presented more clearly by the Supper, properly understood? Because that is the function of the Eucharist: it was instituted so that "pious minds may there duly apprehend Christ, . . . to help the otherwise weak mind of man so that it may rise up to perceive the height of spiritual mysteries."[38] Such an accommodated instrument of grace is absolutely necessary in Calvin's thought in 1543 because of the importance Calvin gives to *understanding* the state and gift of salvation. He says as much clearly when he states, "For we do not eat Christ duly and beneficially except as crucified, when in a living sense we *grasp the efficacy of his death* (emphasis mine)."[39] Thus, for Calvin, union with Christ constitutes salvation, but proper and full understanding of that union is essential to growth in that life together. The physical celebration of eating bread and drinking wine serves the elect and helps them realize that union with Christ is much more real than "mere imagining."[40]

Calvin's New Testament Commentaries, 1546–1556[41]

Calvin first published his commentary on 1 Corinthians[42] in 1546. In this work, Calvin lays out a structure of thought that emphasizes the elements of knowledge necessary to faith. In fact, faith becomes a way of knowing God because the natural pathways to such knowledge have been blocked by humankind's sinfulness. The natural order, God's creation, provides a pure knowledge of God, were humans able to read the universe correctly. However, since human beings are sinful creatures, unable to see the light around them because of their own darkness, God, in order to make himself known, worked around this insufficiency in humanity. Thus, "because the whole world learnt nothing at all from what God revealed of his wisdom in created things," Calvin writes as he comments on 1 Corinthians 1:21, "he then set about teaching men in a different way."[43]

This new way of teaching involves the knowledge of God that comes by and is part of and shores up faith. This is so because, according to Calvin, God *desires* that he be known by his people. Commenting on 1 Corinthians 1:31, Calvin claims that it is humanity's duty to "glory only in the knowledge of [God]." This knowledge, however, is not simply factual knowledge. As Calvin explains, God "wishes to be known in such a way that we may know that it is He who acts in justice, righteousness, and mercy."[44] In other words, Calvin is speaking here not of an objective and detached knowledge of an abstract God but of a saving knowledge of a personal God who acts on behalf of his children.[45]

This saving knowledge of God, which is given as a help to Christians because of their imperfections,[46] is divine in origin. Thus, it must come to the Christian through the work of the Holy Spirit. As Calvin says, "everything which is concerned with the true knowledge of God is a gift of the Holy Spirit."[47] It is only through this medium that the knowledge of God can be assured and sealed in the minds of the believers. Believers should, according to Calvin, know what God has done for them and be sure of it. Therefore, in commenting on 1 Corinthians 2:12, where Paul says that believers "received . . . the Spirit which is of God; that we might know the things that are freely given to us by God," Calvin says:

> The word *know* has been used in order to bring out better the assurance of confidence. However, let us note that it is not obtained in a natural way, or laid hold of by our mental power of comprehension, but it depends altogether of the revelation of the Spirit.[48]

Thus, according to Calvin, the Spirit, through its revelation, imparts a type of assurance about God's blessings that can be termed "knowledge," though it is spiritual knowledge, not natural knowledge.

However, it should be noted that Calvin balances his emphasis on knowledge with an emphasis on the mystery of the Eucharist. There is a spiritual knowledge the Eucharist imparts, but it is also an accommodated knowledge, which means that it is neither full nor complete in that the subject matter cannot be fully comprehended by the human mind. The same can be said of the word; indeed, that seems to be the reason the Eucharist was instituted: to flesh out, so to speak, the accommodated message of the word. Even though God seeks to assure Christians of their salvation through the Eucharist, there are finally things that human minds cannot grasp. The Eucharist helps Christians know *that* they have union with Christ; it does not, however, explain *how* this union takes place. The working of the union falls within the realm of the mysterious and incomprehensible action of the Holy Spirit. To know *how* union takes place is to step outside the bounds of piety. Calvin reminds his readers in his *Acts* commentary that there are limits to what even the Apostles were allowed to know. In speaking of Christ being taken in the clouds during his Ascension (Acts 1:9), Calvin comments:

> This seems to be the reason why the cloud concealed Him before He entered into His celestial glory, so that the disciples, content with what they had seen, might not inquire further. From them we learn that our minds are of too limited capacity to rise to the full measure of the glory of Christ. Therefore, let this cloud be the means of restraining our presumption.[49]

This passage on Christ's glory relates well to Christ's presence in the Eucharist: there are limits to what can be known due to human limitations. Thus, the Eucharist serves as a source of knowledge in that it assures believers of their union with Christ. They know *that* they have such union through the appropriation of the eucharistic symbolism. However, that is the limit of the accommodation and to step beyond what the sacrament assures in order to ask "how" is to step beyond the limits of piety into the realm of speculation.

It is clear that Calvin thinks that, even though there are limits to this knowledge, it is knowledge nonetheless. What is more, it is a knowledge that is saving, as Calvin said. Therefore, it is also a knowledge that functions as a type of spiritual power, helping the Christian grasp the things of God. In fact, Calvin seems to indicate that such a knowledge plays a part in enabling the Christian to partake of the flesh and blood of Christ. Thus, the Eucharist functions not only at the level of knowledge but also at the level of substantial partaking. Calvin's thought on this matter can be seen as he comments on 1 Corinthians 10:4, where Paul explains that the rock that provided drink for the Hebrew children during their sojourn in the desert was, in fact, Christ himself, who provided spiritual drink as well as water. Here Calvin is relying on his theory of the relationship between the two testaments, where he asserts that there is more continuity than discontinuity between the two; that the difference between the two testaments is one of degree rather than kind. Does one enjoy the benefits of Christ only by partaking of his body and blood and thus attaining union with him? Calvin thinks so. Moreover, he believes that such a mode of communication is applicable, indeed, absolutely necessary, for any of God's children in any time or place to commune with God. Therefore, in explaining the passage, Calvin makes it clear that he believes that, just as the Christians who live after Christ partake of his body and blood in substantial communion in order to receive his benefits, so the Hebrew children, those who belonged to God before the birth of Christ, must also partake of that body and blood to receive the benefits of Christ. As Calvin states of the Hebrews, "for their salvation depended on the benefit of the death and resurrection, and for that reason on the flesh and blood, of Christ, so that they might share in the blessing of redemption."[50] Of course, this position carries the problem of historical effect; namely, that Calvin claims that the Hebrew children substantially partook of Christ's body and blood before the incarnation had taken place. He answers that the partaking was of a different degree because the Hebrew children received, through the Holy Spirit, the efficacy of Christ's body and blood though the flesh of Christ was not yet created. On the other hand, the Christian receives the body and blood in such a manner that "the eating is substantial. . . . Christ feeds us with

His flesh."[51] Thus, Christ is given to the believer more fully after the incarnation.

Part of the reason is, of course, because the Christian lives after the fact of the incarnation. However, that seems to be only part of the reason for Calvin. The other part of the reason has to do with the fact that the Christian has the reality at its fullest and clearest rather than in the shadow form of the Old Testament signs. Calvin states that "Christ is now conveyed to us more fully, because of the greater degree of revelation."[52] Since Calvin relates revelation to knowledge,[53] the passage can be interpreted to mean that the Christian substantially partakes of Christ's body and blood not only because the flesh came into existence but also because the Christian can grasp by the revelation of that incarnation the knowledge that God is merciful to the point of joining himself to human flesh in order that, through the mediator, Christians could be joined in communion with him.

These threads of thought related to faith, knowledge, and the substance of Christ come together in Calvin's comments on 1 Corinthians 11:23-29. It is in this passage of 1 Corinthians that Paul describes what he considers to be a proper account of Christ's Last Supper. Once again, the emphasis on the cognitive impact of the Eucharist is strong.

The first thing to note is that, in the Eucharist, Christ has bound together the sign and the reality, the ritual and the substance, knowledge and the promise of union with Christ's body and blood. Thus, even though sign and reality can and should be distinguished, they can never be separated; in fact, the one follows the other something like cause and effect. What is more, Calvin seems to indicate that the reality that the Eucharist signifies, feeding on the body and blood of Christ, depends on the recognition of that event to gain its fullest effect. In his comments on 1 Corinthians 11:24, Calvin asserts that Christ, when promising to give his body to the disciples, at the same time commanded that the bread be taken and eaten. The command must be followed in order to derive benefit from the promise. Calvin states that:

the promise is bound up with the commandment, as if the latter were a condition; the promise therefore only becomes effective if the condition is fulfilled. . . . What we have to do is to obey God's commandment so that He may carry out what He has promised us; otherwise we deprive ourselves of its fulfillment.[54]

Further, in explaining the words, "Take, eat, this is my body," Calvin avers that Christ would have interpreted the words this way: "By sharing in the breaking of bread, according to the order and rite which I have commanded, you will also be sharing in my body."[55] Sign and reality can be distinguished but properly belong together. Therefore, they can be discussed as dialectical parts that make up a whole. These two parts are the reality, which is Christ himself, and the sign, which I take to be an instrument of meaning that carries a gift of knowledge and assurance to the believer so that the reality may be experienced at its fullest.

Though the notion of substantial partaking will be discussed in a separate section, it must be noted here that Calvin believes Christ to be truly given in the sacrament of the Lord's Supper. This is the reality. In the Eucharist, Calvin says, "we really do become sharers in the body of Christ, so far as spiritual power is concerned, just as much as we eat the bread."[56] The body and blood of Christ are "really" and "truly" given in the Supper.[57] Real bread represents a real body. Therefore, as Calvin states, "our souls are fed by the substance of His body, so that we are truly made one with him."[58]

However, as shown, Calvin has declared that fulfillment of the promise is tied to the commandment to eat. Therefore, the sign can never be bare and frigid but works as a symbol "by which the reality is held out to us."[59] But how does the sign work? According to Calvin, it bears witness to the body as food. This testimony is important—it has the ring of legal language by which truth is established. Calvin says that in order for the reality given in the Eucharist to be genuine, then the sign itself must be genuine.[60] Why is this so? Because only if the sign remains as a sign can it maintain its signative power; or better, its cognitive power. The sign bears a resemblance to the thing signified just so it can serve its cognitive function—serving to provide knowledge of Christian existence; that is, that just as bread provides sustenance to the body, likewise Christ's body provides sustenance to the life of the believer.

This cognitive function is made clear over the course of Calvin's exegesis of the next few verses. When the Eucharist is properly celebrated, it exhibits a sign that proclaims a promise, a promise that is heard in proclamation during the celebration of the ritual. Thus, Calvin is able to say in a rather remarkable passage:

> You see bread, and nothing else, but you hear that it is a sign of the body of Christ. Be quite sure that *the Lord will really carry out what you understand the words to mean* (emphasis mine): that His body, which you do not see at all, is spiritual food for you.[61]

The sign and the words are interdependent: the sign reinforces the words, paints a picture of them for the senses. The words explain the sign. Together, they present to the believer the fullest expression of Christ as spiritual food. That is one of the functions of the eucharistic act: to help the believer grasp the knowledge of union with Christ. What is more, through an understanding of that union such as the Eucharist brings its reality is all the more forcefully presented and experienced.

This interpretation of reality and sign as substantial partaking of Christ and the knowledge of that partaking is based on evidence in Calvin's own writings. At 1 Corinthians 11:25, Calvin speaks of two elements in the celebration of the Supper: the covenant itself that Christ makes with his people and the pledge of that covenant that is given in the Supper.[62] These two elements can be interpreted to mean substance and knowledge.

Though Calvin says that he will speak of the covenant itself in a later commentary on the Letter to the Hebrews, there is enough material here to piece together that at least part of what Calvin means by covenant is the reconciliation of the Christian to God through the blood of Christ, shed on the cross. Calvin says that "the blood was poured out to reconcile us to God, and now we drink it spiritually in order to have a share in that reconciliation."[63] Reconciliation through substantial partaking is the covenant of the blood for Calvin.

The cognitive aspect of the eucharistic rite comes as the act of partaking of the signs of bread and wine serves as a reinforcing pledge of the substantial partaking of body and blood. Thus, in this sense, the sacraments provide testimony to God's purpose and good will in Christ Jesus. They act, to quote Calvin, "to make our minds all the surer of it."[64] Thus, they "awaken men's consciences to an assurance of salvation."[65]

That this act of assurance can be called knowledge can be shown from the way Calvin speaks of this assurance. First of all, it is an assurance to the mind; Calvin often speaks of assurance this way. This can be seen throughout Calvin's section on 1 Corinthians 11:23–29: the Eucharist is a memorial given because of human weakness, in order to "stir us up to remember Him";[66] the point of the Supper is to seal consciences in the power of Christ's death, which Calvin explicitly terms a "knowledge";[67] the symbol of the body of Christ is given "to occupy our minds";[68] unworthy eating is a result of the fact that unworthy eaters "do not discern the Lord's body."[69] Discernment here implies an act of the mind.

It should be noted, however, that this knowledge is not natural knowledge; Calvin is no rationalist. He makes it clear that what takes place within the eucharistic celebration is a heavenly act.[70] Thus, both the substantial partaking and the knowledge thereof takes place through the power of the Spirit. The mode of the Spirit's working, however, is a mystery that believers cannot penetrate.

What is more, the knowledge of union with Christ that the Supper gives serves a twofold purpose. The first has been treated extensively here: knowledge serves to heighten the sense of union with Christ, in fact, makes the union more real, increases its depth, and leads to growth in the Christian life. However, the second purpose is just as important. Calvin thinks that the knowledge the eucharistic act imparts is essential, for it leads the Christian believer to "praise [God] openly, so as to let men know, when we are in their company, what we are aware of within ourselves in the presence of God."[71] In other words, the eucharistic knowledge evokes gratitude, which is the chief end of human existence. Since the Eucharist provides the clearest picture of the believer's union with Christ, it should evoke the clearest expression of gratitude, which results in thankfulness to God and love toward fellow creatures.[72]

Conclusion: The Concept of Knowledge in Calvin's Developing Eucharistic Thought

The interdependent structure of faith, knowledge, and the Eucharist that is developed in depth by Calvin in his 1546 *1 Corinthians* work becomes more explicit in later commentaries. I will conclude this section by briefly examining later commentaries for the light they shed on this subject.

Calvin's commentary on the New Testament books traditionally identified as Paul's prison epistles, first published in 1548, provides a clue as to why the concept of knowledge as it relates to faith is important for him. At his discussion of Galatians 1:8, Calvin attacks the Catholic notion of *fides implicita* (implicit faith). "What use was it," Calvin asks, "to profess the Gospel and not know what it meant?" He answers his rhetorical question with the stark assertion, "But with Christians there is *no faith where there is no knowledge* (emphasis mine)."[73] What is more, he relates this question of knowledge also to worship when he states that "The legitimate worship of God, therefore, must be preceded by sure knowledge."[74]

There is no faith where there is no knowledge for Calvin and no legitimate worship of God where there is no sure knowledge. This is because Christianity, for Calvin, has to do with the mind, taken in a spiritual way. If the essence of Christianity for Calvin is union with Christ, which it appears to be, then Calvin's comment on Ephesians 3:17 is telling. He says, "The substance of it is that Christ is not to be viewed from afar by faith but to be received by the embrace of our minds, so that he may dwell in us, and so it is that we are filled by the Spirit of God. "[75] As Calvin has indicated before, this is not a natural knowledge but a spiritual knowledge; thus, it is a knowledge that springs from faith.[76] The certainty of faith is, according to Calvin, a *scientia* that comes from the teaching of the Holy Spirit.[77] As such, this knowledge is "the true life of the soul."[78]

Calvin's emphasis on knowledge can be seen as a reaction against two notions: the Catholic notion of implicit faith and the notion of a bare historical faith, that is, a faith that is simply cognizant of the historical details of Jesus' life. Calvin seems to be reacting to the notion of a simply historical faith when he comments on Paul's meaning in Philippians 3:10:

> He describes the power and nature of faith, that it is the knowledge of Christ, and that, too, not bare or indistinct, but such that the power of his resurrection is felt. . . . Christ is therefore rightly known, when we feel how powerful his death and resurrection are, and how efficacious they are in us.[79]

In other words, we have here to do with the notion, at the heart of the eucharistic liturgy for Calvin, of a personal appropriation of Christ's words of promise. It is not enough to know that Christ died, was buried, and then raised to new life. Calvin is a true disciple of Luther here as he insists that the Christian know and feel that the death, burial, and resurrection are "for me," or as Calvin says above, "in us." Thus, Calvin is insistent that the Christian have a "full and clear perception" of this knowledge, which is given by the Holy Spirit and in which new life consists. This is a knowledge that will "transform the whole man."[80]

Moreover, in Calvin's 1550 *Titus* commentary, he explicitly attacks the Catholic notion of implicit faith.[81] Again, he relates true faith to explicit knowledge of God, which he relates to true worship:

> First, when he calls faith 'knowledge' he is not merely distinguishing it from opinion but from that unformed or implicit faith contrived by the Papists. . . . By saying that

it is of the essence of faith to know the truth, he plainly
shows that there is certainly no faith without knowledge....
In short, the truth is that pure and right knowledge of God
which frees us from every error and falsehood. . . . its
only aim is to further the right worship of God.[82]

To be a Christian is to know what one believes, to know in
whom one believes, to know by whom one believes, and to
know how to properly express thanks for the gifts of God. These
themes, begun in Calvin's *1 Corinthians* commentary, continue
through the material just cited and, indeed, throughout the rest
of his New Testament commentaries as they are written.[83]

Of course, these themes run through the material Calvin
writes on the sacraments. For, after all, the entire reason that
God instituted the sacraments was "to make known His love
towards us."[84] Thus, as Calvin's comments on the passages from
the Last Supper as portrayed by the Synoptics make clear in his
1554 *Harmony of the Three Evangelists,* knowledge is of the
utmost importance in the celebration of the Eucharist.

Much of Calvin's exposition of the Last Supper has to do
with the *teaching* function of the symbols; that is, what knowledge they bring to the believer. Calvin asserts that Jesus, when
he took the bread used at the Last Supper, sanctified it so as to
serve another purpose than that to which it had been originally
ordained by God, the original use being nourishment to the
body. The new purpose of the sanctified bread is to serve the
Christian's spiritual nourishment.[85] However, the bread is not
spiritually nourishing because it carries within itself the body of
Christ but because of its teaching function and symbolism. True
bread is required as a symbol so that the Christian may grasp
that just as true bread nourishes the body, so Christ's flesh
nourishes the soul.[86] It is only as Christians understand the
relation of bread to the physical body that they are able to grasp
the analogy that the Supper teaches; namely, that "The flesh of
Christ is spiritual food, because it is life-giving to us."[87]

Calvin's discussion of baptism in *Acts* sheds considerable
light on the function of the sacraments in Calvin's thought. The
full passage bears repetition here.

But when it comes to the formal cause the Holy Spirit indeed plays the leading role, but an inferior instrument is added, the preaching of the Gospel and baptism itself....

Therefore, since baptism helps our faith to receive remission of sins from the blood of Christ and that alone, it is called the laver of the soul. So when he mentions washing Luke is not describing the cause, *but is referring to Paul's understanding* (emphasis mine), for, by receiving the symbol, he grasped better that his sins were expiated. . . . [he] obtained fresh confirmation of the grace which he had received.[88]

When applied to the eucharistic passages in the Synoptics, several things are affirmed, and Calvin's exegesis at Matthew 26:27 is better explained.

First of all, the formal cause of union with Christ is the Holy Spirit. The eucharistic act itself is an inferior instrument that God has ordained to aid the weakness of human faith. Second, as the rule of metonymy makes clear, just as baptism can be called the laver of the soul, so the bread and wine can be called the body and blood of Christ. Third, and most important here, the eucharistic act itself is given not because the bread and wine carry the body and blood of Christ and can be seen as the "cause" of union with Christ; rather, the eucharistic act as it presents the body and blood of Christ refers to the Christian's understanding, just as Calvin thinks washing in the baptismal exegesis refers to Paul's understanding. Thus, baptism and the Eucharist work toward the same end: to serve as symbols by which one better grasps an understanding of the reality (as Calvin stated of Paul's baptism, by receiving the symbol he better grasped that his sins were expiated). Therefore, by partaking of bread and wine, through which Christ exhibits his body and blood, the Christian grasps that in like manner his soul feeds on the substance of Christ as the only true spiritual food. Thus, the Eucharist can be seen to serve as a "fresh confirmation of the grace which [the Christian] receives."

This explanation and correlation finds support in Calvin's comments on Matthew 26:27. The symbols of bread and wine are to "assure us that our life was established in Him." Calvin goes on to explain how the analogy works. "This body," he writes, "needs both food and drink for nourishment and sustenance. Christ, to teach that He alone is sufficient to give . . . all that belongs to our salvation, makes Himself our food and drink." Such a lesson is necessary because of the simplicity of the Christian's faith.[89]

Therefore, faith, knowledge, and the Eucharist, directed by the Holy Spirit, are bound to one another in such a way that they are interdependent, each strengthening the other, each building the other up, in dialectical relationship that makes for progress in the Christian life. The Holy Spirit illuminates; faith is the gift that enables the Christian subject to receive the illumination; divine knowledge is the result of faithful reception of spiritual illumination; and the Eucharist seals the gift, testifies to its trustworthiness, and assures the believer that what has been promised is so. Thus, the promise of union with Christ, on which all the other promises depend (remission of sin, spiritual benefits, heirs of God's goodness), is exhibited in the most graphic manner so that it may be most fully grasped, perceived, and understood.

With the close of this section, then, it is necessary to move on to what it is the Christian recognizes in the eucharistic act: that union with Christ comes when he is the Christian's spiritual food, when the believer partakes of the substance of Christ's body and blood.

Christ's Real Presence: Substantial Partaking, Its Metaphor, and Its Mode of Communication

In this section, Calvin's view of substantial partaking, its metaphor, and its mode of communication will be explored based primarily on developments that come after 1550. Since it is important for Calvin that the Eucharist serve as a source of knowledge for the Christian's understanding of union with Christ, what Calvin means when he speaks of substantial partaking must now be explicated. The sources to be explored to shed light on this subject are Calvin's treatises against Westphal and his exegesis of John 6.

What one finds as these sources are examined is that much of the problem, particularly in regard to Calvin's polemics with the Gnesiolutherans, is that widely divergent things are meant by "substantial partaking." When Calvin uses the words "to eat the body and blood of Christ" or "to feed on Christ's substance," he uses the controlling metaphors "eat" and "feed" in a different manner than his opponents. Therefore, the mode of communication is different, is able to be different, because of the way Calvin uses these metaphors. What we will find is that, for Calvin, the eating metaphor that is used in the eucharistic act refers primarily to the category of nourishment rather than to the category of manducation. Thus, when Calvin refers to the fact of "eating" Christ, the referent is really that of nourishment and sustenance; what one might call the result of physical eating. The bread and wine do not represent the eating process for Calvin, but rather the nourishing process, that by which life is sustained. Thus, this section will show how the substance of Christ's body, its metaphor, and its mode of communication are developed as Calvin seeks to refute Westphal and as he comments on the sixth chapter of John.

The Concept of Substantial Partaking

By 1539, Calvin had incorporated into his *Institutes* the concept of the substantial partaking of the body and blood of Christ through the power of the Holy Spirit as that which vivifies Christian existence.[90] By 1543, Calvin had included in his *Institutes* the two principles that must guide talk of Christ's presence in the Supper: that nothing should be taken away from Christ's heavenly glory and that nothing be said of Christ's body that does not pertain to a true human body.[91]

After the publication of the *Consensus Tigurinus*, Westphal attacked Calvin on this very point: that the *Consensus* depicts the Eucharist as presenting a phantasm; that it denies the substantial partaking of the body and blood of Christ. Thus, in answer to Westphal's attack, Calvin seeks to clarify and reinforce his position on the true and substantial participation in the body of Christ.[92]

The argument of Calvin's 1556 *Second Defence of the Pious and Orthodox Faith Concerning the Sacraments, in Answer to the Calumnies of Joachim Westphal* hinges on a disagreement over substance. What Calvin argues against is that the bread of the Eucharist is substantially the body.[93] What Calvin argues for is that, in the Eucharist, the substance of Christ's body and blood is shown in the bread and wine. Therefore, the Christian truly communicates in that body and blood through the Spirit, just as the Christian truly eats the symbols of bread and wine. As Calvin says, "For we say that the reality which the promise contains is there exhibited, and that the effect is annexed to the external symbol."[94] Thus, Christians partake of the true substance of the body and blood of Christ in the Eucharist as they partake of the symbols of that reality. However, that reality is enjoyed because of the power of the Holy Spirit to connect heaven and earth, not because the substance of the flesh of Christ is in some manner connected to the physical bread.

In some ways, it may have been Calvin's realistic language that led Westphal to believe that Calvin had changed his colors in the *Consensus*. By 1539, Calvin boldly proclaims that the Christian substantially partakes of the flesh and blood of Christ. The *Consensus*, however, does not speak of the Eucharist as a substantial partaking of Christ's body and blood.[95] Therefore, Calvin must do two things: establish that the Christian, through the Eucharist, does truly communicate in the body and blood of Christ and derive life from it, and establish how it is that such realistic language does not imply that the substance of Christ's flesh is present in the bread. Thus, Calvin must emphasize substantial partaking while distinguishing between that substance and the bread of the Eucharist.

This feat is accomplished by Calvin's notion of the virtue, or power, of Christ's flesh. It is in the Westphal treatises that Calvin fully develops the notion and uses it explicitly to explain a full body and blood substantial partaking that does not require that the substance be tied to the physical elements of bread and wine or that the substance intermingle with the substance of believers. In his *Second Defence* against Westphal, Calvin states, "But when I inculcate that the reality is conjoined with the signs, I mean the virtue of the sacrament, not the substance of the flesh."[96] With this distinction, Calvin is able to assert that "our souls receive nourishment from the very body of Christ in the same way as the body eats earthly food."[97] Thus, there is the emphasis that it is the flesh of Christ that is life-giving to the Christian. However, the distinction also serves to protect the human dimension of Christ's body, so that, as a human body, it may remain in one place—heaven—while its power, through the Spirit, may be majestically displayed throughout the world.[98] Therefore, Calvin is able to assert, "It is one thing to say that the substance of Christ is present in the bread to give life to us, and another to say, that the flesh of Christ gives us life, because life flows from its substance to our souls."[99] For Calvin, then, to be given the body of Christ is one thing, to say that his substance is under the bread is quite another.[100]

Perhaps the most important development in regard to substantial partaking of the body and blood of Christ during the early to mid-1550s is that Calvin develops an explanation for the importance of substantial partaking, other than simply saying it is necessary for the life of the soul. He develops a rationale for *why* such participation is necessary. The most developed argument for the necessity of communication with the flesh of Christ comes in the commentary Calvin writes on the gospel of John. What is more, the development of this argument for substantial participation in the body and blood of Christ provides one with clues to the Westphal treatises in terms of exposing two other opponents against which Calvin writes in these treatises: the docetists and Caspar Schwenkfeld.

It should not be surprising that the explanation Calvin develops is an instrumental one: Christ's flesh is life-giving to the soul of the believer because that is the instrument God has chosen to bestow new life on his children. In commenting on John 6:27, where Jesus speaks of working for the meat that abides unto eternal life, given by Jesus and sealed by God, Calvin says that God ordained Christ to the purpose of serving as spiritual food to the believer.[101] At his exegesis of John 6:51, where Jesus calls himself the living bread, Calvin lays out explicitly the hierarchy of salvation and how it is accommodated to human capacity through a series of instruments, the end result of which is to present Christ's flesh as the living bread that serves as spiritual food to the believer.

First, righteousness comes from God alone. There is no other source of salvific righteousness than God. However, as second person of the Trinity, Christ also shares in the Godhead, and thus can be seen also as the one from whom righteousness springs. But, in order to bring that righteousness to human beings, Christ, the second person of the Trinity, became incarnate in the person of Jesus Christ. It is in his office as mediator that Christ brings righteousness to his people and all its benefits. Yet, as mediator, Christ is fully human as well as fully divine, which means he has true flesh. Moreover, it was in that flesh that salvation was accomplished—for it was in the flesh that Christ was sacrificed to atone for sin. Thus, the righteousness of Christ then is transferred from his divinity, where righteousness intrinsically belongs, to his flesh. It is there in the flesh, thus, that the righteousness of God and its offer to his people is most fully manifested. Therefore, that flesh "communicates to us a life that it borrows from elsewhere."[102] It is in this sense, then, that Christ's flesh can be considered life-giving. Righteousness flows to the Christian then through a hierarchy of instruments: from God (which includes the second person of the Trinity), to the mediator, and from the divine essence of the mediator to his flesh. Calvin then is able to conclude: "Therefore it follows that in it [the flesh of Christ] are placed all the parts of life, so that none can rightly complain that he is deprived of life because it is hidden and far off."[103]

If the instrumental nature of Christ's flesh is not emphasized heavily enough by the above explication, Calvin makes it absolutely clear later that he does, in fact, view Christ's flesh in instrumental terms. He does so as he explicates John 6:63, where Jesus proclaims that it is the Spirit that quickens, therefore the flesh profits nothing. How does Calvin explain the passage? In a way that is reminiscent of the manner in which he deals with the power of the Eucharist, where the instrument is dead and lifeless without the quickening effect of the Spirit. In regard to the flesh, Calvin states:

> For where does the flesh get its quickening power, but because it is spiritual? . . . But those who raise their eyes to the power of the Spirit with which the flesh is imbued, will feel from the effect itself and the experience of faith that quickening is no empty word.
>
> We now understand how the flesh is meat indeed and yet profits nothing. It is meat in that, by it life is procured for us, in it God is reconciled to us, and in it we have all the parts of salvation accomplished. It profits nothing if considered in its origin and nature; for the seed of Abraham, which in itself is subject to death, does not give life, but receives its power of feeding us from the Spirit. Therefore we also must bring the spiritual mouth of faith that we may be truly nourished by it.[104]

As in the Eucharist, the instrument is made alive and effective by God through the Spirit, whose task it is to enliven all God's instruments and creatures. Therefore, according to Calvin, Christ's flesh is life-giving because it has been ordained as an instrument of God for that purpose.[105] Thus, Calvin insists that the Christian must partake of the substance of Christ's body and blood.

This emphasis of Calvin's also explains why he is so insistent that the body of Christ retain its human nature: it is intrinsically linked to the means of salvation. To strip Christ's flesh of its human nature is to make nil God's salvation, for it denies the instrument God has chosen to give salvation to his children. This explains Calvin's insistence on Christ's flesh remaining in heaven: it is the nature of flesh so to do, and to change that nature so that it can be everywhere at once in fact changes the nature of the body in such a way that it makes it seem less human, thus more remote (and therefore, for Calvin, nonsalvific). It must retain its full human nature, including specificity of place, if it is to serve as an instrument that seems near at hand for humans rather than at a distance.[106] Thus, when Calvin speaks of partaking of the flesh of Christ, full body and blood communion, he literally means participation in real and true human flesh. To speak of eating the body and blood of Christ means for Calvin that the Christian is nourished by and gains union with a real human body. There is, literally, a fleshly body involved in the Christian's feeding on Christ. That is why Calvin insists on substantial partaking of the body and blood of Christ in the Eucharist.

The Eating Metaphor

However, though true participation in Christ involves a literal body, it does not involve literal eating of a physical nature. The physical elements of bread and wine in the Eucharist are, for Calvin, figures of the body and blood of Christ: they exhibit on a natural plane what is given in a spiritual manner—the true body. This is a recognized maxim in treatments of Calvin's eucharistic teaching. What is less recognized, but made explicit by Calvin in his *John* commentary and in his Westphal treatises, is that the process of eating is also a figure. Therefore, not only is the substance of the Eucharist figured by the elements but the activity of union with Christ is figured by the action of eating and drinking. The point of the sacred meal has as its reference sustenance, nourishment, and aliment, not chewing, digesting, and swallowing. The figure of food is used because of the notion that it sustains physical life, not because there is some similarity between union with Christ and the eating activity as such. In other words, Calvin believes that the Eucharist shows forth Christ as food because food is nourishing, not because it can be eaten. The metonymy is between union with Christ and the *result* of physical eating, life sustenance, not the process of eating.

Calvin states in *John* that everything that relates to the new life of the Christian is called "food."[107] Moreover, he explains that when Jesus uses the word "bread" what he means to convey is the notion of "nourishment."[108] Therefore, when Christ speaks of his flesh as meat, what does it mean? Does it mean that the flesh should be torn as a steak? No. Calvin says, "[Christ] means that souls are starved if they lack that food. You will only find life in Christ when you seek the substance of life in His flesh."[109] For Calvin, this means, thus, that "there is no other way for Him to become ours than by our faith being directed at His flesh."[110] It is in this sense, then, in terms of the eating metaphor, that faith can be called the "mouth and the stomach of the soul."[111] Faith is that which receives and makes possible the eating of the flesh and blood, that is, its real communication to the believer. By his flesh "life is procured for us, in it God is reconciled to us, and in it we have all the parts of salvation accomplished."[112] Union with that flesh enables these things to become the Christian's possession. That union Calvin calls, metaphorically, "eating."

Calvin is correct in a sense when, in his polemics against Westphal, he claims that "the whole dispute relates to the definition."[113] In a sense, however, Calvin and Westphal are closer to agreeing on the definition of flesh than they are on agreeing on a definition of eating. When Calvin speaks of souls being "spiritually fed by the substance of the flesh of Christ,"[114] the use of the word "spiritually" utterly changes what the word "fed" means. This may be more truly at issue than the notion of substance, or even of mode (to be discussed in the next section) of communication, which is directed by what Calvin means by eating.

In his *Second Defence*, Calvin makes explicit his definition of eating, supplementing the work he had written in *John*. He says:

> Our exposition is, that the flesh of Christ is spiritually eaten by us, because he vivifies our souls in the very manner in

which our bodies are invigorated by food: only we exclude
a transfusion of substance. According to Westphal, the flesh
of Christ is not vivifying unless its substance is devoured.
. . . I did not begin only three days ago, to say that we eat
Christ by believing, because being made truly partakers of
him, we grow up into one body, and have a common life
with him.[115]

Here Calvin delineates how, in fact, the eating of the flesh of
Christ is unlike the process of physical eating: there is no
devouring (chewing, swallowing, etc.) and there is no transfusion of substance (digestion). He then explicates how eating the
flesh of Christ is like the *result* of physical eating: it is vivifying,
that is, it provides nourishment so that life may continue.
Moreover, Calvin sets out the fact that such vivification comes
from a union with Christ in which the believer shares a common
life with him. That life-giving common life and its maturing into
full participation is what Calvin means by "eating."

This sentiment is greatly expanded in Calvin's *Last
Admonition* to Westphal. When speaking of eating in the
eucharistic act, Calvin claims the authority of Augustine to deny
that there is any physical eating involved—there is a flat denial
that Christ can be chewed by the teeth or swallowed by the
stomach.[116] Therefore, what must be posited, according to
Calvin, is a spiritual eating that has nothing to do with the
stomach but consists entirely of a secret force of the Spirit.[117]
What is it to eat by the secret force of the Holy Spirit? It means
to be engrafted into Christ, so that the fullness of his life resides
in believers.[118] Calvin himself sets up the contradistinction
between the act of physical eating and the act of spiritual eating
as an act akin to the nourishing effect of physical eating when he
poses the question: "Are we fed by the flesh and blood of
Christ, when by them he infuses life into us; or is it necessary
that the substance of his flesh should be swallowed up by us in
order to be meat, and that the blood should be substantially
quaffed in order to be drink?"[119] That Calvin believes the former
to be the case is plainly answered later in the document, where

he most clearly lays out what he believes it to mean to say that the Christian eats and drinks the body and blood of Christ:

> Therefore, the eating and drinking which [Christ] mentions does not at all require the teeth, palate, throat, or stomach, but hungering of the soul; for we do not, in compliance with that commandment of Christ, eat his flesh or drink his blood in any other way than by being made one with him by faith, so that he, dwelling in us, may truly give us life. Why he claims the office of nourishing for his flesh and blood is by no means obscure. It was to let us know that our life is to be sought nowhere else than in the sacrifice by which he has reconciled the Father to us.[120]

Eating the body and blood of Christ is, for Calvin, the same as mystical union with Christ. That union is the source of the Christian's life. Moreover, the emphasis is on union with the flesh of Christ, for it was in the flesh that Christ accomplished the function of redemption. That is why Calvin indicates in his earlier treatise against Westphal that "to rob Christ of his human nature . . . [is to] divest him of his office of Redeemer."[121]

Because of the difference between Westphal and Calvin on what it means to "eat," there is the difference between them on unworthy partaking of the body of Christ. Westphal believed that all partook of the body of Christ in the Eucharist; Calvin thought only believers received the body of Christ, while unbelievers received only the sign of bread.[122] If the eucharistic act is thought to consist of an actual act of eating, then if Christ is truly present in the Eucharist, he would truly be eaten. However, in this case Christ would be eaten as poison would be eaten—he would be received by the mouth to the person's detriment, not salvation. However, if the eucharistic act is thought of as a figure for the nourishing process, rather than the eating process, then, as Calvin claims, there can be no true partaking by unbelievers. This is so, not because Christ is not truly given in the Eucharist, but because unbelievers by their unbelief deprive themselves of the nourishment of Christ's flesh, which is, as shown above, salvation. Calvin asks the question of Westphal, "Do unbelievers become substantially partakers of the flesh of

Christ?"[123] The answer, for Calvin, can only be "no." For substantial partaking, the eating of Christ's body and blood, is by definition nourishment unto eternal life. Therefore unbelievers cannot receive the body. This position is defensible based on Calvin's notion of the figurative nature of the eucharistic eating. To eat is to receive the life of Christ.

The Mode of Participation in the Life-Giving Flesh of Christ

Since Calvin has defined eucharistic eating as spiritual union with and nourishment from Christ's flesh, he is able to deal with the mode of participation in a manner consistent with that interpretation.[124] His definition of eucharistic eating has made any notion of the ubiquity of Christ's flesh unnecessary. The only requirement for the mode of communication is that it in fact bring the life of Christ to the Christian. Though Calvin had in place by the 1539 *Institutes* a doctrine of the Holy Spirit's work in the Lord's Supper, it is in his Westphal treatises that he most clearly defines the role of the Spirit in the communication of Christ's body and blood to the believer. Moreover, Calvin is clearer about the limits of what can be said about this communication.

Calvin states that the eucharistic action is a heavenly action and therefore to be considered a spiritual mystery.[125] That being the case, the following maxim can be assumed: the action itself is incomprehensible to the human mind; faith, however, enables the Christian to grasp what God has chosen to reveal to believers concerning that action. As is characteristic with Calvin, this means that the Christian can (and should) know that something is the case without knowing why or how it is the case. In this instance, believers are assured that through the power of the Holy Spirit they are united to Christ in bodily communion; what they cannot know is how the Spirit does this or why this is the medium that has been chosen.

It is clear that Calvin believes the Holy Spirit to be the channel through which Christ communicates his body to believers. Though he claims the process to be a mystery, the believer can know the fact and experience of the Holy Spirit's work as a medium of grace. However, Calvin does go so far as to use an illustration of the process that he thinks exemplifies how the mode of the Holy Spirit brings the grace of true partaking to the believer. This is, of course, the famous "sun" illustration. "Christ dwelling in us," Calvin says, "raises us to himself, and transfuses the life-giving vigour of his flesh into us, just as we are invigorated by the vital warmth of the rays of the sun."[126] This image is important for two reasons. The first is that it makes clear that Calvin believes the power of Christ's flesh can be equated to the flesh itself; that is because the power emanates from the body itself and nowhere else. Though a distinction can be made between the sun and its rays as the difference between source and power, still few would say there is an essential difference between the two; rather, the substance of the source is simply carried to the recipient as energy. The second reason the image is important is that it reinforces what has been said above about eating as primarily an image for nourishment; Calvin speaks of the rays of the sun as a life-giving, sustaining force. He uses the image as a parallel to the eating metaphor, and thereby he makes it clear that the point of the eucharistic act is the life-sustaining image. Therefore, it is probably inaccurate to refer to Calvin's doctrine as mere "virtualism," for the emphasis is not on the energy of Christ as such but on the way that power unites believers to their Lord so that nourishment from the flesh of Christ may be a reality.

Beyond this explanation, Calvin resolves only to assert the fact of the Spirit's function as the instrument by which believers are united to the flesh of Christ. Explanations of the mode of participation are, in fact, more like assertions than explanations.[127] Indeed, when explaining the mode, Calvin asserts that the best way of understanding the mode of participation in Christ is the notion of "communion." For Calvin, the word implies the engrafting of the Christian into the life of Christ in order to share Christ's life.[128] Thus, Calvin is arguing here from the general state of Christian existence to the Eucharist. He avers that, just as the Spirit joins the Christian to Christ as body to head in holy fellowship, so the Eucharist does the same thing, and thus the mode is the same: the secret working of the Holy Spirit.

For Calvin, the work truly is a secret (arcanum). As stated above, he thinks the fact of the work of the Spirit can be known, but the how and the why is clouded in mystery. The secret action of the Spirit that unites Christians to Christ to partake of his life, the work of the Spirit that unites things distant in space, "transcends the reach of the human intellect."[129] Thus, according to Calvin, God reveals the mode but not its actual operation. Therefore, there is both revealing and hiding, knowledge and mystery, involved in the Spirit's work in uniting Christ with his people.

Conclusion: The Role of Faith in Understanding Eucharistic Substance, Eating, and Mode

Calvin declares that everything he teaches about the Supper is in order to "make the sacred ordinance of the Supper conformable to the rule of faith."[130] What this means for Calvin is that Christ can be sought properly only by faith: a trust and confidence in the promises of God. To seek Christ in any other way is anathema. It is through the vehicle of faith that Christ is received and made present. In other words, faith works as an instrument prior to and with the eucharistic instrument.[131] It is that by which the eucharistic meaning can be appropriated.

It is for this reason that Calvin is able to distinguish between believing and eating: he calls eating the effect of faith.[132] Thus, though the two are related, they can be distinguished as cause and effect. Moreover, the two can be distinguished in terms of justification and sanctification. Faith is the instrument by which the Christian obtains the unmerited grace of God. Once the Christian has been justified, there is growth in the Christian life: sanctification. Of course, these two things cannot be separated, but they can be distinguished. The Christian is always in need of justification. Yet, growth in the Christian life depends on growing more and more into Christ. This process can be seen as dialectical. Faith in Christ prepares one for reception of Christ. Reception of Christ involves union with Christ. Union with Christ enables growth into Christ. This communion is helped by the Eucharist in that, for those engrafted in Christ, through the sacrament they become "united to him more and more."[133] By becoming more and more united to Christ, faith is helped and grows. As faith grows, the Christian's capacity to receive Christ grows, and so union with Christ is enhanced.

The Eucharist as a Means of Grace: Accommodation and Instrumentality in Calvin's Writings from the 1550s

It is only through the instrumental activity of God that any knowledge of God or union with Christ is possible. When one leaves the period of the early to mid-1540s, one begins the period of Calvin's intense concentration on biblical exegesis. From the mid-forties[134] until the year of his death, Calvin produced commentaries on all the books of the New Testament, except Revelation, and on most of the Old Testament. Though Calvin had in place by the time of his 1539 *Institutes* concepts of accommodation and instrumentality, it is in the commentaries that Calvin fully develops these concepts, particularly as they relate to the sacraments. Of course, this sacramental view is based on how Calvin perceives God relating to the human world in general.[135] In the period of the 1550s, one can see the full development of Calvin's notions of accommodation and instrumentality, especially in Calvin's writings against Westphal, his *John* commentary, and in his Old Testament commentaries. It is in the Old Testament commentaries in particular that Calvin develops his fully mature notion of how God interacts with his people; there he works from the general to the particular, from the Old Testament manifestations of God to the Christian sacraments.

It has already been shown how it is that Christ's flesh serves as an instrument of salvation. In *John*, Calvin sets up a hierarchy of instruments to serve as channels by which righteousness is poured into the believer. Part of the instrumental motion can be attributed to Calvin's doctrine of the Trinity, which sees action starting with God, proceeding through the Son, and being completed in the Holy Spirit. However, for this action to reach the Christian, the person of the mediator is essential: thus, there is a motion from the divine to the human instrument. This human instrument is used in accommodation to human weakness: there can be no excuse that God is "far off."[136]

However, it is not simply a matter of rendering human beings without excuse. Calvin's basic assumption is that humanity can have no direct communication with God. This assumption is based on both divine and human attributes. Calvin reminds his readers that "our understanding cannot attain the height of God."[137] Moreover, because of the sinful nature of humanity, immediate contact with the holiness of God would destroy any human being because of God's "incomprehensible brightness."[138] Thus, there can be no hope of direct human knowledge of or contact with God;[139] there can only be a mediated knowledge and a mediated presence.

God accommodates knowledge of himself and his presence through the use of earthly signs. Because of humanity's condition, this has been God's modus operandi from the beginning. Calvin states that "God from the first manifested himself by visible symbols that he might gradually raise believers to himself, and conduct them by earthly rudiments to spiritual knowledge."[140] It is because God has, in Calvin's opinion, always worked in this accommodated manner with fallen humanity that he is able to state with such assurance that "in Scripture the name of God is everywhere transferred to the visible symbol of the presence of God."[141] Thus, the metonymy Calvin sees at work in the Eucharist he sees at work in all of Scripture: the sign, as an accommodated instrument of God's presence and activity, has the name of God transferred to it on that account.[142]

In a sense, the world and all that is in it serve as a means of accommodation; the cosmos is an instrument in the hands of God that points to his glory and majesty. Yet, because of sinful humanity, the vast accommodated instrument of the universe must be seen through the eyes of faith in Jesus Christ in order to work; this is not because of a defect in the instrument but in humanity. Thus, Jesus is the instrument par excellence of God's communication with human beings, accommodated in flesh and blood.[143]

Yet, neither does the church have direct access to Jesus Christ. His presence and the knowledge thereof are also mediated through accommodated instruments since his ascension into heaven. Word and sacrament serve as such instruments. Calvin is thus able to proclaim, "in this sense, the preaching of the Gospel is called the kingdom of heaven, and the sacraments can be called the gates of heaven, because they admit us into the presence of God."[144] Of course, as has been shown, even these means are of no use without the empowerment of the Holy Spirit. But with the work of the Spirit, word and sacrament serve as the ordained and established means by which the Christian communicates with God through Jesus Christ. To speak of the Eucharist as an accommodated instrument is, for Calvin, to speak of God's usual way of communicating knowledge of himself to the Christian believer. Such an accommodation is a gift and vitally necessary for Christian life. For after all, it is God who has decided that the Eucharist is the best means to convey knowledge of communion with the body and blood of Jesus Christ, through whom life with God is possible. It is also one of the ways God has chosen to effectively exhibit and give that communion to the believer.

It is with this understanding, then, that Calvin warns that neither too much nor too little should be attributed to the Eucharist. He insists that the instrument of the Eucharist is necessary for Christians in their fallen state. The Eucharist, for Calvin, is an instrument that takes Christians out of the world, in a sense, into the heavenly sphere where they enjoy union with

Christ. In order for that ascension of the soul to take place, however, the sign of the Eucharist is imperative. Calvin flatly states, "this [ascension] cannot take place without the help of a figure or sign."[145] It is in this helping sense, then, that the name of body is transferred to bread: so that the figure may work to bring about the transition from the earthly to the heavenly.

Such a transfer of name, however, requires that the believer be clearly taught that it is, in fact, the function of such signs to raise the believer to God's presence. Therefore, the sign must retain its own nature rather than its reality being collapsed into the divine nature—in which such Calvin thought Westphal's doctrine of ubiquity resulted. Otherwise, Christ is brought down rather than the soul being elevated.

Finally, it must be remembered that there is a hierarchy of instrumentality involved in the way God accommodates himself to his elect. In *John*, for example, we saw how the lowest level to which God stooped to accommodate himself was taking on flesh in the person of the Mediator. Through this instrument, then, the Christian is able to partake of that in which righteousness properly dwells, God himself. However, this sharing in the righteousness of God is not direct but is mediated through a series of accommodations.

It is in this sense, then, that Calvin can refer to the Eucharist as an inferior instrument. Calvin reminds readers that in and of themselves, apart from a higher power, the sacraments are empty and useless. They are at the bottom of the hierarchy of accommodated instrumentality and depend on the "higher rungs of the ladder," so to speak, to raise the Christian to heaven. However, in Calvin's eyes this is not to denigrate the sacraments but to recognize them for what they are: God's act of accommodation to the human need for visible signs. In his *Second Defence*, he states that "For while . . . things standing to each other in the relation of superior and inferior are not contradictory, an inferior sealing of grace by the sacraments is not denied, while the Spirit is called the prior and more internal seal."[146] By so stating the case Calvin has, in his mind, put the Eucharist in its proper position in relation to the higher instruments of God.

However, just because the power of sealing is not inherent in the Eucharist does not mean that it is dispensable; no more so than Christ's flesh being dispensable because the righteousness of God does not properly dwell in it. In fact, just as the flesh of Christ, the Eucharist is indispensable to the Christian because God uses it as a visible, earthly approach to his children to show that he is near at hand, not far away. This assurance helps the Christian grow in knowledge and possession of Christ. And that, after all, is the point of the Eucharist for Calvin.

Conclusion

What this chapter has established is that, in relation to the themes of knowledge, substantial partaking, and accommodated instrumentality, Calvin's eucharistic thought underwent significant refinement in the period 1541–1557. Many of these refinements involve explanations by Calvin as to *why* these themes are important. Before 1541, he established that he believed these topics to be essential to correct eucharistic doctrine; after 1541, he provides a rationale why this is the case.

In relation to the Eucharist and the way it provides assurance to believers, it becomes clear during these years that Calvin thinks knowledge and faith are intimately linked. In fighting notions such as implicit faith, Calvin asserts one of the important tenets of Reformation faith: the importance of correct doctrine and its proper appropriation. In the act of the Eucharist, Calvin avers, a personal knowledge of God and his action toward the believer is presented in a heightened fashion; namely, through all the senses, not just hearing. This is why Calvin believes the Mass to be an abomination: it clouds what should be revealed—knowledge of union with Christ.

In terms of substantial partaking, Calvin's development of eucharistic doctrine in this period answers at least two questions: why substantial partaking is important and why Christ's bodily substance must reside in heaven. Participation in the true flesh and blood of Christ is necessary because in that substance resides salvation; the flesh is literally "God with us" in its most accessible form. In the flesh of Christ and nowhere else is salvation. Thus, there is the necessity of communication with the flesh of the mediator in order to obtain salvation.

Moreover, the incarnation means that God has committed salvation to human flesh. Therefore, it must remain human flesh. Any attempt to introduce a doctrine of ubiquity is seen as a danger by Calvin; not just because Christ's body has ascended but because of the nature of human flesh. If the flesh loses its "humanness," then humanity is moved further away from salvation.

In addition, Calvin makes it clear during these years what it means to "eat" Christ—to be united to him by the power of the Holy Spirit. Here is a refinement of a concept that enables Calvin to affirm substantial partaking. As long as "to eat" meant "devour" Calvin had to deny substantial partaking, as he did in the 1536 *Institutes*. However, with the affirmation of the true participation in the substance of Christ during the years 1537-1541 came the need to explain such substantial participation without implying a mingling of substances as takes place in physical eating. The development of the metaphorical use of the term "eat," so that it means essentially "nourishment," and its explicit explication overcomes this problem for Calvin's eucharistic theology.

Finally, Calvin's work on accommodation and instrumentality during this period sets in place a notion of how God works in the world. With the full development of this concept, it is possible for Calvin to affirm the Eucharist as a means of grace (which he had denied in 1536) without transferring the power from the principal cause (God) to the instrument. Moreover, such a development allows Calvin to insist fully on the absolute necessity of the Eucharist while still maintaining its position as an inferior instrument. This development, with its varied expressions throughout this period, can be seen as Calvin's own "Against the Heavenly Prophets," as he joins with Luther in denying immediate revelation from God. It is here that Calvin gives the reasons why no direct communication with God is possible: as long as the Christian is in this earthly life, a mediated God is the only God to which the believer has access. Moreover, it is God himself who has chosen the means of mediation. Therefore, even if in theory God could choose other ways of communicating himself, Christians have no such liberty. They have access to God only through his chosen instruments, of which the Eucharist is a prime means.

With these themes thoroughly developed and explored, we are now in a position to examine Calvin's final eucharistic writings.

Notes

1. See *Inst. '36*, p. 104; OC 1:120-21; OS 1:139.

2. See "Draft of Ecclesiastical Ordinances," in Dillenberger, ed., *John Calvin: Selections from His Writings*, p. 238; OC 10:25. Since there were three parishes, it was set up so that the Eucharist was celebrated in the town of Geneva once per month; that is, three parishes celebrated four times per year.

3. (Le ministre) "Quelle est la principal fin de la vie humaine?" (L'enfant) "C'est de congnoistre Dieu." OC 6:9. The answer of the later Latin translation is a bit less succinct, though the meaning is the same: "Ut Deum, quo conditi sunt homines, ipsi noverint." OC 6:10. The translation from Calvin, *Selected Works* 2:37, edited and translated by Henry Beveridge, ("To know God by whom men were created.") is based on the Latin at this point. It should be pointed out that the Latin word Calvin uses that is translated "know" (novisse) is a word that is only used in regard to knowing a *person*. Thus, Calvin is speaking, from the beginning, about a personal knowledge of God, not an abstract, impersonal knowledge.

4. It is interesting to note that, in the original catechism of 1542 and 1545, Calvin includes under this section material on Scripture and preaching. Beza later inserted the title "On the Word of God" before this material and moved the title "On the Sacraments" so that it appeared just before Calvin asks the question, "What is a sacrament?" See OC 6:107/108, n. 2 and 111/112, n. 2; OS 2:127, n. "s" and 130 n. "q." Beveridge retained the erroneous title heads in his translation

of the catechism; see *Selected Works* 2:81, 83. Beza may well have thought it more logical to place the heading "On the Word of God" before the material on Scripture and preaching so that people were not led to believe Calvin considered Scripture and preaching to be sacraments. However, there are ways in which Scripture and its exposition might be considered "sacramental"—they consist of signs (words and language) with promises that must be sealed by the work of the Holy Spirit to be effective. I will not argue that issue here, but I will point out that the *concern* of the section "On the Word of God" (as Beza labeled it) is consonant with the concern of the strictly and properly sacramental section that Beza labeled "On the Sacraments." In both there is a concern for religious knowledge. In speaking of Scripture and its exposition, the Catechism says, "truth itself teaches . . . that this is eternal life to know one true God . . . to know him, I say, in order that we may pay due honour and worship to him." This knowledge is like a "door by which we enter his heavenly kingdom." This knowledge is possible only "by the gift of [God's] spirit." Moreover, Calvin equates continual instruction with being "the disciples of Christ to the end, or rather without end." See *Selected Works* 2:82–83; OC 6:107/108–111/112; OS 2:128–30.

5. Calvin, *Selected Works* 2:84; OC 6:111/112; OS 2:130. The translation of Beveridge is from the Latin edition of 1545; the French edition of 1542 says simply that the sacraments render the promises more certain ("et nous en rendre plus certains"). The meaning, however, is the same.

6. Calvin, *Selected Works* 2:84; OC 6:113/114; OS 2:131.

7. Calvin, *Selected Works* 2:84; OC 6:113/114; OS 2:131.

8. Calvin, *Selected Works* 2:85; OC 6:115/116; OS 2:133.

9. Calvin, *Selected Works* 2:86; OC 6:115/116; OS 2:133.

10. Calvin, *Selected Works* 2:89; OC 6:123/124; OS 2:137.

11. Calvin, *Selected Works* 2:89. The actual wording of the question is translated from the 1545 catechism, where Calvin asks, "Ergone corpore Domini et sanguine vescimur?" OC 6:124; OS 2:138. The 1542 catechism used less realistic language; instead of asking about actually "eating" the flesh and blood, here Calvin had asked if the believer was made to "truly communicate" in the body and blood. ("Entens-tu qu'il nous faille communiquer vrayement au corps et au sang du Seigneur?" OC 6:123.) Though the 1545 language is the stronger, in terms of traditional understanding of partaking of the body and blood of Christ, both 1545 and 1542 seem stronger to me than the language of 1537, where Calvin had said that "the Savior presents to

us the true communication of his body and of his blood, but spiritually." (". . . le Seigneur nous presente la vraye communication de son
corps et de son sang, mais spirituelle.") OC 22:70; OS 1:412.

12. Calvin, *Selected Works* 2:89; OC 6:123/124; OS 2:138.

13. Calvin, *Selected Works* 2:90; OC 6:125/126; OS 2:138.

14. Calvin, *Selected Works* 2:90; OC 6:125/126; OS 2:139.
"Scire," to know or understand, is used in the 1545 edition; the 1542
French edition speaks simply of the sacrament "certifying" reconcilia-
tion.

15. Calvin, *Selected Works* 2:90; OC 6:125/126; OS 2:138.
Again, the translation is from the Latin edition; whereas in 1545 the
controlling verb is "agnoscire," in the 1542 edition it is "croyer."

16. Calvin, *Selected Works* 2:91; OC 6:129/130; OS 2:140.
Again, there is a discrepancy between '42 and '45. In the '42 French
edition, Calvin uses the word "cueurs" (hearts); in the Latin, he uses
"mentes" (minds).

17. Calvin, *Selected Works* 2:93; OC 6:131/132; OS 2:143.
Again, the translation is made from the Latin edition; the 1542 French
version speaks instead of the conjoining of the preaching of the word
and the administration of the sacraments.

18. Calvin's liturgies, along with others, are examined at length
in William D. Maxwell, *The Liturgical Portions of the Genevan Service
Book* (Edinburgh: Oliver and Boyd, 1931). The intent of Calvin's
liturgy is analyzed extensively in James H. Nichols's "The Intent of the
Calvinistic Liturgy," in *The Heritage of John Calvin*, edited by John H.
Bratt (Grand Rapids: Eerdman's, 1973), pp. 87–109. Calvin's "theory"
of the liturgy is examined in Peter Rodolphe, "Calvin et le liturgie
d'après l'*Institution*," *Études théologiques et religieuses* 60, no. 3
(1985): 385–401.

19. Calvin, *Selected Works* 2:121. The word used in the liturgy
that has been translated as "minds" is "espritz." OC 6:200; OS 2:48.
However, "espritz," while it can mean "spirit," can also mean "mind"
or "intelligence." Given the context of the word, I would argue that
Calvin here means "mind" rather than "spirit." This argument is based,
in part, on the context of the passage. However, it is also based on
Calvin's instruction for the use of the 1545 eucharistic liturgy, which
is discussed in the next paragraph.

20. "Il baille donques vrayement son corps avecques le pain et
avecques le calice son sang. Pourquoy? En la remission des pechez, et
la confirmation du nouveau Testament." OC 6:196. The summary of

the four things Calvin thinks a congregation should be taught before celebrating the Eucharist are all summarized here at page 196.

21. ". . . ces deux choses nous sont données pour deux raysons, pour la remission de pechez, et pour augmenter la vie le Christ en nous: c'est à dire la confirmation de l'alliance nouvelle." OC 6:196.

22. ". . . afin que nous congnoissions combien il est necessaire que Christ vive en nous, et nous en luy." OC 6:196.

23. Calvin uses the phrase "we are assured" ("nous summes asseurez") when speaking of the function of the Eucharist throughout this instructional section; see OC 6:193–95 passim.

24. This is because Augustine's definitions of a sacrament ("a visible sign of a sacred thing" or "a visible form of an invisible grace") are obscure in their brevity. Thus, Calvin says since the case arises that "many of the ignorant are confused, I want to give a fuller statement with more words so that the matter does not remain in doubt." (". . . multi rudiores hallucinantur, volui pluribus verbis pleniorem reddere sententiam, ne quid dubitationis haereret.") *Inst. '43* 16.1; OC 1:939.

25. "Now, if we were incorporeal, as Chrysostom says, he would give to us these things themselves, naked and incorporeal. Now, since we have souls inserted into bodies, he conveys the spiritual under visible things." ("Nam si incorporei essemus, ut Chrysostomus ait, nuda et incorporea nobis haec ipsa daret. Nunc qui corporibus insertas habeamus animas, sub visibilibus spiritualia tradit.") *Inst. '43* 16.3 (chapter and section numbers are given); OC 1:940. Thus, once again, Calvin emphasizes the accommodated nature of the sacraments—that they are absolutely necessary given the type of existence human beings lead.

26. It should be remarked here that Calvin makes it perfectly clear that the word, in and of itself, is like the sacrament in that it needs the empowerment of the Holy Spirit to function positively. In other words, the word as an instrument is as dependent upon the enlivening work of the Holy Spirit as the sacrament is. Thus, Calvin quotes Augustine with approval: "For the word itself, as a passing noise, is one thing, the power remaining is another." ("Nam et in ipso verbo aliud est sonus transiens, aliud virtus manens.") *Inst. '43* 16.4; OC 1:940. Calvin's relationship to Augustine in terms of their eucharistic theology has been traced in Joachim Beckmann, *Vom Sakrament bei Calvin: Die Sakramentslehre Calvins in ihren Beziehungen zu Augustin* (Tübingen: J.C.B. Mohr, 1926); and in Joseph Fitzer, "The Augustinian Roots of Calvin's Eucharistic Teaching," *Augustinian Studies* (1976): 69–98.

27. "Ergo quum de verbo sacramentali fieri mentionem audimus, promissionem intelligamus, quae clara voce a ministro praedicata plebem eo manu ducat, quo signum tendit ac nos dirigit." *Inst.* *'43* 16.4; OC 1:940.

28. "Quantum igitur tum ad veram Christi intelligentiam in nobis fovendam, confirmandam, augendam, tum ad eum plenius possidendum, fruendasque eius divitias, illorum ministerio adiuvamur, tantum apud nos efficaciae habent. Id autem fit, ubi quod illic offertur, vera fide suscipimus." *Inst.* *'43* 16.6; OC 1:949. In 1553, Calvin changed "intelligentiam" (understanding) to "notitiam" (knowledge), thus rendering the phrase "knowledge of Christ" rather than "understanding of Christ."

29. In other words, only in the Eucharist are all the senses utilized to convey the message of union with Christ.

30. "illustrius ac luculentius." *Inst.* *'43* 16.26; OC 1:958.

31. "significatione augustiora, virtute praestantiora." *Inst.* *'43* 16.26; OC 1:958. Here Calvin is again quoting Augustine. The other large sections of new material in Chapter 16 include expanded discussions on the distinction between matter and sign and the insistence that the power of the sacrament resides in Christ, not in the sign. However, these sections are included by Calvin to make the point that it is the *truth* that the sacrament brings that is important; thus, "the sacrament is a void thing, if it is separated from its truth." (". . . sacramentum rem esse nihili, si a veritate sua separatur." *Inst.* *'43* 16.16, OC 1:949.) Yet, the distinction is important, not because of the need for an emphasis on distinction as such, because Calvin always holds in contrast to distinction the necessity that sign and reality not be separated, but so that his emphasis on the cognitive function of the sacrament is not overwhelmed by the materiality of the sign. In other words, it is a concern of Calvin to make sure that the mind is not held captive by the material elements: "The second [vice] is, by not raising up our minds beyond the visible sign, that we transfer to it the praise for those good things that are not conferred to us except by Christ alone." ("Alterum, dum mentes ultra visibile signum non erigendo, ad ipsum transferimus eorum bonorum laudem, quae non nisi ab uno Christo nobis conferuntur.") *Inst.* *'43* 16.16; OC 1:950.

32. ". . . nos ea vita sustineat ac conservet in quam nos verbo suo genuit." *Inst.* *'43* 18.1; OC 1:991, n. 2.

33. ". . . nobis confirmet, corpus Domini sic pro nobis semel esse immolatum, ut nunc eo vescamur ac vescendo unici illius sacrificii efficaciam in nobis sentiamus." *Inst.* *'43* 18:1; OC 1:991, n. 2.

34. ". . . vivificae illius mortis virtutem vigere nunc in nobis certo confidamus." *Inst. '43* 18.1; OC 1:991, n. 2.

35. ". . . illic testimonium habent, Christum sic nobis coadjunatum, sic nos illi vicissum insertos esse, adeoque in unum corpus cum ipso coaluisse, ut quidquid ipsius est nostrum vocare liceat." *Inst. '43* 18.2; OC 1:991, n. 2.

36. *Inst. '43* 18.2; OC 1:991. This section is quite interesting in that Calvin speaks of the Eucharist as a *testimony* and an *assurance* of a state the Christian already enjoys: the partaking of Christ and his benefits. The section basically delineates what it is to be one with Christ and what the benefits he brings entail. However, this section, primarily a radical reworking in 1543 of material implicit in 1536, is labeled in the McNeill-Battles English edition of the 1559 work "Union with Christ as the special fruit of the Lord's Supper" (*Inst.* 4.17.2). Thus, McNeill and Battles have carried over Weber's heading without realizing that it misrepresents the point of the section. The section under consideration simply does not state that union with Christ is the special fruit of the Eucharist; what it says is that the Eucharist is a special testimony and assurance of that union.

37. "Id fit, cum per evangelium, tum illustrius per sacram coenam, ubi et se ipse cum bonis suis omnibus nobis offert et nos fide eum recipimus." *Inst. '43* 18.5; OC 1:994, n. 1.

38. "Christum illic rite apprehendant piae animae . . . mentem hominis infirmam alioqui adiuvare, ut ad percipiendam spiritualium mysteriorum altitudinem sursum assurgat." *Inst. '43* 18.32; OC 1:1012.

39. "Neque enim Christum rite et salutariter manducamus nisi crucifixum, dum efficaciam mortis eius vivo sensu apprehendimus." *Inst. '43* 18.4; OC 1:993.

40. "nudam imaginationem" *Inst. '43* 18.14; OC 1:1000.

41. During the period 1546–1556, Calvin produced most of his New Testament Commentaries. The only ones that fall outside this period are: *Romans* (1540), which was dealt with in Chapter IV with the 1539 *Institutes*; *First and Second Peter*, first published in French in 1545; and *Jude*, first published in 1542, which has only a brief line that relates to the Eucharist in terms of the necessity for charity but sheds no light on the issue at hand.

In assessing scholarly research on Calvin's commentaries, David Steinmetz places that research in the broader context of Reformation studies in general when he says, "I think it is no secret that the history of biblical exegesis in the sixteenth century represents one of the last, great, virtually unexplored frontiers of Reformation history." Stein-metz, "The Theology of Calvin and Calvinism," in *Reformation Europe: A Guide to Research*, edited by Steven Ozment (St. Louis: Center for Reformation Research, 1982), p. 215; see pp. 217–18 for the (short) list of those who have written on Calvin as an exegete.

42. Calvin, *The First Epistle of Paul the Apostle to the Corinthians*, translated by John W. Fraser, in the series *Calvin's New Testament Commentaries*, edited by David W. Torrance and Thomas F. Torrance (Edinburgh: Oliver and Boyd, 1960; repr. ed., Grand Rapids: Eerdmans, 1980); OC 49:292–574. Hereafter cited as *1 Corinthians*.

43. Calvin, *1 Corinthians* 1:21, p. 39; OC 49:326. In speaking of the "knowledge of God," Calvin uses the word "notitia," which implies a personal knowledge, as of an acquaintance. When speaking of the act of knowing, a verbal construction, he uses "cognoscere." He also, in other passages, uses "scire."

44. Calvin, *1 Corinthians* 1:31, p. 47; OC 49:332.

45. Calvin uses the term "saving knowledge" in his comments at *1 Corinthians* 1:21, p. 39; OC 49:326; the emphasis on "personal" knowledge comes when Calvin exegetes 1 Corinthians 8:2, where he says, "For the foundation of true knowledge (verae scientiae) is personal knowledge of God." *1 Corinthians*, p. 172; OC 49:429; finally, at 12:3, Calvin makes the distinction between "mere factual knowledge" and the "gift of regeneration," which, from the context, is associated with the "true knowledge of God." *1 Corinthians*, p. 259; OC 49:497.

46. See Calvin's comments at *1 Corinthians* 13:9, where he speaks of knowledge as a gift given "precisely because we are imperfect." Once the imperfection has disappeared, so will the gift, which is temporary. This comment is given in context of the Pauline statement of 1 Corinthians 13:12, which states that "For now we see in a mirror darkly; but then face to face." *1 Corinthians*, p. 280; OC 49:513. The knowledge of which Calvin speaks here, then, is "the likeness of God in the Word, in the sacraments, and, in short, in the whole ministry of the Church." *1 Corinthians*, p. 281; OC 49:514.

47. Calvin, *1 Corinthians* 12:3, p. 259; OC 49:497.

48. Calvin, *1 Corinthians* 2:12, p. 59; OC 49:342. The Latin word here translated "know" is "scientia," which is used throughout this section of Calvin's commentary.

49. Calvin, *Acts, 1–13*, p. 33; OC 48:12.

50. Calvin, *1 Corinthians* 10:4, p. 205; OC 49:455.

51. Calvin, *1 Corinthians* 10:4, p. 205; OC 49:455–56.

52. Calvin, *1 Corinthians* 10:4, p. 205; OC 49:455.

53. See Calvin's comments at *1 Corinthians* 1:21, p. 40, OC 49:326; 2:6–7, p. 53, OC 49:337; 2:10, p. 57, OC 49:340–41; 2:12, p. 59, OC 49:342; and 13:9–12, pp. 280–81, OC 49:513–15, all of which relate revelation to knowledge.

54. Calvin, *1 Corinthians* 11:24, p. 244; OC 49:485.

55. Calvin, *1 Corinthians* 11:24, p. 244; OC 49:485. It should be noted that Calvin, as most Reformation figures, apparently had no trouble collating the eucharistic passages, so that to talk of one included discussion of all of them. This is apparent in his discussion here, for in the Corinthian passage Paul does not use the exact words, "Take, eat, this is my body"; the words he hands down as coming from Jesus are, "This is my body which is for you. Do this in remembrance of me." The words Calvin actually exegetes, "Take, eat, this is my body," are found in Matthew 26:26.

56. Calvin, *1 Corinthians* 11:24, p. 245; OC 49:487.

57. Calvin, *1 Corinthians* 11:24, p. 246; OC 49:487.

58. Calvin, *1 Corinthians* 11:24, p. 246; OC 49:487.

59. Calvin, *1 Corinthians* 11:24, p. 245; OC 49:486.

60. Calvin, *1 Corinthians* 11:24, p. 246; OC 49:487.

61. Calvin, *1 Corinthians* 11:24, p. 247; OC 49:488.

62. Calvin, *1 Corinthians* 11:25, p. 249; OC 49:489.

63. Calvin, *1 Corinthians* 11:25, p. 249; OC 49:489.

64. Calvin, *1 Corinthians* 11:25, p. 249; OC 49:489. The word translated "minds" is "animis." "Animus," though it is often translated as soul, is, in fact, probably best translated as mind in this context on certainty. In classical Latin, the word means soul in the sense of the *rational* soul.

65. Calvin, *1 Corinthians* 11:25, p. 249; OC 49:490.

66. Calvin, *1 Corinthians* 11:24, p. 248; OC 49:489.

67. Calvin, *1 Corinthians* 11:26, p. 250; OC 49:490. "Cognitio" is the word Calvin uses here.

68. Calvin, *1 Corinthians* 11:26, p. 250; OC 49:491. The word translated as "minds" is "mentes."

69. Calvin, *1 Corinthians* 11:29, p. 253; OC 49:493.

70. Calvin, *1 Corinthians* 11:24, p. 247; OC 49:488.

71. Calvin, *1 Corinthians* 11:26, p. 250; OC 49:490.

72. Calvin, *1 Corinthians* 11:24, p. 243, OC 49:485; 11:26, p. 250, OC 49:490.

73. Calvin, *The Epistles of Paul the Apostle to the Galatians, Ephesians, Philippians and Colossians*, translated by T.H.L. Parker,

in the series *Calvin's New Testament Commentaries*, edited by David W. Torrance and Thomas F. Torrance (Edinburgh: Oliver and Boyd, 1965; repr. ed., Grand Rapids: Eerdmans, 1980), p. 14; OC 50:173. The full Latin text of *Galatians* is found in OC 50:161–268. Citations will be made to the individual books in the English translation.

74. Calvin, *Galatians* 4:8, p. 76; OC 50:229.

75. Calvin, *Ephesians* 3:17, p. 168; OC 51:187. The Latin text of this commentary can be found in OC 51:141–240.

76. Calvin, *Ephesians* 3:18, p. 168; OC 51:187.

77. Calvin, *Ephesians* 3:19, p. 169; OC 51:188.

78. Calvin, *Ephesians* 4:18, p. 188; OC 51:205. Given the rationale for sometimes rendering "animus" as "mind," this passage could be translated so as to speak of the knowledge of God as "the true life of the mind."

79. Calvin, *Philippians* 3:10, p. 275; OC 52:50. The Latin text of the Philippians commentary is found in OC 52:1–66.

80. See Calvin's comments at *Colossians* 2:2, p. 325, OC 52:99; and *Colossians* 3:10, p. 349, OC 52:121.

81. "Calvin also disallowed the term *implicit faith* as it was propounded by the Roman theologians to refer to a kind of pious submission to the collective judgment of the church. True faith rests not on ignorance but on knowledge. It is not enough to embrace what someone else has declared to be true; we must penetrate further to the personal knowledge of God the Father through Jesus Christ His Son." George, *The Theology of the Reformers*, pp. 224–25.

82. Calvin, *The Second Epistle of Paul to the Corinthians, and the Epistles to Timothy, Titus, and Philemon*, translated by T. A. Smail, in the series *Calvin's New Testament Commentaries*, edited by David W. Torrance and Thomas F. Torrance (Edinburgh: Oliver and Boyd, 1964; repr. ed., Grand Rapids: Eerdmans, 1980); *Titus* 1:1, pp. 352–53; OC 52:404–5. The Latin text of Titus is found in OC 52:401–36.

83. For examples of the themes we have dealt with that continue in Calvin's commentaries, see his *1 Peter* commentary, where at 1:14 Calvin equates progress in the Christian life with progress in the knowledge of God. Calvin, *Hebrews and I and II Peter*, translated by W. B. Johnston, in the series *Calvin's New Testament Commentaries*, edited by David W. Torrance and Thomas F. Torrance (Edinburgh: Oliver and Boyd, 1963; repr. ed., Grand Rapids: Eerdmans, 1980), p. 245; OC 55:222; and the extensive treatment of these themes in the *Acts* commentary: at 17:24 Calvin asserts that the true rule of godliness

is to have a clear grasp of who God is (Calvin, *The Acts of the Apostles, 14-28*, translated by John W. Fraser, in the series *Calvin's New Testament Commentaries*, edited by David W. Torrance and Thomas F. Torrance (Edinburgh: Oliver and Boyd, 1966; repr. ed., Grand Rapids: Eerdmans, 1980), p. 112; OC 48:410); at 17:26 Calvin declares that people were made so that they could acquire a knowledge of God (p. 116; OC 48:414); and at 17:27 Calvin insists that this knowledge requires a "special gift" of God (p. 119; OC 48:416).

84. Calvin, *Acts, 1-13*, 7:8, p. 179; OC 48:135.

85. Calvin, *A Harmony of the Gospels Matthew, Mark and Luke*, 3 vols., translated by A. W. Morrison, in the series *Calvin's New Testament Commentaries*, edited by David W. Torrance and Thomas F. Torrance (Edinburgh: St. Andrew Press, 1972; repr. ed., Grand Rapids: Eerdmans, 1980); comments are based on exegesis of Matthew 26:26-30 and parallel Synoptic passages, 3:134; OC 45:706.

86. Calvin, *A Harmony of the Gospels*, 3:135; OC 45:707.

87. Calvin, *A Harmony of the Gospels*, 3:136; OC 45:708.

88. Calvin, *Acts, 14-28*, 22:16, p. 218; OC 48:496-97.

89. Calvin, *A Harmony of the Gospels*, 3:138; OC 45:710.

90. For an example, see *Inst.* '*39* 12.17.18-19, p. 297; OC 1:1009, where Calvin states, "In short, [Christ] feed his people with his own body, the communion of which he bestows upon them by the power of his Spirit."

91. *Inst.* '*43* 18.22; OC 1:1004-5. If these guidelines are observed, Calvin asserts that "But, these absurdities having been removed, I willingly admit whatever can be made to express the true and substantial communication of the body and the blood of the Lord, which is exhibited to the faithful under the sacred symbols of the Supper. ("Caeterum, his absurditatibus sublatis, quidquid ad exprimendam veram substantialemque corporis ac sanguinis Domini communicationem, quae sub sacris coenae symbolis fidelibus, facere potest, libentur recipio.") *Inst.* '*43* 18.22; OC 1:1005.

92. Calvin's first answer to Westphal has been analyzed as part of Chapter II; therefore, for this section, I will concentrate on Calvin's last two treatises against Westphal. Moreover, I have skipped from the 1543 *Institutes* to the Westphal treatises because the 1550 edition of the *Institutes* provides virtually no new material in the sections on the sacraments in general and on the Eucharist in particular. Major additions to these sections do not come until the 1559 edition, to be discussed in Chapter VI.

93. Calvin, *Selected Works* 2:248-49; OC 9:47.

94. Calvin, *Selected Works* 2:275; OC 9:68.

95. Article 23 of the *Consensus*, "Of the Eating of the Body," speaks of eating the flesh as a figure but does not use the word "substance" in a positive sense; indeed, it is used only to negate the notion of a mingling of substances. Article 19, which speaks of communication with Christ, does not speak of communion in the body and blood of Christ but only of communication with Christ, which could as well be taken to mean the Spirit of Christ. Calvin, *Selected Works* 2:219, 218; OC 7:742, 741; OS 2:252, 251. Compare these emphases to the emphasis of the 1539 *Institutes* quoted above, "In short, he feeds his people with his own body."

96. Calvin, *Selected Works* 2:280; OC 9:72. On the notion of the virtue or power of Christ's body in relation to the body itself, see Joachim Rogge, *Virtus et Res: Um die Abendsmahlwirklichkeit bei Calvin*, Arbeiten zur Theologie, series 1, no. 18 (Stuttgart: Calwer Verlag, 1965).

97. Calvin, *Selected Works* 2:281; OC 9:73.

98. Calvin, *Selected Works* 2:285; OC 9:76.

99. Calvin, *Selected Works* 2:293; OC 9:81.

100. Calvin, *Selected Works* 2:298; OC 9:86.

101. Calvin, *The Gospel According to St. John, Part 1, 1–10*, translated by T. H. L. Parker, in the series *Calvin's New Testament Commentaries: A New Translation*, edited by David W. Torrance and Thomas F. Torrance (Edinburgh: Oliver and Boyd, 1961; repr. ed., Grand Rapids: Eerdmans, 1980), p. 154; OC 47:140.

102. Calvin, *John, Part 1*, 6:51, p. 167; OC 47:152–53.

103. Calvin, *John, Part 1*, 6:51, pp. 167–68; OC 47:153.

104. Calvin, *John, Part 1*, 6:63, p. 175; OC 47:159.

105. As we have noted, the word "flesh" denotes for Calvin more than the body; it means the unregenerated human being. However, the concept of flesh *includes* the notion of body, though flesh is not completely defined by that reality. When God uses "flesh" as an instrument, the bodily aspect is certainly included. Calvin is saying that the flesh has no power of its own for salvation, but when enlivened by the Spirit of God it is made to serve the needs of Christian spiritual nourishment.

As can be ascertained from David Steinmetz (Steinmetz, "Scripture and the Lord's Supper in Luther's Theology," in *Luther in Context* (Bloomington: Indiana University Press, 1986), pp. 75–76), neither Luther nor Zwingli shares Calvin's view of John 6:63. Zwingli denies that the flesh can ever serve to feed the spirit. The physical can not nourish the spiritual. Thus, Zwingli read "the flesh profits nothing" quite literally.

Luther, however, thinks that, though "flesh" can mean body in some cases, in John 6:63 it does not. In this context, Luther thinks the flesh is a reference to the human's self-centered nature. Moreover, Luther denies that this passage has anything to do with the Eucharist. Thus, both Luther and Zwingli deal with the text quite differently than Calvin because of differences in exegetical assumptions.

For Zwingli's use of John 6 in discussing eucharistic doctrine, particularly in relation to the flesh of Christ, see Zwingli, "Das dise wort Iesu Christ: 'Das ist min lychnam . . . ,' ewigklich den alten eynigen sinn haben werden, etc.", in *Corpus Reformatorum*, vol. 92, *Huldreich Zwinglis Sämtliche Werke*, vol. 5, edited by Emil Egli et al. (Leipzig: M. Heinsius Nachfolger, 1934), pp. 805–977. For Luther's view of 6:63, see his comments in *Luther's Works*, vol. 23: *Sermons on the Gospel of St. John, Chapters 6–8*, edited by Jaroslav Pelikan (St. Louis: Concordia Publishing House, 1959), pp. 118–25. Also helpful here are Luther's remarks in "That These Words of Christ, 'This is My Body,' etc., Still Stand Firm against the Fanatics," in *Luther's Works*, vol. 37, edited by Robert H. Fisher (Philadelphia: Muhlenberg Press, 1961), pp. 13–150, especially p. 113. In speaking of Christ's flesh as body, Luther much prefers to work from Matthew 26:26, "This is my body." For an analysis of Luther's exegesis of this passage, see Jaroslav Pelikan, *Luther's Works: Companion Volume: Introduction to the Exegetical Writings* (St. Louis: Concordia: 1959), pp. 137–56.

106. Thus, one sees at John 6:55 and 56 Calvin's warning that "they are false interpreters who lead souls away from Christ's flesh" and "if you want to have anything in common with Christ you must especially take care not to despise the flesh." Calvin, *John, Part 1*, pp. 170–71; OC 47:155–56. This perspective explains not only Calvin's attitude toward Westphal's insistence on ubiquity but also his constant references to the heresy of Marcion, which in this context refers to docetism, the doctrine that Christ only appeared to have a fully human body. See especially Calvin, *Selected Works* 2:329; OC 9:108. The emphasis on the flesh of Christ as fully human may also be in reaction to Schwenkfeld who, with his doctrine of the celestial flesh of Christ, presented as dangerous a threat to Calvin's notion of salvation through the instrument of the fully human flesh of Christ as did Westphal's notion of ubiquity and the communication of natures. Thus, Calvin's indignity shows in refuting Westphal's claim that Calvin should be

grouped with the Schwenkfeldians. See Calvin, *Selected Works* 2:266 and 333; OC 9:62 and 111.

107. Calvin, *John, Part 1*, 6:27, pp. 153–54; OC 47:139.

108. Calvin, *John, Part 1*, 6:35, p. 160; OC 47:145.

109. Calvin, *John, Part 1*, 6:55, p. 170; OC 47:155.

110. Calvin, *John, Part 1*, 6:56, p. 171; OC 47:156.

111. Calvin, *John, Part 1*, 6:56, p. 171; OC 47:156.

112. Calvin, *John, Part 1*, 6:63, p. 175; OC 47:159.

113. Calvin, *Last Admonition*, in *Selected Works* 2:485; OC 9:244.

114. Calvin, *Selected Works* 2:484; OC 9:243.

115. Calvin, *Selected Works* 2:283; OC 9:74–75.

116. Calvin, *Selected Works* 2:362; OC 9:154.

117. Calvin, *Selected Works* 2:276; OC 9:69.

118. Calvin, *Selected Works* 2:376; OC 9:164.

119. Calvin, *Selected Works* 2:402; OC 9:183.

120. Calvin, *Selected Works* 2:426–27; OC 9:201.

121. Calvin, *Selected Works* 2:385; OC 9:171.

122. See, for example, Calvin's distinction between "spiritual eating" in the sacrament, which is how Calvin designates proper reception of Christ's substance in the Eucharist, and "sacramental eating," which is the external reception of the elements. Christians participate in both kinds of eating; indeed, they are conjoined. However, unbelievers only eat sacramentally, devoid of the reality. Calvin, *Selected Works* 2:373–74; OC 9:162.

123. Calvin, *Selected Works* 2:305–6; OC 9:90.

124. Calvin states in his *Last Admonition* to Westphal that the only quarrel between the two of them is the mode of eating. See Calvin, *Selected Works* 2:493; OC 9:250. However, it is the difference in the definition of "eating" that is crucial; the mode of eating flows from what each of them considers eating to be.

125. Calvin, *Last Admonition*, in *Selected Works* 2:443; OC 9:213.

126. Calvin, *Second Defence*, in *Selected Works* 2:279; OC 9:72.

127. "I only explain the manner, viz., that Christ overcomes the distance of space by employing the agency of his Spirit to inspire life into us from his flesh." Calvin, *Selected Works* 2:287; OC 9:77–78. "Christ, by his Spirit, infuses into us the vivifying virtue of his flesh and blood." *Second Defence*, in *Selected Works* 2:329; OC 9:109. Elsewhere, Calvin refers to Christ's presence as presence in "grace" and "majesty." Calvin, *Last Admonition*, in *Selected Works* 2:384, 389;

OC 9:170, 173. Because the action of the Spirit is involved, he calls Christ's presence a "celestial" or heavenly mode of presence. *Last Admonition*, in *Selected Works* 2:387, 443; OC 9:172, 213. Calvin also refers to the Spirit as the "bond" of the union. *Last Admonition*, in *Selected Works* 2:445; OC 9:215.

128. Calvin, *Last Admonition*, in *Selected Works* 2:414; OC 9:192.

129. Calvin, *Second Defence*, in *Selected Works* 2:249; OC 9:48. Later, he states, "Still I deny not that there is a mystery, surpassing human comprehension, in the fact, that Christ in heaven feeds us on earth with his flesh." *Selected Works* 2:291; OC 9:81.

130. Calvin, *Second Defence*, in *Selected Works* 2:282; OC 9:74.

131. In speaking of Christ's presence and the role of faith, Paul Jacobs reminds his readers that, in the Eucharist, "Here faith is no condition [of Christ's presence], but the gift which is given with it." ("Der Glaube ist hier keine Bedingung, sondern die mitgeschenkte Gabe.") Jacobs, "Die Gegenwart Christi im Abendmahl nach reformiertem Verständnis und das römisch-katholische Gegenbild," in *Gegenwart Christi: Beitrag zum Abendmahlsgespräch in der Evangelischen Kirche in Deutschland*, edited by Fritz Viering (Göttingen: Vandenhoeck und Ruprecht, 1960), p. 29. David Willis agrees when he states, "it is not our faith that makes Christ really present. Rather, it is by Christ's fresh action by the power of his Spirit that the covenant is kept and Jesus Christ joins himself to the signs." Willis, "A Reformed Doctrine of the Eucharist and Ministry and Its Implications for Roman Catholic Dialogues," *Journal of Ecumenical Studies* 21, no. 2 (Spring 1984): 300. In another place, Willis states that Christ is present in the Eucharist "because he freely is faithful to his own promises." Willis, "Calvin's Use of Substantia," in *Calvinus Ecclesiae Genevensis Custos: Die Referate des Internationalen Kongresses für Calvinforschung vom 6. bis 9. September 1982 in Genf*, edited by W. H. Neusner (Frankfurt: Peter Lang, 1984), p. 300.

132. See Calvin, *Second Defence*, in *Selected Works* 2:283, 284; OC 9:75; besides speaking of faith and eating as cause and effect, Calvin also speaks of the two, respectively, as former and latter (prius et posterius). Calvin, *John, Part 1*, 6:47, p. 166; OC 47:151.

133. Calvin, *Second Defence*, in *Selected Works* 2:336; OC 9:114.

134. With the exception of the first edition of the *Romans* commentary, which was published in 1540, and the *Jude* commentary, published in 1542.

135. Especially helpful in regard to Calvin's commentaries and the concepts of accommodation and instrumentality are T. H. L. Parker, *Calvin's Old Testament Commentaries* (Edinburgh: T. & T. Clark, 1986); and Ronald S. Wallace, *Calvin's Doctrine of the Word and Sacrament* (Edinburgh: Oliver and Boyd, 1953; repr. ed., Tyler, Tex.: Geneva Divinity School Press, n.d.).

136. Calvin, *John, Part 1*, 6:51, p. 168; OC 47:153.

137. ". . . ad Dei altitudinem non perveniant sensus nostri." Calvin, *Psalm* 86:8, OC 31:749.

138. "incomprehensibilis fulgor." Calvin, *Exodus* 33:20, OC 25:111.

139. As Forstman says of Calvin, "His view of God is so high and his view of man so low that the problem of communication of knowledge is severe." H. Jackson Forstman, *Word and Spirit: Calvin's Doctrine of Biblical Authority* (Stanford: Stanford University Press, 1962), p. 9.

140. Calvin, *Second Defence*, in *Selected Works* 2:296; OC 9:84.

141. Calvin, *Second Defence*, in *Selected Works* 2:266; OC 9:62.

142. Hunter's caution drawn from his study of Calvin is appropriate: "Grace comes with the sacraments, not from them." A.M. Hunter, *The Teaching of Calvin: A Modern Interpretation*, 2d edition (London: James Clark and Co., 1950), p. 168.

143. "God never revealed himself without Christ." Calvin, *John, Part 1*, 5:23, p. 128; OC 47:115. Battles, in discussing Calvin's understanding of God's incarnation in the person of Jesus Christ, speaks of that act as God's "supreme act of condescension." Battles, "God Was Accommodating Himself to Human Capacity," *Interpretation* 31 (January 1977); reprinted in *Readings in Calvin's Theology*, edited by Donald McKim (Grand Rapids: Baker Book House, 1984), p. 23.

144. ". . . hoc sensus evangelii praedicatio vocatur regnum coelorum, et sacramenta dici possunt coelorum portae, qui in Dei conspectum nos admittunt." Calvin, *Genesis* 28:17, OC 23:394.

145. Calvin, *Last Admonition*, in *Selected Works* 2:373; OC 9:162.

146. Calvin, *Second Defence*, in *Selected Works* 2:344; OC 9:119.

VI

Calvin's Mature Eucharistic Theology

This chapter will explore the three expressions of Calvin's most mature eucharistic theology: the 1559 *Institutes*, the 1561 treatise against Tileman Heshusius, *The True Partaking of the Flesh and Blood of Christ*, and *The Best Method of Obtaining Concord, Provided the Truth Be Sought Without Contention.*[1] The emphasis in this exposition will be the additions Calvin made to the 1559 *Institutes* and how those additions are consonant with and reinforce the gains he had made in his eucharistic theology. The two treatises will be considered in conjunction with the themes treated in the '59 edition.

There will follow a section on the interpretation of Calvin's eucharistic theology as found in the '59 *Institutes*. In this section the development of the themes of knowledge, substantial partaking, and accommodative instrumentality will be reviewed. Finally, the necessity of the Eucharist will be analyzed in relation to criticisms of Calvin's eucharistic theology. What we will find is that, given the proper understanding of the context of Calvin's development, there is a twofold eucharistic gift that makes a vital contribution to Christian life; indeed, which makes Christian life possible.

Knowledge, True Partaking, and Instrumentality in
Calvin's Mature Eucharistic Theology

Almost all of the additions to Calvin's 1559 *Institutes* in the chapters on the sacraments in general (4.14) and the Eucharist in particular (4.17, 18) can be grouped under the headings of knowledge, true partaking, and instrumentality. This is not surprising, given the fact that these themes had been extensively developed and dealt with in Calvin's treatises against Westphal and his commentaries. However, as Calvin worked these themes into the new structure of the final Latin edition of his *Institutes*, he adds not only the emphases of these themes but also, in some cases, clarifies further the implications of the proper appropriation of those themes.

The Necessity of Eucharistic Knowledge

In the very first section of the eucharistic chapter of the 1559 *Institutes*, material new to '59 makes it clear that the category of knowledge is of concern to Calvin. The opening sentences of 4.17.1 describes God as the good father who nourishes his children through the life-giving bread of his only-begotten son. Moreover, the son himself instituted the sacrament to attest to that fact. Calvin then follows with an emphasis that has become characteristic in his eucharistic thought: "The knowledge of this high mystery [union with Christ] is very necessary, and in view of its greatness it demands a careful explanation."[2] How does Calvin explain this great mystery of union with Christ? By explaining the sacrament of the Eucharist. Thus, knowledge about the sacrament, which it is Calvin's purpose to disclose, leads to the sacrament serving its function as a source of knowledge about union with Christ. Therefore, Calvin follows the new '59 material on the necessity of knowledge with material original with 1543, where he asserts that, since the "mystery of Christ's secret union with the devout is by nature incomprehensible, he shows its figure and image in visible signs best adapted to our small capacity."[3] In explaining the Eucharist, Calvin clears the way for the Eucharist to serve its proper function as an accommodated instrument of knowledge of union with Christ[4]: a thing so incomprehensible to human nature it must be brought down and exhibited in physical terms so that human senses might perceive it.

In other words, by speaking of Calvin's explanation of the sacrament, we are speaking of doctrine—holy teaching. Calvin believes himself to be delivering true doctrine about the Eucharist to his readers. His belief is that, once this doctrine is delivered and believed, the Eucharist can serve its function as a source of knowledge. In Chapter 14, in Calvin's discussion of the sacraments in general, he makes this correlation explicit: God links sacramental signs to doctrine "without which our senses would have been stunned in looking at the bare sign."[5] Thus, proper teaching (doctrine) about the sacrament is a requirement for its functioning. However, once the requirement is met, the sacrament can assume its proper function: to serve in an accommodated way to present the clearest promises of the Gospel. Or, as Calvin says for the first time in the '59 *Institutes*, by the sacraments God "attests his good will and love toward us more expressly than by word."[6]

That Calvin sees this attestation as a function of the Eucharist can be seen in the way he speaks of Christ's presence. He is adamant that the Christian has Christ's presence as the source of life; therefore, it must be continual rather than occasional. Thus, though the Supper does serve as a source for communion with the body of Christ, it is one among several means (though not quite, as we shall see in the conclusion).[7] Yet, the Supper serves as the extraordinary means for presenting the knowledge of that union in such a way that it can be best appropriated by the believer. As Calvin says, Christ "our Mediator is ever present with his own people, and in the Supper reveals himself in a special way."[8] Or, as Calvin indicates against Heshusius, the Eucharist is a special confirmation of Christ's presence.[9] Thus, what is unique to the Supper is the graphic presentation of Christ's body and blood as nourishment to the soul. It enables the Christian to grasp wherein lies life. Such knowledge is necessary for growth in Christian life.

True Partaking: Union with Christ

By the time of the 1559 *Institutes*, it is clear that Calvin believes that in the Supper one truly partakes of the flesh and blood of Christ through the power of the Holy Spirit. What is more, the emphases that have been developed, particularly in the Westphal treatises, are reinforced in the last Latin edition of the *Institutes*. Indeed, much of the new material in Book 4, Chapter 17, "The Sacred Supper of Christ, and What It Brings To Us," comes from Calvin's Westphal treatises.[10] Again, the idea of true partaking can be discussed under the headings of substance, the eating metaphor, and the mode of communion, all of which point to union with Christ as the goal of the eucharistic act.

When Calvin speaks of partaking of the substance of Christ's body and blood in the Holy Supper, it is clear that he does mean Christ's literal body. As has been shown, in his opposition to the various theories of Westphal, what he calls the Marcionite heresy, and, perhaps, Schwenkfeld's idea of celestial flesh, Calvin emphasizes that the flesh of the ascended Christ is true human flesh. He charges in the 1559 work that, without that flesh, Christ is no more than a "phantasm."[11] Without that flesh, Christ is no longer present in his office as mediator, and thus salvation is imperiled. For that reason, Calvin, when speaking of partaking of Christ, emphasizes that it must be a partaking of that same flesh and blood in which Christ accomplished salvation. He asserts that any feeding that takes place through the Eucharist is of the *substance* of Christ's body and blood.[12] By saying this, Calvin establishes that the body of which he speaks in the Eucharist is Christ's body, a real human body. In speaking of Christ's resurrection appearances, Calvin quotes Christ's words that he uses to assure his disciples that in his post-resurrection state he is no ghost: "See and touch, for a spirit has no flesh and bones." Calvin then goes on to conclude, "Observe that the truth of the flesh is proved by Christ's own lips because he can be touched and seen. Take these away and flesh now ceases to be."[13] Thus, if one takes away the physical properties of the natural body, then a new definition of body is required. With this sort of logic, Calvin believes he has refuted any notion that Christ's true human body was obliviated by his divinity after the resurrection.[14]

Such an emphasis on the flesh of Christ as human flesh is further strengthened by Calvin as he, in his mature writings, distinguishes the flesh from the spirit and distinguishes substantial partaking from faith. Calvin makes clear that the body serves as the referent in matters eucharistic. First of all, he had been charged by Heshusius as being an energist—one who believed communion with Christ involved the energy of the flesh but not the flesh itself. Calvin denies such an accusation in his treatise against Heshusius and carries the clearest statement of the distinction between the energy and the body in his reply. This is a development in the sense that, in his treatises against Westphal, Calvin did speak of the Christ being fed from the energy of the body, just as the rays of the sun feed and nourish the earth. Though, as we noted, the emphasis is on the substance as the source of the energy, there is some room for confusion: is it the body or its energy that feeds the Christian? In his *The True Partaking of the Flesh and Blood of Christ*, Calvin answers Heshusius's accusation by moving the question from the reality to the mode. He asks, "When I teach that the body of Christ is given us for food by the secret energy of the Holy Spirit, do I thereby deny that the Supper is a communion of the body?" Calvin obviously thinks not. Communion with Christ is with his body and blood through the energy of the Spirit; the feeding is not derivative, in the sense of feeding on the energy generated by the body. A substantial communion is declared.[15]

The basis for this declaration lies, in part, in a new section of the '59 *Institutes*. Calvin, in commenting on a passage from Augustine, claims that a distinction must be made between the essence of Christ's flesh and the power of the Spirit.[16] It is the essence of the flesh that gives life; it is the function of the Spirit to join by its power the Christian to that source of life over the vast distance that separates Christ's flesh from earthly existence. Thus, though the flesh of the Christ and the Spirit obviously belong together,[17] they can, indeed should, be distinguished; just as reality and mode of reception, though they belong together, can and should be distinguished.[18]

The same distinction holds in the earthly realm as much as within the heavenly realm. Thus, Calvin gives his clearest expression on the distinction between Christ's flesh and faith. If the Spirit is the divine mode by which the reality of the flesh is given to the elect, then faith is that quality by which Christians are enabled to receive the reality. Calvin is unwilling that the reality be collapsed into the divine mode of giving; neither is he willing that the reality be collapsed into the human mode of reception: faith. In fact, Calvin seems to deny the idea of eating the flesh of Christ as being simply faith for the same reason that he denies that the eating of Christ's flesh requires a doctrine of ubiquity. As Calvin says, "the substance of the flesh is no more found under the bread than in the mere virtue of faith."[19] Thus, the reality of the Supper of which the believer partakes is the human flesh of Jesus Christ.

If Calvin has become more insistent and, at least in one sense, more clear on the flesh of Christ as the reality of the Supper, as that of which the Christian truly partakes, he also strengthens his notion of eating as a metaphorical concept. One can run through the material new to the 1559 edition of the *Institutes* to see how much new material, much of it with its genesis in the Westphal dispute, concentrates on exactly this issue. Calvin speaks of the nourishing aspect of the Supper; that it is an analogy that works from bread and wine as nourishment to the body to Christ's flesh as nourishment to the soul. The nourishment takes place through union with Christ; that indeed is what Calvin seems to mean when he speaks of eating and drinking Christ: union with him.[20]

That the eating and drinking process is a metaphor for this union with Christ and the nourishment derived therefrom is made clear by the additions to the '59 edition. Calvin insists that the word "is" in "This is my body" must be taken as a metonym;

and by '59 his extensive study and exegesis of biblical texts provides his foundation.[21] This section is followed by material new to '59 that insists that a literal interpretation of the words of institution is impossible,[22] thus bringing about the necessity for an *interpretation* of the passage.[23]

Calvin makes it clear that such a move toward interpretation is not a "rationalist" approach to the sacrament. He claims that only faith could reveal to the Christian that one is joined to Christ's flesh through the marvelous transportation of the Holy Spirit.[24] Indeed, Calvin, for the first time, states that it is against the nature of the sacrament to test the words by common rule and grammar.[25] If one is "trapped" by the letter, and the gift of interpretation taken from the church, then one is led into absurdities, the prime one being the deduction of physical eating from the words of Christ. But, if that deduction is allowed to take place, then other corollaries are necessary that do not have the strict letter as a foundation: such as the idea of a visible and invisible body of Christ.[26] The alternative, and the correct doctrine in Calvin's opinion, is a notion of eating that is figurative. Thus, just as bread and wine figure body and blood, so eating figures the nourishing process. Calvin views this solution as the only one that allows for the substance of Christ's flesh to breathe life into souls without allowing Christ's flesh to enter the Christian as any other food would.[27] Christians are said to eat the flesh of Christ because his flesh nourishes the Christians' souls in "the same way that bread and wine nourish our bodies."[28] However, another way Calvin speaks of true partaking of Christ is to speak of the fellowship between head and members, what Calvin calls a "substantial fellowship."[29] In fact, this term probably gets at what Calvin means by true partaking better than does the eating language; the term "substantial fellowship" at least presents the notion of true partaking as a type of union with Christ that Calvin seems to have at the heart of his theology (not just his eucharistic theology).

The 1559 *Institutes* have no new material on the Holy Spirit as the mode or channel of communication between Christ and his people. The Spirit's role in this matter had been spelled out by Calvin as early as the 1539 *Institutes*. However, the final refinements to be made to this notion come during this last period of Calvin's writings in his two treatises. The Spirit's essential role as the channel of the grace of Christ's flesh is maintained, but the way Calvin speaks of it falls in line with his most developed thoughts on the eating metaphor. If eating means a type of substantial fellowship with Christ, then the mode of that eating will be one that emphasizes union, not manducation. For example, when discussing how the Spirit joins things apart in space, the emphasis is on union rather than how one substance is made available to another for eating. Thus, when discussing the Spirit's role in the Eucharist, Calvin says that Christ unites with the believer so that they may be joined in the same life, "in the same way in which head and members unite to form one body."[30] Therefore, what is involved is not a transferral of substance but the secret work of the Spirit by which "he infuses his life into us from heaven."[31] Here again, one can see that the controlling metaphor is something other than "eating"; moreover, it makes sense of the Christian's experience in that the head can control, guide, lead, and, in a sense, give life to the body without being moved from its position above the body to be intermingled with the parts below it.

Calvin, in one of his last writings on the Eucharist, states that "the only way we are conjoined to Christ is by raising our minds above the world."[32] Since such an act is beyond the reach of humanity, the Holy Spirit must perform the divine action that unites believers to Christ. In any case, Calvin has made it clear by his last writing that an act of the Spirit is essential if the Christian is to be moved from this world to the heavenly realm. That, really, is the most important development in his thought on the matter of mode: that the Spirit does not simply connect things distant in space but also serves to start the Christian on a journey that will end in life in the eternal and heavenly kingdom of God.

The Eucharist as an Accommodated Instrument: *"Intermediate Brilliance"*

In the 1539 *Institutes*, Calvin wrote:

> Therefore, word and sacraments confirm our faith when they fix in front of our eyes the good will of our heavenly Father toward us. It is by the knowledge of him that the whole firmness of our faith exists and increases in power. The Spirit confirms it when, by engraving this confirmation on our minds, he makes it effective.[33]

Word and sacrament confirm and strengthen faith because they present a knowledge of God's good will. The Spirit makes operative these instruments of knowledge. Calvin then adds in the 1559 *Institutes* a sentence to follow this paragraph that sums up beautifully his view of the Eucharist as an accommodated instrument: "Meanwhile," Calvin writes, "the Father of Lights cannot be hindered from illumining our minds with a sort of intermediate brilliance through the sacraments, just as he illumines our bodily eyes by the rays of the sun."[34] By speaking of the sacraments as "brilliance," Calvin associates them with the "Father of lights," seeming to say they bring to the believer something of the essence of God. This way of speaking of the sacrament can be taken in two ways, which relates to the two functions of the sacrament. The first is that the passage obviously relates to knowledge; brilliance is used as a reference to the illumination of the mind. In this sense, it can be related to the idea of "shedding light" upon a subject; namely, a way of clarifying and making more sure knowledge of a subject. The second way the passage can be taken, though implicit, is that by sharing his "brilliance" God shares his essence, insofar as humankind is able to receive it through the accommodated instrument of the flesh of Christ. The sun analogy in this case brings to mind that same analogy as Calvin uses it to describe substantial partaking of the essence of Christ's flesh.

Moreover, the word "intermediate" is important: it connotes the fact that both knowledge and substance are brought to the believer through a secondary source rather than being given directly by God to the believer. "Intermediate" implies intermediary channels that serve to bring the gifts of God to the believer. Again, this notion, by the time of the '59 *Institutes*, has been well established, particularly in the commentaries. Drawing on the developments in his thought on instrumentality, Calvin adds several new sections to the '59 *Institutes* that bring out fully his notion of the "intermediate" as it relates to the accommodated instrument of the Eucharist.

Calvin makes clear that the sacrament, as "intermediate brilliance," is part of the process of salvation and righteousness, not its cause.[35] The only cause of salvation is God's work in Jesus Christ and no other. The task of the Eucharist is to make clear that work and join the Christian to the source of that work: the mediator himself. In emphasizing that the Eucharist is a part of salvation rather than its cause, Calvin is asserting that the Eucharist as an instrument must be recognized as an instrument, as something used by God, so that the honor and glory are not transferred from the cause to the instrument. The only proper celebration of the Eucharist is one that does not detract from God's original activity as source of salvation.[36]

If one keeps this distinction between source and instrument in mind, then the Eucharist is free to serve its function as an "intermediate brilliance." In fact, when properly understood, the Eucharist's brilliance shines forth brighter than any other light available to the Christian believer in this life. It is the "appropriate means" God chose "to lift us to himself."[37] In so saying, Calvin links both the earthly and divine instruments in the "appropriate means" of the Eucharist. The Spirit is the divine force that enlivens the Eucharist; the signs of bread and wine are the earthly elements through which the Spirit works. Both are essential for the proper and effective work of the eucharistic instrument. Calvin emphasizes this conjunction when he states, "We say Christ descends to us both by the outward symbol and by his Spirit, that he may truly quicken our souls by the substance of his flesh and blood."[38] Since Calvin, further along in another addition new with the '59 *Institutes*, says that Christ is in fact not brought down to the Christian but instead raises the Christian to himself through the working of the Holy Spirit,[39] he seems to contradict himself. However, when Calvin says that Christ descends to the Christian through the symbol and the Spirit, he means that Christ has accommodated himself to human weakness through the instruments of Spirit and sign, so that those very instruments of "descent" (literally, coming down to the human level) might work to raise the Christian to heaven. Thus, the Eucharist is an instrument that comes down to the human level in its presentation of Gospel truth so that, as human understanding is strengthened by that presentation, it might be raised to heavenly knowledge of union with Christ. The process itself serves to strengthen that heavenly union between Christ and his elect. In other words, it is the instrument, not the reality, that descends; by such a descent the instrument is the channel by which the Christian is raised up to Christ and heavenly glory.

Moreover, the knowledge of this union and the actual partaking of its reality that comes through the intermediate brilliance of the Eucharist is seen as a "school" by Calvin. The Eucharist is an instrument accommodated to human weakness so that it might serve to teach Christians about their Christian existence and strengthen them in that existence. In his treatise against Heshusius, Calvin makes clear that the Eucharist belongs to the realm of sanctification—it is for those who have been justified by faith in Christ. Growth into Christ is a gradual process. Calvin states that "for if Christ dwells in us by faith, it is certain that he in a manner grows up in us in proportion to the increase of faith."[40] Union with Christ increases with the growth of faith; the growth of faith depends upon the sure knowledge of salvation as promised by God; the Eucharist presents the clearest picture of the union promised by God and thereby increases faith. The faith that justifies the Christian is necessary before growth can take place. However, once justified, the Christian's faith can be enlarged by the knowledge the Eucharist presents; as faith grows, union with Christ grows; as union with Christ grows, the Christian can better grasp the significance of the eucharistic instrument. All of God's instruments then converge to work together in the celebration of the Eucharist: Christ and his life-giving flesh; the faith that enables initial union with that flesh; the accommodated knowledge of God that is shown forth in the Eucharist; and the work of the Holy Spirit that controls and gives life to God's instruments. Thus, the intermediate brilliance that is presented in the complete working of the eucharistic act grows as the Christian grows in faith. Finally, upon full entry into the heavenly kingdom of God, the Christian sees "face to face" that brilliance of God that before had only been known, could only be known, through instruments.

What we see, then, in Calvin's last eucharistic writings is the completion of a journey. At the beginning of his career, as he wrote on the Eucharist in his 1536 *Institutes*, Calvin flatly and unequivocally denied substantial partaking of Christ in the Eucharist. He claimed that the Eucharist could not, in fact, be thought of as an instrument of grace. Moreover, he delineated no clear eucharistic gift. As has been shown, over a period of twenty-three years, Calvin's eucharistic theology matured. It developed in such a way that Calvin claimed as essential those very elements that he had originally denied as part of his eucharistic doctrine. Furthermore, Calvin refined and developed those concepts so that they were strengthened and incorporated fully into his eucharistic theology. He goes from denying substantial partaking to strongly affirming it, linking that participation in the body of Christ to the very means of salvation, Christ the mediator in his flesh and blood. Calvin advances from denying the Eucharist as an instrument of grace to claiming for it the highest honor—an intermediary brilliance sent and used by God to illumine Christian existence. Finally, Calvin moves from no affirmation of a gift to asserting that there is presented by the Eucharist a twofold gift: Jesus Christ himself, on the one hand, and the clearest picture possible for sinful human creatures of the promises of God on the other. This movement can be attributed to Calvin's desire that the Christian, first of all, know what it is that makes a Christian—union with Christ. The true celebration of the sacrament, for Calvin, stands as a stark repudiation of the Catholic notion of implicit faith, for there is no faith where there is no knowledge. Second, Calvin believes that the true celebration of the Eucharist brings to the believer knowledge of the power of union with Christ, that it is "for you." Calvin thinks the Eucharist exhibits God's love in its most personal, most intense, most experienced form. Thus, Calvin has set the Eucharist up as not just a "bare knowledge" of union with Christ, as simply information. Rather, Calvin views the Eucharist as a type of knowledge that works alongside Christ's union with the believer to mold the believer's life.

Conclusion

François Wendel asks, "What does the Supper give us that we cannot obtain otherwise?"[41] He asks the question in the context of Calvin's claim that union with Christ takes place outside the eucharistic activity: in the preaching of the word, reading of Scripture, or prayer. Though Calvin emphasizes the utility of the sacrament, Wendel finally finds Calvin's eucharistic doctrine baffling in that he questions how in the Eucharist one really receives the body and blood of Christ.[42]

Kilian McDonnell also faults Calvin on this issue. He claims that for Calvin the "eucharistic moment is a particularization of a union with Christ in faith through the Holy Spirit."[43] However, as McDonnell reads Calvin's theology, God "does not need them [the sacraments] to bring nourishment to man."[44] Thus, McDonnell is able to conclude, "For Calvin . . . there is no specific eucharistic gift, no object, person, effect, or grace given in the Eucharist which is not given in faith outside of the Eucharist."[45] Both Wendel and McDonnell, therefore, give the impression that Calvin's eucharistic teaching makes the Eucharist somewhat superfluous to Christian existence, in the sense that it is not necessary.

However, after tracing Calvin's eucharistic teaching over the course of his career, one sees that the Eucharist is absolutely necessary for the Christian in this life. For, after the elements of the Holy Spirit and union with Christ are in place by the time of the 1539 *Institutes*, one finds that Calvin's further developments come along the lines of knowledge, substantial partaking of the flesh and blood of Christ, and accommodated instrumentality. As has been shown, the three are linked. The mistake that Wendel and McDonnell make are in looking at the issue solely in terms of presence, or a special type of union with Christ. Calvin, however, joins the issue of presence with the need for certainty. Thus, in his eucharistic theory, the Eucharist serves as an instrument by which the Christian not only is joined to Christ but also knows the goodness of God in a way most fully accommodated to the weaknesses of the faithful. Though the two concepts may be distinguished, they work together in Calvin's eucharistic theology and may not be separated. Together, they form the gift of the Eucharist. According to Calvin, a gift given by God is to be accepted with thanks, not questioned about its utility in relation to other gifts.

It is at this point that Nevin was right in his instincts: there is a eucharistic gift in Calvin. It is *Christ* and the *knowledge* of his presence. The gift, in a sense, cannot be a special presence, for Calvin has set up his theology so that the definition of being a Christian is to be in union with Jesus Christ. In that sense, McDonnell and others have asked Calvin a question foreign to his outlook. Calvin does say, however, that one does not have all of Christ all at once, so in the word, in Scripture reading, in prayer, in the sacraments that union is, in fact, strengthened. This is what growth in the Christian faith means for Calvin: to grow more and more into Christ Jesus. Once justification has taken place, the Christian is wed permanently to the person of Jesus Christ, body and blood. What Calvin calls the "mystical and incomprehensible operation of the flesh"[46] is the focal point of his notion of union with Christ. Thus, there cannot be a different or separate type of presence in the Eucharist than what the Christian already has; it can only be strengthened and confirmed.

Because of the dialectical hermeneutic Calvin sets up between word and sacrament, the word as a source of knowledge about the Eucharist enables the Eucharist itself to become a source of knowledge. The eucharistic event, as it makes plain the relationship of the believer to Christ, enables the believer to enjoy more fully the reality of union with Christ and see it grow. There is a revelation by God in the Eucharist in which he accommodates the truth of his good will toward humanity, his nourishment of the Christian with the very body and blood of Jesus Christ. The Eucharist is one of the chosen instruments by which God makes this revelation. It relies on the word, it is powerless without the Spirit, and there is no positive effect if the believer is not already in union with Christ. However, once these qualifications are met, that is, when the Eucharist is appropriately celebrated, there is no clearer indication from God as to his relationship to his chosen people. It is thus through this clear mirror then that God has chosen to most fully reveal his grace to the full range of human senses in order that Christian faith may grow. Therefore, part of the eucharistic gift is knowledge. The Eucharist is the chosen instrument accommodated in the best and clearest way to present knowledge of God's gracious action in Christ.

"Nearly all the wisdom we possess," Calvin states, "that is to say, true and sound wisdom, consists of two parts: the knowledge of God and of ourselves."[47] A developmental view of Calvin's eucharistic teaching leads one to affirm that this wisdom is given in the Eucharist in a heightened fashion. The Lord's Supper serves as an instrument of meaning, where one knows in a special way what it is to be a sinful human creature, what marvelous grace God has extended to his people, and what life as a Christian is all about.

However, it would be remiss to end the discussion of Calvin's eucharistic theology with an emphasis on knowledge as such. In addition to knowledge, there is mystery. And there is nothing more mysterious to Calvin than the union of Christ with his faithful. The eucharistic gift of knowledge is related in such a way to the more general gift of union with Christ that the gift of union is effected so as to be considered, in a manner, as "special."

Calvin makes it clear in *The Best Method of Obtaining Concord* that the gift of the Eucharist is Christ himself. He says, "For certainly the reality and substance of the sacrament is not only the application of the benefits of Christ, but Christ himself with his death and resurrection."[48] Moreover, Calvin declares that the Eucharist, aside from being an instrument of knowledge, is also an instrument that gives the gift of Christ, body and blood, to believers: "under the bread and wine we receive an earnest which *makes us partakers of the body and blood of Christ* (emphasis mine)."[49] Thus, though Calvin does not admit a different sort of communion with Christ in the Eucharist, he does see it as one means God uses to effect and strengthen that union. This general eucharistic gift, combined with the more specific eucharistic gift of knowledge, results in a heightening of the general gift of union that can be termed, in its own way, a eucharistic "more." In other words, the substantial partaking of the life-giving body and blood of Christ does gain a degree of "specialness" in the Eucharist that is not to be found elsewhere.

The argument on which this conclusion is based is as follows. The reception of Christ in the Eucharist is not limited to the Eucharist; Christ can be and is received substantially through other instruments. Yet, the presence is intensified in the eucharistic act because of the special type of knowledge the Eucharist brings: the presentation of union with Christ in its most graphic and appropriate form for sinful humans. Therefore, the general gift of presence changes as a result of the cognitive experience; not in kind, certainly, but in degree. This reasoning is based on Calvin's own arguments about the Old Testament patriarchs as it has been presented in this work. For the Old Testament elect, Christ was also given in sacraments available to them. However, the Christian has an advantage in the sense that, because of fuller revelation, because of the greater knowledge Calvin associates with the New Testament revelation, the Christian enjoys more fully the reality of Christ.[50] For Calvin, this means that the reality is not different; indeed, it must be the same. However, the degree of enjoyment of the reality is increased. Thus, Calvin makes the comparison between having Christ in shadow form under the old dispensation, while those living under the new dispensation have Christ in fully exhibited colors, a picture of brilliant intensity.

Likewise, one could argue that the revelation of knowledge the Eucharist gives works along the same lines. It serves to heighten the intensity of a reality received elsewhere. It paints a picture that is fuller to the human eye than the drawings of the word. Therefore, there is the greater recognition of what it is that is enjoyed, Christ himself. Though the reality given through other instruments is of the same sort as that given in the Eucharist, there is a difference in degree. Thus, the Eucharist gives not only the clearest picture of union with Christ, but enables the fullest partaking of that reality in this life.[51] How can such a gift be considered superfluous? To consider it such would be to exhibit ingratitude to the greatest degree.

That is, indeed, why Calvin links the Eucharist and gratitude to such a degree in his eucharistic thought. That which reveals and extends God's grace to such a great degree should evoke the greatest gratitude. Thus, as Calvin proclaims, the Eucharist should evoke "sacrifices of praise." "What is the chief end of human life?" Calvin would ask his students. "To glorify God," the student would answer. According to Calvin, there is no greater instrument than the Eucharist by which to direct Christians to that end of human life.

Notes

1. Bibliographic information on the '59 *Institutes* has been given in note 2 of the Introduction. The treatise against Heshusius carries the Latin title *Dilucida explicatio sanae doctrinae de vera participatione carnis et sanguinis Christi in sacra coena ad discutiendas Heshusii nebulas*, OC 9:457–518, hereafter cited *The True Partaking of the Flesh and Blood of Christ. The Best Method of Obtaining Concord* carries the Latin title *Optima Ineundae concordiae Ratio, si extra contentionem Quaeratur Veritas*. This work, written in 1560, was published at the end of the treatise against Heshusius in 1561. The Latin text is found in OC 9:517–24. Both works have been translated in Calvin, *Selected Works* 2:496–572.

2. *Inst.* 4.17.1.

3. *Inst.* 4.17.1.

4. Peter Barth, in discussing both baptism and the Eucharist, applies to them the very appropriate phrase "salvation-training instruments" ("heilspädagogische Instrumente"). Barth, "Calvins Stellung im Abendmahlsstreit," *Die christliche Welt* 43 (1929): 928.

5. *Inst.* 4.14.4.

6. *Inst.* 4.14.6. Calvin had said in 1536 that the sacraments attest God's good will toward Christians (*Inst. '36*, p. 88; OC 1:103; OS 1:119). Thus, the new addition in the '59 edition is the phrase "more expressly than by word." Here, in a nutshell, is a summary of the developmental process from 1536–1559 in Calvin's eucharistic theology in terms of the cognitive function of the Lord's Supper. This emphasis on knowledge, however, is always balanced by Calvin's emphasis on the mystery of the Supper. On the one hand, Calvin believes that as a result of the celebration of the Eucharist, the believer *knows* that he is in union with Christ. On the other hand, how that union takes place will always remain a mystery. Thus, when speaking of the knowledge the sacrament imparts to the believer, one must always remember that in Calvin's thought that emphasis is part of a dialectic, the other pole of which is mystery.

7. For examples of Calvin's comments on communion with Christ outside the eucharistic act, see *The True Partaking of the Flesh and Blood of Christ*, in Calvin, *Selected Works* 2:523, 530–31, 538, 539, 559, and 560 (OC 9:481, 487, 493, 494, 509, respectively); in these passages it is clear that union with Christ is a perpetual state for the believer and that the union is with the flesh and blood of Christ.

8. *Inst.* 4.17.30.

9. Calvin, *The True Partaking of the Flesh and Blood of Christ*, in *Selected Works* 2:524; OC 9:482.

10. McNeill suggests that, particularly in sections 20–34, Calvin has Westphal in mind. See *Inst.*, p. 1382, n. 67.

11. *Inst.* 4.17.7.

12. *Inst.* 4.17.24.

13. *Inst.* 4.17.29. As part of the nature of a human body, in order for it to remain a human body, even in a glorified state, the finite nature must remain. See *Inst.* 17.4.26.

14. *Inst.* 4.17.29.

15. Calvin, *The True Partaking of the Flesh and Blood of Christ*, in *Selected Works* 2:501–2; OC 9:466.

16. *Inst.* 4.17.28.

17. Calvin states that, in terms of Christ as mediator, Christ incarnate is never present without the Spirit. See *The True Partaking of the Flesh and Blood of Christ*, in *Selected Works* 2:569; OC 9:516.

18. Given all the citations to Calvin's statements on Christ's flesh that have been given in this work, one wonders how a scholar such as Gregory Dix can so confuse Spirit and flesh as to be able to say of Calvin: "This, then, is his [Calvin's] final meaning—that in the Eucharist Jesus bestows his Spirit on the spirit of the individual who believes in Him as Redeemer and partakes of the bread and wine as he had commanded." Dix, *The Shape of the Liturgy*, with additional notes by Paul V. Marshall (San Francisco: Harper and Row, 1982), p. 633.

19. Calvin, *The True Partaking of the Flesh and Blood of Christ*, in *Selected Works* 2:560; OC 9:509.

20. *Inst.* 4.17.10.

21. *Inst.* 4.17.22.

22. *Inst.* 4.17.23.

23. *Inst.* 4.17.25.

24. *Inst.* 4.17.24.

25. *Inst.* 4.17.20.

26. *Inst.* 4.17.25.

27. *Inst.* 4.17.32. Calvin's thoughts on the eating process in the Eucharist as something other than a literal, physical event can be seen in *The True Partaking of the Flesh and Blood of Christ*, in *Selected Works* 2:507, 510, 516–18, 522, 541, 549, and 550 (OC 9:470, 472, 477–78, 481, 495, and 501, respectively).

28. Calvin, *The Best Method of Obtaining Concord*, in *Selected Works* 2:577; OC 9:521.

29. Calvin, *The Best Method of Obtaining Concord*, in *Selected Works* 2:577; OC 9:521.

30. Calvin, *The True Partaking of the Flesh and Blood of Christ*, in *Selected Works* 2:507; OC 9:470.

31. Calvin, *The True Partaking of the Flesh and Blood of Christ*, in *Selected Works* 2:518–19; OC 9:478.

32. Calvin, *The Best Method of Obtaining Concord*, in *Selected Works* 2:579; OC 9:522.

33. "Confirmant ergo fidem nostram et verbum et sacramenta, dum bonam patris coelestis erga nos voluntatem nobis ob oculos ponunt. Cuius cognitione, et tota fidei nostrae firmitudo consistit, et robur augescit. Confirmat spiritus, dum, eam animis nostris confirmationem in sculpendo, efficacem reddit." *Inst.* '39 10.7.22–26, p. 264; OC 1:945.

34. *Inst.* 4.14.10.

35. *Inst.* 4.14.16.

36. *Inst.* 4.14.17. "But we contend that, whatever instruments he uses, these detract nothing from his original activity."

37. *Inst.* 4.17.15.

38. *Inst.* 4.17.24.

39. *Inst.* 4.17.31.

40. Calvin, *The True Partaking of the Flesh and Blood of Christ*, in *Selected Works* 2:534; OC 9:490.

41. Wendel, *Calvin*, p. 353.

42. Ibid., p. 354.

43. McDonnell, *John Calvin, the Church and the Eucharist*, p. 70

44. Ibid., p. 169.

45. Ibid., p. 179. Werner Krusche would seem to agree: "The proper gift of the Lord's Supper, communion with Christ, is according to him [Calvin] not a specific gift of the Lord's Supper." ("Die eigentliche Gabe des Abendmahls: die Gemeinschaft mit Christus, ist bei ihm gerade keine spezifische Gabe des Abendmahls.") Krusche, *Das Wirken des Heiligen Geistes nach Calvin* (Göttingen: Vandenhoeck und Ruprecht, 1957), p. 272.

46. Calvin, *The True Partaking of the Flesh and Blood of Christ*, in *Selected Works* 2:560; OC 9:509.

47. *Inst.* 1.1.1.

48. Calvin, *The Best Method of Obtaining Concord*, in *Selected Works* 2:578; OC 9:522.

49. Calvin, *The Best Method of Obtaining Concord*, in *Selected Works* 2:574; OC 9:519.

50. "I must briefly remind them that everything is subverted when he makes the fathers equal to us in the mode of eating; for though they had Christ in common with us, the measure of revelation was by no means equal. Were it otherwise, there would have been no ground for the exclamation, Blessed are the eyes which see the things which ye see." Calvin, *The True Partaking of the Flesh and Blood of Christ*, in *Selected Works* 2:532; OC 9:488.

51. J. K. S. Reid says that "In the Eucharist we have, as cannot be said of simply the Word of God, offered to us the body of Jesus Christ and the blood of Christ." Reid, "Gospel and Eucharist—a Reformed Exposition," in *Evangile et sacrement*, edited by Günter Grassman and Vilmos Vajta (Paris: Cerf, 1970), p. 218. The conclusion I present agrees fully with Reid's analysis if one means having in

the Eucharist the body and blood of Christ in a higher degree rather than in a different manner.

SELECTED BIBLIOGRAPHY

Primary Sources

Calvin, John. *Calvini opera selecta.* Edited by Peter Barth and Wilhelm Niesel. 5 vols. Monachii: Kaiser Verlag, 1926–1936. [Cited as OS.] Each passage is cited by volume and page number.

——. *Iohannis Calvini opera quae supersunt omnia.* Edited by Wilhelm Baum, Edward Cunitz, and Edward Reuss. 59 vols. Brunsvigae: C. A. Schwetscke, 1863–1900. Vols. 29–87: *Corpus Reformatorum.* [Cited as OC.] Each passage is cited by volume (1–59) and column number.

——. *Institutes of the Christian Religion of John Calvin 1539: Text and Concordance.* 4 vols. Edited by Richard F. Wevers. Grand Rapids: The H. Henry Meeter Center for Calvin Studies, 1988. [Cited as *Inst. '39*] Each passage is cited by Chapter, Paragraph, and Line number, followed by page number.

Zwingli, Huldreich. "Das dise wort Iesus Christi: Das ist min lychnam, ewigklich den alten eynigen sinn haben werden, etc." In *Corpus Reformatorum*, vol. 92: *Huldreich Zwinglis Sämtliche Werke*, vol. 5. Edited by Emil Egli and others. Leipzig: M. Heinsius Nachfolger, 1934. Pp. 805–977.

Translations

Cajetan. *Cajetan Responds: A Reader in Reformation Controversy.* Edited and translated by Jared Wicks. Washington, D.C.: The Catholic University of America Press, 1978.

Calvin, John. *Calvin's New Testament Commentaries.* Edited by David W. Torrance and Thomas F. Torrance. Grand Rapids:

Eerdmans, 1980. (This is a reprint edition; the original publisher and date of publication are given in the note citations.) Vol. 3: *A Harmony of the Gospels Matthew, Mark and Luke; James and John*, translated by A. W. Morrison; Vol. 4: *The Gospel According to St. John, Part One 1-10*, translated by T. H. L. Parker; Vol. 6: *The Acts of the Apostles, 1-13*, translated by W. J. G. McDonald; Vol. 7: *The Acts of the Apostles, 14-28*, translated by John W. Fraser; Vol. 9: *The First Epistle of Paul the Apostle to the Corinthians*, translated by John W. Fraser; Vol. 10: *The Second Letter of Paul to the Corinthians, and the Epistles to Timothy, Titus, and Philemon*, translated by T. A. Smail; Vol. 11: *The Epistles of Paul the Apostle to the Galatians, Ephesians, Philippians, and Colossians*, translated by T. H. L. Parker; and Vol. 12: *Hebrews and I and II Peter*, translated by W. B. Johnston.

————. *John Calvin: Selections from His Writings.* Edited by John Dillenberger. Missoula: Scholars Press, 1975. Originally published by Anchor Books, 1971.

————. *Institutes of the Christian Religion.* 2 vols. Edited by J. T. McNeill and translated by Ford Lewis Battles. Philadelphia: Westminster Press, 1960. [Cited as *Inst.*] This is the standard English translation of the 1559 *Institutes*. Each passage is cited by Book, Chapter, and Section.

————. *Institutes of the Christian Religion, 1536 edition.* Translated and annotated by Ford Lewis Battles, revised by M. Howard Rienstra. Grand Rapids: Wm. B. Eerdmans and the H. Henry Meeter Center for Calvin Studies, 1986. [Cited as *Inst. '36*] Each passage is cited by page number. Originally published by John Knox Press, Atlanta, 1975.

————. *Selected Works of John Calvin: Tracts and Letters.* 7 vols. Edited and translated by Henry Beveridge and Jules Bonnet. Grand Rapids: Baker Book House, 1983. [Cited as *Selected Works*] Originally published by the Calvin Translation Society, 1849.

————. *Theological Treatises.* Translated, with introductions and notes by J. K. S. Reid. Philadelphia: Westminster Press, 1954.

Luther, Martin. *Luther's Works*. Edited by Jaroslav Pelikan and Helmut T. Lehmann. Vol. 23: *Sermons on the Gospel of St. John, Chapters 6–8*. Edited by Jaroslav Pelikan. St. Louis: Concordia Publishing House, 1959. Vol. 37: *Work and Sacrament III*. Edited by Robert H. Fisher. Philadelphia: Muhlenberg Press, 1961.

———. *Sermons of Martin Luther*. Edited and translated by John Lenker. 7 vols. 1907; repr. ed. Grand Rapids: Baker Book House, 1988.

Schwenkfeld, Caspar. "An Answer to Luther's Malediction." In *Spiritual and Anabaptist Writers*. Edited by George H. Williams and Angel M. Mergal. Philadelphia: Westminster Press, 1957. Pp. 163–81.

Zwingli, Ulrich. *Zwingli and Melancthon*, edited by G. W. Bromiley. Philadelphia: Westminster Press, 1953.

———. *Commentary on True and False Religion*, edited by Samuel Jackson. Durham, N.C.: The Labyrinth Press, 1981.

———. *On Providence and other essays*. Edited by Samuel Macauley Jackson. 1922; repr. ed., Durham, N.C.: Labyrinth Press, 1983.

Bibliographies

Barth, Peter. "Fünfundzwanzig Jahre Calvinforschung, 1909–1934." *Theologische Rundschau* (1934): 161–267.

DeKlerk, Peter. "Calvin Bibliography." *Calvin Theological Journal* (1972-). Annual bibliographies in the no. 2 issue of each volume since 1972.

Erichson, Alfred. *Bibliographia Calviniana*, with chronological listing of publications. Nieuwkoop, 1960. Reprint of 1900 edition.

Fraenkel, Peter. "Petit supplement aux bibliographies calviennes, 1901-1963." *Bibliotheque d'Humanisme et Renaissance* 33 (1977): 385-414.

Kempff, Dionysius. *A Bibliography of Calviniana 1959-1974.* Studies in Medieval Thought, 15. Leiden: Brill, 1975.

Tylenda, Joseph. "Calvin Bibliography, 1960-1970." *Calvin Theological Journal* 6, no. 2 (November 1971): 156-93.

The H. Henry Meeter Center for Calvin Studies, Calvin College and Seminary, Grand Rapids, Michigan, publishes a *Newsletter* that lists recent publications (books, articles, reviews, and dissertations) on Calvin. The *Newsletter* first appeared in Spring 1988 and is published twice per year.

Secondary Sources

Abba, Raymond. "Calvin's Doctrine of the Lord's Supper." *The Reformed Theological Review* 9, no. 2 (Winter 1950): 1-12.

Aron, Raymond. *Introduction to the Philosophy of History: An Essay on the Limits of Objectivity.* London: Weidenfeld and Nicolson, 1961.

Barclay, Alexander. *The Protestant Doctrine of the Lord's Supper: A Study in the Eucharistic Teaching of Luther, Zwingli and Calvin.* Glasgow: Jackson, Wylie, and Company, 1927.

Barth, Peter. "Calvins Stellung im Abendmahlsstreit." *Die christliche Welt* 43 (1929): 922-29.

Battles, Ford Lewis. "Calculus Fidei." In *Calvinus Ecclesiae Doctor: Die Referate des Internationalen Kongresses für Calvinforschung vom 25. bis 28. September 1978 in Amsterdam,* edited by W. H. Neusner. Kampen: J. H. Kok, 1978. Pp. 85-110.

————. "God Was Accommodating Himself to Human Capacity." *Interpretation* 31 (January 1977): 19-38. Reprinted in *Readings in Calvin's Theology*, edited by Donald K. McKim. Grand Rapids: Baker Book House, 1984. Pp. 21-42.

Battles, Ford Lewis, and Stanley Tagg, editors. *The Piety of John Calvin: An Anthology Illustrative of the Spirituality of the Reformer.* Grand Rapids: Baker Book House, 1978.

Battles, Ford Lewis, assisted by John Walchenbach. *Analysis of the Institutes of the Christian Religion.* Grand Rapids: Baker Book House, 1980.

Bavinck, Herman. "Calvijn's Leer over het Avondmaal." *Vrije Kerk* 13 (1887): 459–86. Also in the author's *Kennis en leven: Opsteelen en Artikelen uit vroegere jaren.* Kampen: J. H. Kok, 1922. Pp. 165–83.

————. "Calvin and Common Grace." Translated by Geerhardus Vos. In *Calvin and the Reformation*, edited by William Park Armstrong. Grand Rapids: Baker Book House, 1980. Pp. 99–130. Reprinted from the 1909 edition issued by the Princeton Theological Review Association.

Beckmann, Joachim. *Vom Sakrament bei Calvin: Die Sakramentslehre Calvins in ihren Beziehungen zu Augustin.* Tübingen: J.C.B. Mohr, 1926.

Benoit, Jean-Daniel. "The History and Development of the Institutio: How Calvin Worked." In *John Calvin*, edited by G. E. Duffield. Courtenay Studies in Reformation Theology, 1. Appleford, England: The Sutton Courtenay Press, 1966. Pp. 102-17.

Bizer, Ernst. *Studien zur Geschichte des Abendmahlsstreit im 16. Jahrhundert.* In Beiträge zur Förderung christliche Theologie, 2. Reihe: Sammlung wissenchaftlicher Monographien, 46. Band, edited by Paul Althaus. Gütersloh: C. Bertelsmann, 1940.

Bornert, René. *La Réforme protestante du culte a Strasbourg au XVIᵉ siècle (1523-1598): Approche sociologique et interprétation théologique.* Studies in Medieval and Reformation Thought 18, edited by Heiko Oberman. Leiden: E. J. Brill, 1981.

Bosc, Jean. "L'Eucharistie dans les Églises de la Réforme." *Verbum Caro* 22, no. 85 (1968): 36-47.

Bouvier, André. *Henri Bullinger, réformateur et conseiller oecuménique, le successeur de Zwingli: d'apres sa correspondance avec les reformes et les humanistes de langue française.* Neuchatel: Delachaux et Niestlé; Paris: Librarie E. Droz, 1940.

Bouwsma, William. *John Calvin: A Sixteenth Century Portrait.* New York and Oxford: Oxford University Press, 1988.

Cadier, Jean. *La doctrine calviniste de la sainte cène.* Montpelier: Études théologiques et religieuses, 1951.

Chavannes, Henry. "La présence réelle chez saint Thomas et chez Calvin." *Verbum Caro* 13, no. 50 (1959): 151-70.

Courvoisier, Jaques. "Bucer et l'oeuvre de Calvin." *Revue de Théologie et Philosophie* 21 (1936): 66–77.

———. "Reflexions a propos de la doctrine eucharistique de Zwingli et de Calvin." In *Festgabe Leonhard von Muralt, zum siebzigsten Geburtstag, 17 Mai 1970, überricht von Freunden und Schulern.* Zurich: Berichthaus, 1970. Pp. 258-65.

Dankbaar, W. F. *De Sacramentsleer van Calvijn.* Amsterdam: H. J. Paris, 1941.

Dix, Gregory. *The Shape of the Liturgy,* with additional notes by Paul V. Marshall. San Francisco: Harper and Row, 1982. Preface and additional notes copyrighted by Seabury Press, 1982. First published in 1945 by A. & C. Black Publishers, 1945.

Doumergue, Emile. *Jean Calvin: Les hommes et les choses de son temps; tome cinquième: La pensée ecclésiastique et la pensée politique de Calvin.* Lausanne: Georges Bridel et Cie, 1917.

Ebrard, Johann Heinrich August. *Das Dogma vom heilige Abendmahl und seine Geschichte*, 2 vols. Frankfort: Heinrich Zimmer, 1845-46.

Emery, Pierre Yves. "The Teaching of Calvin on the Sacrificial Element in the Eucharist." *The Reformed and Presbyterian World* 26 (1960): 109-14.

Engel, Mary Potter. *John Calvin's Perspectival Anthropology.* American Academy of Religion Academy Series, 52. Atlanta: Scholars Press, 1988.

Fitzer, Joseph. "The Augustinian Roots of Calvin's Eucharistic Teaching." *Augustinian Studies* (1976): 69-98.

Forstman, H. Jackson. *Word and Spirit: Calvin's Doctrine of Biblical Authority.* Palo Alto, Calif.: Stanford University Press, 1962.

Gadamer, Hans-Georg. *Truth and Method.* New York: Crossroad, 1982.

Gäbler, Ulrich. "Das Zustandekommen des Consensus Tigurinus im Jahre 1549." *Theologische Literaturzeitung* 104/5 (1979): 321-32.

Ganoczy, Alexandre. "L'action sacramentaire de Dieu par le Christ selon Calvin." In *Sacrements de Jésus-Christ*, edited by Joseph Dore. Paris: Desclée, 1983. Pp. 109-29.

———. *Calvin: Théologien de l'Église et du Ministère.* Unam Sanctum 48. Paris: Cerf, 1964.

———. "Calvin als paulinischer Theologe." In *Calvinus Theologus: Die Referate des Europäischen Kongresses für Calvinforschung vom 16. bis 19. September 1974 in Amsterdam*, edited by W. H. Neusner. Neukirchen-Vluyn: Neukirchener Verlag, 1976.

———. *The Young Calvin.* Translated by David Foxgrover and Wade Provo. Philadelphia: Westminster Press, 1987.

George, Timothy. "John Calvin and the Agreement of Zurich (1549)." In *John Calvin and the Church: A Prism of Reform*, edited by Timothy George. Louisville: Westminster/John Knox Press, 1990. Pp. 42–58.

————. *Theology of the Reformers*. Nashville: Broadman Press, 1988.

Gerrish, Brian A. "The Flesh of the Son of Man: John W. Nevin on the Church and the Eucharist." In *Tradition in the Modern World: Reformed Theology in the Nineteenth Century*. Chicago: University of Chicago Press, 1978. Pp. 49-70.

————. "Gospel and Eucharist: John Calvin on the Lord's Supper." In *The Old Protestantism and the New: Essays on the Reformation Heritage*. Chicago: University of Chicago Press, 1982. Pp. 106–17.

————. "The Pathfinder." In *The Old Protestantism and the New: Essays on the Reformation Heritage*. Chicago: University of Chicago Press, 1982. Pp. 27–48.

————. "Sign and Reality: The Lord's Supper in the Reformed Confessions" In *The Old Protestantism and the New: Essays on the Reformation Heritage*. Chicago: University of Chicago Press, 1982. Pp. 118–30.

Gleason, Ronald N. "Calvin and Bavinck on the Lord's Supper." *Westminster Theological Journal* 45, no. 2 (Fall 1983): 273-303.

Gollwitzer, Helmut. *Coena Domini: Die altlutherische Abendmahlslehre in ihrer Auseinandersetzung mit dem Calvinismus dargestellt an der lutherischen Frühorthodoxie*. Munich: Chr. Kaiser Verlag, 1937.

Grass, Hans. *Die Abendmahlslehre bei Luther und Calvin: Eine kritische Untersuchung*. In Beiträge zur Förderung christlicher Theologie, 2. Reihe: Sammlung wissenschaftlicher Monographien, 47. Band. Gütersloh: C. Bertelsmann, 1954.

Hartvelt, G. P. *Verum Corpus: Een Studie over een Centraal Hoof dstuk uit de Avondmaalsleer van Calvijn.* Delft: W. D. Meinema, 1960.

Heron, Alasdair I. C. *Table and Tradition: Toward an Ecumenical Understanding of the Eucharist.* Philadelphia: Westminster Press, 1983.

Hodge, Charles. "Doctrine of the Reformed Church on the Lord's Supper." *Princeton Review* 20 (April 1848): 227, 275-77, 278.

Hunter, A. Mitchell. *The Teaching of Calvin: A Modern Interpretation.* Second, revised edition. London: James Clarke and Co., 1950.

Jacobs, Paul. "Die Gegenwart Christi im Abendmahl nach reformiertem Verständnis und das römisch-katholische Gegenbild." In *Gegenwart Christi: Beitrag zum Abendmahlsgespräch in der Evangelischen Kirche in Deutschland*, edited by Fritz Viering. Göttingen: Vandenhoeck und Ruprecht, 1960. Pp. 23-33.

Janssen, Heinrich. "Die Abendmahlslehre Johannes Calvin." *Una Sancta* 15, no. 2 (1960): 125-38.

Jolivet, Régis. *La Notion de Substance: Essai historique et critique sur le développement des doctrines d'Aristote à nos jours.* Bibliotheque des Archives de Philosophie. Paris: Beauchesne, 1929.

Kolfhaus, Wilhelm. *Christusgemeinschaft bei Johannes Calvin.* Neukirchen, 1939.

Krusche, Werner. *Das Wirken des Heiligen Geistes nach Calvin.* In Forschungen zur Kirchen- und Dogmengeschichte, Band 7. Göttingen: Vandenhoeck und Ruprecht, 1957.

Maxwell, William D. *The Liturgical Portions of the Genevan Service Book.* Edinburgh: Oliver and Boyd, 1931.

McDonnell, Kilian. *John Calvin, the Church and the Eucharist.* Princeton: Princeton University Press, 1967.

McGrath, Alister E. *A Life of John Calvin*. Oxford: Basil Blackwell, 1990.

McLelland, Joseph C. "Meta-Zwingli or Anti-Zwingli? Bullinger and Calvin in Eucharistic Concord." In *Huldrych Zwingli, 1484-1531: A Lively Legacy of Reform*, edited by Edward J. Furcha. ARC Supplement 2. Montreal: McGill University Faculty of Religious Studies, 1985. Pp. 179-96.

Meyer, Boniface. "Calvin's Eucharistic Doctrine: 1536-39." *Journal of Ecumenical Studies* 4 No. 1 (1967): 47-65.

Nevin, John Williamson. "Doctrine of the Reformed Church on the Lord's Supper." In *The Mystical Presence and other Writings on the Eucharist*, edited by Bard Thompson and George H. Bricker, pp. 267-401. Volume four of Lancaster Series on the Mercersburg Theology. Philadelphia and Boston: United Church Press, 1966. Originally published as Volume II, no. 5 of the *Mercersburg Review*, 1850.

————. *The Mystical Presence: A Vindication of the Reformed or Calvinistic Doctrine of the Holy Eucharist*. Hamden, Conn.: Archon Books, 1963. Facsimile of original edition, Philadelphia: J. B. Lippincott & Co., 1846.

Nichols, James H. "The Intent of the Calvinistic Liturgy." In *The Heritage of John Calvin*, edited by John H. Bratt. Heritage Hall Lectures, 1960-1970. Grand Rapids: Wm. B. Eerdmans, 1973. Pp. 87-109.

————. "The Reformed Doctrine of the Lord's Supper Recovered." In his *Romanticism in American Theology: Nevin and Schaff at Mercersburg*. Chicago: University of Chicago Press, 1961. Pp. 84-106.

Niesel, Wilhelm. *Calvins Lehre vom Abendmahl im Lichte seiner letzen Antwort an Westphal*. Second edition. Munich: Chr. Kaiser Verlag, 1935.

Oberman, Heiko. "The 'Extra' Dimension in the Theology of Calvin." In *The Dawn of the Reformation*. Edinburgh: T. & T. Clark, 1986. Pp. 234–58.

––––. "Fourteenth-Century Religious Thought: A Premature Profile." In *The Dawn of the Reformation*. Edinburgh: T. & T. Clark, 1986. Pp. 1–17.

––––. "The Shape of Late Medieval Thought." In *The Dawn of the Reformation*. Edinburgh: T. & T. Clark, 1986. Pp. 18–38.

Parker, T. H. L. *Calvin's New Testament Commentaries*. Grand Rapids: Eerdmans, 1971.

––––. *Calvin's Old Testament Commentaries*. Edinburgh: T. & T. Clark, 1986.

––––. "Calvin the exegete: change and development." In *Calvinus Ecclesiae Doctor: Die Referate des Internationalen Kongresses für Calvinforschung vom 25. bis 28. September 1978 in Amsterdam*, edited by W. H. Neusner. Kampen: J. H. Kok, 1978. Pp. 35–46.

––––. *John Calvin*. London: J. M. Dent and Sons, 1975; repr. ed., n.p., Lion Publishing Co., 1987.

Pauck, Wilhelm. "Calvin und Butzer." *Journal of Religion* 9 (1929): 237–56.

Pelikan, Jaroslav. *Luther's Works: Companion Volume: Introduction to the Exegetical Writings*. St. Louis: Concordia: 1959.

Peter, Rodolphe. "Calvin et la liturgie d'apres l'*Institution*. *Études théologiques et religieuses* 60, no. 3 (1985): 385-401.

Pruett, Gordon E. "A Protestant Doctrine of the Eucharistic Presence." *Calvin Theological Journal* 10, no.2 (November 1975): 142–74.

Raitt, Jill. *The Eucharistic Theology of Theodore Beza: Development of the Reformed Doctrine.* AAR Studies in Religion, 4. Chambersburg, Pennsylvania: American Academy of Religion, 1972.

Reid, J. K. S. "Gospel and Eucharist—A Reformed Exposition." In *Evangile et sacrament,* edited by Günter Grassman and Vilmos Vajta. Paris: Cerf, 1970. Pp. 212–39.

Rogge, Joachim. *Virtus und Res: Um die Abendmahlswirklichkeit bei Calvin.* Arbeiten zur Theologie, series 1, no. 18. Stuttgart: Calwer Verlag, 1965.

Rorem, Paul. "Calvin and Bullinger on the Lord's Supper, Part I. The Impasse." *Lutheran Quarterly* 2, no. 2 (1988): 155–84.

———. "Calvin and Bullinger on the Lord's Supper, Part II. The Agreement." *Lutheran Quarterly* 2, no. 3 (1988): 357–89.

Schaff, Philip. *The Creeds of Christendom.* 3 vols. Sixth edition. New York: Harper and Brothers, 1931.

Schreiner, Susan. "Exegesis and Double Justice in Calvin's Sermons on Job." *Church History* 58, no. 3 (September 1989): 322–38.

Smedes, Lewis B. "Calvin and the Lord's Supper." *The Reformed Journal* 4, no. 6 (June 1954): 5-7; no. 7 (July-August 1954): 4-5.

Smits, Luchesius. *Saint Augustin dans l'Oeuvre de Jean Calvin, I: Étude de Critique Litteraire.* Assen: Van Gorcum, 1956.

Steinmetz, David C. "Scripture and the Lord's Supper in Luther's Theology." In *Luther in Context.* Bloomington: Indiana University Press, 1986. Pp. 72–84.

———. "The Theology of Calvin and Calvinism." In *Reformation Europe: A Guide to Research,* edited by Steven Ozment. St. Louis: Center for Reformation Research, 1982. Pp. 211–32.

Strohl, Henri. "Bucer et Calvin." *Bulletin de Histoire du Protestantisme française* 87 (1938): 354–56.

Thurian, Max. "The Real Presence." In *Christianity Divided*, edited by Daniel J. Callahan et al. New York: Sheed and Ward, 1961. Pp. 203-22.

Tylenda, Joseph N. "The Calvin—Westphal Exchange: The Genesis of Calvin's Treatises Against Tylenda." *Calvin Theological Journal* 9, no. 2 (November 1974): 182-209.

———. "Calvin and Christ's Presence in the Supper—True or Real." *Scottish Journal of Theology*, 27 (1974): 65-75.

———. "Calvin on Christ's True Presence in the Lord's Supper." *The American Ecclesiastical Review* 155 (November 1966): 321-33.

———. "The Ecumenical Intentions of Calvin's Early Eucharistic Teaching." In *Reformatio Perennis*, edited by Brian A. Gerrish. Pittsburgh: Pickwick Press, 1981. Pp. 27–47.

Walker, Williston. *John Calvin: The Organiser of Reformed Protestantism, 1509–1564.* New York: G.P. Putnam's Sons, 1906; repr. ed., New York: AMS Press, 1972.

Wallace, Ronald S. *Calvin's Doctrine of the Word and Sacrament.* Edinburgh: Oliver and Boyd, 1953; repr. ed., Tyler, Tex.: Geneva Divinity School Press, n.d.

Warfield, Benjamin B. "Calvin's Doctrine of the Knowledge of God." In *Calvin and the Reformation*, edited by William Park Armstrong. Princeton: Princeton Theological Review Association, 1909; repr. ed., Grand Rapids: Baker Book House, 1980. Pp. 131–214.

———. *The Literary History of The Institutes of the Christian Religion by John Calvin.* Philadelphia: Presbyterian Board of Publication, 1909.

Wendel, François. *Calvin: The Origins and Development of His Religious Thought.* Translated by Philip Mairet. London: William Collins and Sons Co., 1963.

Willis, E. David. "Calvin's Use of Substantia." In *Calvinus Ecclesiae Genevensis Custos: Die Referate des Internationalen Kongresses für Calvinforschung vom 6. bis 9. September 1982 in Genf,* edited by Wilhelm H. Neusner. Frankfurt: Peter Lang, 1984. Pp. 289-301.

———. "A Reformed Doctrine of the Eucharist and Ministry and its Implications for Roman Catholic Dialogues." *Journal of Ecumenical Studies,* 21, no. 2 (Spring 1984): 295-309.

Wolf, Hans Heinrich. *Die Einheit des Bundes: Das Verhältnis von Altem und Neuem Testament bei Calvin.* Second edition. In Beiträge zur Geschichte und Lehre der Reformierten Kirche, edited by Paul Jacobs et. al. Neukirchen: Verlag der Buchhandlung des Erziehungsvereins, 1958.

Index

accommodation, 123–25, 146, 183, 184, 214, 201

Acts (Calvin's commentary), 65n., 157, 165–66, 195n.

Agreement of Zurich see *Consensus Tigurinus*

Aron, Raymond, 69

assurance, 8, 102, 110, 120, 125–28, 142, 147, 150, 151, 154, 156, 160, 162, 181, 184, 191

Augsburg Confession, 35

Augustine, Saint, 175, 189, 190, 205

Barclay, Alexander, 33–35, 94n.

Battles, Ford Lewis, 5, 10n., 12n., 63n., 73–74, 77

Bavinck, Herman, 23, 24, 70, 71

Bern Articles, 37

Bern, Synod of, 32

Beza, Theodore, 33, 40, 44, 56, 186–87n.

Bouvier, André, 32, 40

Bouwsma, William, 9, 126

Bucer, Martin, 22, 42, 43, 45, 92n., 103, 106, 133n., 147

Bullinger, Heinrich, 21, 23, 29, 30, 32–40, 42–44, 46, 55

Capito, Wolfgang, 103

Catechism, Genevan, 1537 edition, 101–3

Catechism, Genevan, 1542 and 1545 editions, 148–50, 186n., 187n.

Catechism, Genevan, 1545 edition, 54

certainty, 66, 85, 108, 120, 121, 126–28, 139, 142, 147, 149, 150, 153, 164, 193, 214

Christ, Jesus, ascension, 49, 55, 68, 157, 182, 183; body, 4, 5, 7, 8, 17, 20, 22, 24, 27, 38, 39, 41, 43, 44, 47–49, 52–54, 56, 66–68, 70–74, 77, 80–83, 89–93, 98–105, 109–15, 117, 118, 122–25, 127–29, 131, 132, 142, 149, 151, 154, 158–62, 165–70, 172, 173, 175–79, 182, 183, 185, 187, 188, 193, 195–197, 203–8, 212–16, 218, 220, 221; benefits, 16, 17, 48–50, 53, 72, 73, 80–84, 89, 90, 92, 93, 98, 100–103, 110, 115, 128, 129, 139, 151, 154, 158, 167, 171, 191, 216; the bread of life 54, 66, 67, 111, 112; communion/communication, 16, 17, 38, 39, 53, 47–50, 54, 56, 99, 100, 102–5, 109, 110, 112, 114, 115, 122–25, 127, 128, 146, 148, 149, 151, 153, 158, 159, 167, 168, 170, 173, 174, 177, 180–82, 185, 195–97n., 203–5, 207, 216, 218n., 220n.; crucified, 111, 120, 155; divinity, 17, 65, 91, 100, 171, 200, 205; food for the soul, 80, 93n., 103, 112, 124, 154, 160, 161, 165–67, 170, 171, 173–75, 205, 207; incarnation, 112, 113, 132, 158, 159, 171, 185, 200, 219; his life, 9, 17, 18, 21, 40–42, 45, 70, 81, 83, 88, 90, 101, 111, 112, 115, 118, 133, 147, 175, 178, 179, 208, 212; life-giving flesh, 17, 42, 48, 49, 53, 80–84, 93, 100–104, 107, 109–15, 125, 142, 158–59, 165, 169–78, 169–78, 181–85, 196–97n., 198, 204–10, 212; presence, 15, 16, 18–20, 25, 38, 54, 70, 76, 78, 81–83, 86, 99, 102, 105, 109, 110, 114, 115, 117, 125, 128, 146, 157, 163, 167, 168, 181–83, 203, 214, 216; his spirit, 80, 99, 109, 110, 112, 196; spiritual communion with, 17, 102; his substance, 4, 22, 23, 42, 48, 53, 71–73, 82, 83, 86, 104, 109, 117, 122, 123, 125, 159–61, 163, 166–70, 172–75, 178, 179, 184, 185, 204–8, 210, 215; substantial partaking of, 7, 8, 19–20, 51–54,

Index

Index

Index